Praise for THEATER KID

"Seller, the producer of such lauded musicals as *Rent, In the Heights,* and *Hamilton,* chronicles his path from Michigan to Broadway in this graceful memoir. . . . He is bracingly forthright about the harsh realities of the industry, as when he mentions a producer who was more upset about a star losing his voice than about a promoter who had just died by suicide."

—*The New Yorker*

"It's hard to beat Moss Hart's *Act One* for best Broadway memoir, but Jeffrey Seller's *Theater Kid* is very much in the running. . . . Like Hart's classic, Seller's book ends on a high note."

—*AirMail*

"Art imitates life in this peek behind the curtain from the award-winning producer of *Hamilton* and *Rent.* After an early life marred by poverty and trauma, Seller helped define the modern age of Broadway with shows about rebels, strivers and outsiders much like himself."

—*The New York Times Book Review*

"The 60-year-old's path from theater-loving Midwesterner to Broadway impresario is also packed with insider nods and insight. . . . *Theater Kid* will resonate with any reader who has tried to manifest their dream job via sheer pluck and commitment. . . . After decades overseeing such endeavors from the wings, Seller earns his moment to step into the spotlight and take a bow."

— *The Washington Post*

"[A] candid and affectionate debut . . . Seller provides colorful, behind-the-scenes peeks into the challenges and joys of producing a musical. . . . Theater buffs would do well to check this out."

—*Publishers Weekly*

"Well-written and compulsively entertaining . . . Anyone who loves theatrical memoirs will cherish—and reread—this book."

—NPR

"In this candid and engaging memoir, [Seller] blends his personal and professional stories to deftly capture his childhood dreams and challenges and his eventual journey to a successful career on Broadway. As an adopted child of a dysfunctional family coming to terms with his sexuality and living on the wrong side of town, musical theater is his saving grace. An entertaining and heartfelt look at what it takes to find your true self and not only survive but thrive amidst the neon lights on Broadway."

—*Booklist*

"Seller is an engaging storyteller and as passionate about directing summer camp theater as he is about producing award-winning Broadway shows. Highly recommended."

—*Library Journal* (starred review)

"[Seller] writes *Theater Kid* with the vividness of a graphic novel, the immediacy of a play, the intensity of a big-screen movie. Candid, sometimes explicit about his sexual awakening, fearless about revealing his family's chaos and conflicts and yet filled with love for even his volatile father, *Theater Kid* reads like the autobiography of someone who has lived with hard truths and made peace with them through his artistry."

—*Detroit Free Press*

"A must-read for grown-up theater kids."

—*New York Theater* (blog)

"Lightning struck twice for theater producer Jeffrey Seller, whose creative eye and business acumen are behind two of the most successful musicals of all time: *Rent* and *Hamilton*. In his touching memoir, *Theater Kid*, Seller gets real about growing up outside of Detroit, coming to terms with his sexuality, living through the height of the AIDS crisis, and his rocky rise to fame in the business of Broadway."

—*Queerty*

"In this searing and inspiring memoir, Jeffrey Seller writes the book he wishes he'd had as a kid; about a wildly brilliant, closeted young man from tough circumstances in Detroit who finds his way into the wilds of New York and helps develop and support some of the most innovative musical theater of the twentieth and twenty-first century. It belongs on your shelf next to *Act One* by Moss Hart—if you can manage to put it down; I certainly couldn't."

—Lin-Manuel Miranda

"I loved reading the wonderful, inspiring adventures of Jeffrey Seller's life and career. If you feel like an outsider from the poorest part of town, take heart: your dreams can come true."

—Bernadette Peters

"One of the great American coming-of-age stories, *Theater Kid* exhilarates and transports. The family Jeffrey Seller portrays here is as unique and indelible as any in American literature. Courageous, honest, and compulsively readable, this book will join the very short shelf of indispensable books on the American stage."

—Oskar Eustis, artistic director, The Public Theater

THEATER KID

KID

A BROADWAY MEMOIR

JEFFREY SELLER

SIMON & SCHUSTER PAPERBACKS

NEW YORK   AMSTERDAM/ANTWERP   LONDON
TORONTO   SYDNEY/MELBOURNE   NEW DELHI

Simon & Schuster Paperbacks
An Imprint of Simon & Schuster, LLC
1230 Avenue of the Americas
New York, NY 10020

This is a work of nonfiction. Some names and identifying details have been changed.

First Simon & Schuster trade paperback edition May 2026

SIMON & SCHUSTER PAPERBACKS and colophon are registered trademarks of Simon & Schuster, LLC

Simon & Schuster strongly believes in freedom of expression and stands against censorship in all its forms. For more information, visit BooksBelong.com.

For information about special discounts for bulk purchases, please contact Simon & Schuster Special Sales at 1-866-506-1949 or business@simonandschuster.com.

The Simon & Schuster Speakers Bureau can bring authors to your live event. For more information or to book an event, contact the Simon & Schuster Speakers Bureau at 1-866-248-3049 or visit our website at www.simonspeakers.com.

Interior design by Wendy Blum

Manufactured in the United States of America

1   3   5   7   9   10   8   6   4   2

Library of Congress Cataloging-in-Publication Data is available.

ISBN 978-1-6680-6418-4
ISBN 978-1-6680-6419-1 (pbk)
ISBN 978-1-6680-6420-7 (ebook)

Scan here to get book recommendations,
exclusive offers, and more delivered to your inbox.

In memory of my mother and father,
Caroline and Mark Seller

CONTENTS

Act One

Act Two

Act Three

THEATER KID

ACT ONE

ACT ONE

Chapter One

THE ACCIDENT

CARDBOARD VILLAGE. That's what the kids at school call my neighborhood. I hate that name, coined by a child poet to describe the tar shingles that cover our small houses, built fast and cheap on concrete slabs with no basements to protect us from tornadoes in Oak Park, Michigan, the poor enclave in a rising Jewish suburb just north of Detroit. It's the neighborhood where the parents have less: less money, less education, less stability. And the kids are deemed less: less smart, less cooperative, less likely to succeed.

On the first day of middle school, my new locker mate looks over at me and asks, "You live in The Village?"

I freeze. My heart speeds up. Blood pumps to my head and ears.

"What?"

"Cardboard Village," he says.

Caught, as if I'm in trouble, I blurt out one syllable.

"Yep."

"What's it like?" he asks.

"What's what like?" I act like I don't know what he's talking about.

"You know, tornadoes. Where do you hide? You're kind of like the little pig in the house made of straw."

I don't have an answer. I don't want to hide. I want to escape the neighborhood that makes me ashamed. I want to escape the poverty that entraps me and my dark, dour family. Mom frowns, Dad erupts, and my

3

fourteen-year-old older sister, Laurie, hides in her bedroom smoking cigarettes. They all fit together. They are tall and heavy; I'm paper-thin. They have dark hair and eyes; I'm blond-haired and blue-eyed. I'm the adopted son who looks and acts different. While they watch Detroit Lions football games, I write plays and make paper cutouts of trees and leaves and sunbursts to tape to my wall. I'm the answer to the *Sesame Street* quiz, "One of these things is not like the other."

And yet.

I'm also the favorite. The light of the family. The boy everyone wants to be with even when I don't want to be with them.

JUMP BACK TO JUNE 1974. I'm nine years old.

"Wanna serve some papers?" asks my dad. We have just finished dinner with Mom and Laurie. It is still light outside on this late spring night.

I do not want to go with my dad to serve papers, but I'm afraid to hurt his feelings.

"Um, I think I need to get ready for school tomorrow." It's a lame excuse and doesn't stop him.

"Come on, keep me company, it's only two papers," he says.

"Go with your father," says Mom. "Keep him company."

"Sure," I say.

We walk to the side drive, cracked like a broken plate, with weeds invading, and open the doors to his Ford LTD station wagon, bought used a couple years ago. I get in the passenger seat, pushing aside dirty napkins and an empty quart of buttermilk from Guernsey Farms, his favorite roadside dairy stand. He can drink a quart of buttermilk a day.

"Just throw that stuff on the floor," says Dad as he drops his weight onto the front seat, which bounces the car toward him like a rowboat about to tip. Dad is a giant next to my small nine-year-old body—he's six-foot-three and 250 pounds. His sword-like eyebrows burn red and the curly crimson hair on his head is receding, but still forms its own burning bush. He's an enormous man, whose size provides safety and entertainment. There is a picture in our small family collection of my sister and me on his shoulders, visiting the zebras at the Detroit Zoo. I love this photograph. Riding his shoulders is also the best vantage point for watching the annual Hudson's Thanksgiving Day Parade. His height lets me soar over the other onlookers, and his expansive shoulders and hands warm my legs and feet. His enormity can also terrify because when this giant loses his temper, he is like another tornado from which we cannot hide.

He backs down the driveway, swerves around the small island in front of our house, and heads toward Detroit.

Driving in the car with Dad, I look straight ahead or out my window, and try not to wince or make funny sounds as he bounds through the streets as if they are his own personal highways. Making a left turn is a game of chicken. For the passenger sitting closest to the oncoming car, it is a terrifying death sport.

"So, what's happening, son?"

"School's out in two weeks," I say.

"Looking forward to summer?"

"Sort of," I say. I like school more than summer vacation. It's more fun than being at home.

"Where we going tonight?" I ask.

"Let's see here," he says, looking down and taking out of his large brown folder a white summons that is attached to a legal complaint. I shouldn't have asked. He pays more attention to the paper than the road.

"We need to get this guy. I've had no luck. He's never home when I show up."

"What's the deal?" I ask.

"It says here he owes a year of child support. Here, take a look at the complaint."

I like reading the complaints.

"It says this guy left town for a year and tried to pass for dead," I say.

"A man who treats his children like that should be in jail," he says.

"Well, I guess they found him," I say.

"And now we're gonna get him."

We're driving on Eight Mile Road, the dividing line between Detroit and the suburbs. The businesses change as we move east through the city. Dress shops and cleaners give way to boarded-up storefronts.

"So, what's happening, son?" Dad asks.

He already asked that question. But he doesn't remember. "School's out in two weeks," I say.

"What are you doing this summer?"

Same question he just asked. "Going to day camp with Bruce, and we're playing T-ball," I say.

"I loved going to B'nai B'rith camp when I was a kid," he says.

A guy pulls into our lane, cutting off Dad.

"What the fuck?" He steps on the gas pedal and swerves into the lane next to the other car. "Roll down your window," he says to me.

"What?" I can hear him, but I don't want to roll down my window.

"Roll down your window," he says. I do what I am told.

"Hey! Asshole! Learn how to drive," shouts Dad.

"Kiss my ass," says the other driver as he gives Dad the finger. He roars away. I can see Dad revving up, about to start chasing him, but then he changes his mind and slows down.

"Sorry about that," he says.

Some silence.

The neighborhood changes again. It becomes middle class, but there are no bagel factories or kosher delicatessens, just lots of liquor stores and churches. This is the East Side, which is 100 percent gentile, while we are from the West Side, which is more Jewish. We arrive at a white brick ranch house with a bow window in the front. The grass is unmown and has a lot of dandelions coming up, kind of like our house. There are no bushes or flowers around the edges. All the windows are covered with bedsheets of different colors and patterns. Dad parks on the street in front, takes out the paper, and opens his door.

"Stay put, son, I'll be right back."

I watch him walk toward the front door, the summons in his back pocket. Some process servers carry handguns, but Dad doesn't believe in guns. I'm not even allowed to play with toy guns. He doesn't need one though. He walks fearlessly through life. He is a Jewish Paul Bunyan, in search of deadbeat dads, prospective divorcees, and delinquent mortgage holders—the kind of people who don't want to see a giant walking up their driveway with a legal-size paper in his hand. He reaches the door and rings the bell. Stands there. No answer. He knocks on the door. Hard. No answer. He peers in the living room window. No luck. He returns to the door, banging his hand over and over. I start to worry. Why isn't he giving up? He starts banging on the glass of the window, as if he might break it. Finally, the door opens a crack. He is talking to someone, a woman. She is wearing a long yellow T-shirt like a dress and looks like he woke her up. She is shaking her head no, but he won't leave. A man comes around the side of the house—he is short and pudgy. He is wearing a black T-shirt and jeans. His belly hangs over his waistband. Dad sees him. The man starts running a little. Dad paces after him. Though Dad doesn't run, his legs are very long, and he quickly catches up with the guy and puts his hand on his shoulder to stop him. He starts talking to the guy and I roll my window down a little so I can hear what they are saying.

"Sorry, that's not me," says the man.

"I think it is," says Dad. "I have your photo."

A man from the house next door opens his door and comes out to his porch.

"Hey, leave him alone," says the neighbor.

"Is this your next-door neighbor, Bill McBride?" says Dad.

"None of your business," says the neighbor.

The man tries to walk away. Dad grabs him by the arm.

"That's assault," says the man. He doesn't put up a fight with this process server who stands many inches over his head.

Dad tucks the summons under the man's shirt. "Mr. McBride, my name is Mark Seller. I've been appointed by the court to serve

you this summons. Please read it carefully and show up on your appointed court date."

Mr. McBride drops the paper on the sidewalk and hustles down the street away from his house.

"Get the hell out of here," says the neighbor from his porch. "You're a fucking pig."

"What did you call me?" Dad strides toward the neighbor on the porch as if he is going to demolish him. Or his house. The man jumps inside and slams the wooden door that has a glass window at the top in the shape of a half circle. Dad punches his fist through the window, breaking the glass.

"Don't ever talk to me like that," says Dad, who calmly turns around and walks to the car. His knuckles are bloody, but his mood is triumphant.

"Got 'em," says Dad as he sits down in the driver's seat. "Mission accomplished."

"What about the summons he dropped?" I ask.

"He'll go back and get it. Or he'll go to jail."

Shaking a little, heart beating fast, I'm relieved to get out of there. Dad has just earned twenty dollars. He explains that if he serves five papers a day, he'll make a hundred bucks, which will keep us housed, fed, and clothed.

"Son, hand me the napkins on the floor."

The napkins are soiled with ketchup and mustard, but they will do. He wraps them around his knuckles like a bandage.

As it begins to get dark, we start our drive home.

"Let's try one more. It's on the way."

I nod, afraid to say I'd like to get the heck out of these scary situations.

"You OK?" he says.

"Fine," I reply.

"It sure is nice to have your company," he says. "So, what are you doing this summer?"

"The regular. Camp, T-ball."

"Sounds great," he says.

We drive a few miles and reach a dingy apartment complex that consists of multiple two-story brown brick buildings, each with a gray metal entrance door in the center. There is a bent gutter hanging off the roof. Kids are playing outside. People are sitting on lawn chairs in the small grassy area between the buildings and the parking lot. Dad takes one more paper and rises out of the car.

"Be right back." He goes into the building with the hanging gutter.

I stay in the car with the windows rolled up; the people from the neighborhood glare at me from their lawn chairs, beer and cigarettes in hand. Being alone in the car while Dad is out of sight is almost scarier than watching him in action. But he returns quickly.

"Success?" I ask.

"You're my good luck charm," says Dad.

"No problem," I say.

"Wanna get some ice cream?" he asks.

"Sure," I say.

We stop at Baskin-Robbins on Nine Mile Road.

"Whatever you want, son." I order two scoops of chocolate chip on a regular cone. I love ice cream—the cold temperature, the hard texture, the sweet vanilla, and the bittersweet chocolate chips. It erases the anxiety of being Dad's junior process server—a job I do not like and a job I do not want. I'm always afraid he'll be shot by angry subpoena recipients. I hate the dirty car that smells like spoiled buttermilk and burnt gas because of the broken heat ducts. Most of all, I hate answering the same questions that Dad asks every time we are together. At only thirty-seven years old, he can't remember what I told him yesterday, a result of The Accident five years before.

When I was four, we lived at 26703 Northview, a friendly street in the middle-class section of Oak Park, where the trees made a canopy over the safe neighborhood. I never forgot the address, though we moved out before second grade. Our home was my playground, complete with a red jungle gym in the living room. I loved running in circles through the house with my cousins and passing through my sister's bedroom, which connected the back hallway to the kitchen and family room. Her tiled floor had speckles that made the sound of sparklers crackling. My sister and I often played in the finished basement that had wood paneling and a long bar our parents never used—a family of eaters not drinkers—that we transformed into a stage for puppets. The family room behind the kitchen housed the big color television on which we watched Neil Armstrong walk on the moon. The kitchen had a walk-in pantry that was filled with fresh bread and chocolate chip cookies that the Awrey man delivered every week. If the front door was locked, I could climb into the house through the milk chute in the kitchen.

Dad owned Poucher Gage and Tool, an industrial tool business he inherited from his father. Mom played mah-jongg two days a week. We had a beloved housekeeper named Tina, who had taken care of Dad's house when he was growing up. Every day a station wagon picked up my next-door neighbor and best friend, Pam, and me, and took us to Huntington Woods Nursery School. I loved the playground, which had a miniature log cabin we could hide in, and I loved playing with the other kids, one of whom taught me how to tie my shoes with two bunny ears.

In the fall of 1969, two weeks before my fifth birthday, Laurie and I were playing Candy Land on the floor of the den and watching *The Brady Bunch*, a new show on TV. We loved this big family with six fun kids who all shared one big bathroom with two sinks. It was getting dark outside, and the rain shrouded the house with the ominous sound of water pounding the roof and dripping down the gutters. Our board game was illuminated by the light shining from the kitchen, where Mom was making dinner. Dad was not home. The phone rang and, after a short, clipped conversation, Mom told us that she needed to go out. Something was wrong. Pam's mother, Mrs. Myers, came over a few minutes later to babysit.

The next moment I remember was going to a hospital to visit Dad two months later. As Mom drove into the parking lot of St. Joseph's

Hospital in Ann Arbor, I spotted a white station wagon with lots of flashing red lights and a blaring siren. I asked what that was.

"An ambulance," said my sister.

"I want to ride in an 'alacadence,'" I said.

My new word, *alacadence*, became part of the story of The Accident. Mom explained that an "alacadence" had rescued my father.

We walked through the door of a cold hospital room, and lying in bed was a large man with white gauze bandages wrapped around his head. It was Dad. He couldn't talk.

Dad had crashed while riding a motorcycle. Mom didn't know he owned a motorcycle. She also didn't know he was in a motorcycle gang. Barreling toward Kalamazoo on I-94 on a Friday night in October with his gang and his girlfriend, June, riding on the back of his bike—Mom didn't know about June either—his front tire blew out and he slammed into the pavement headfirst. June escaped with cuts and bruises while Dad was rushed to the hospital. When Mom arrived, the doctor prepared her for his probable death. The doctors performed emergency brain surgery, drilling holes into the right and left sides of his temple to stop the bleeding and relieve the pressure.

Against the odds, he survived. Though his body would recover over many months of convalescence, he was permanently brain-damaged. He had a form of dementia and couldn't use the left side of his body, a disability made more complicated because he was a lefty. His personality devolved. He lost his spark, his charisma, his verbal dexterity. He gained an explosive temper. At dinner one night, soon after coming home, he started eating meat loaf and mashed potatoes with his hands. Mom encouraged him to use his fork and knife, but he couldn't hold them. Enraged, he flung his utensils down, threw his plate at the wall, and stumbled away to their bedroom. Laurie and I huddled in fear and silence while Mom tried to comfort us.

The Accident was the euphemism everyone used to describe the motorcycle crash that changed our family forever. An aunt said to me years later, "It was as if your dad died in that crash because, let me tell you, the man who came back was not the same man I knew before."

He didn't work for a year. Poucher Gage and Tool had gone bankrupt months before The Accident, a result of Dad's overspending. Broke, we went on welfare. Friends and family brought groceries. The milkman continued bringing milk, eggs, and butter even though we couldn't pay. Someone was secretly paying on our behalf. Mom, who had never worked before, got a job at McDonald's. Grandma Louise, Dad's mother, moved in to help pay the bills. She took my room, and I shared Laurie's, which meant sleeping in the room with the floor that crinkled whenever anyone stepped on it. I liked that sound. Dad started working odd jobs. He took me with him once when he drove a potato chip delivery truck. A high school friend, who was a district court judge, gave him a part-time job serving court papers. That led to a full-time job serving papers for lawyers across southeastern Michigan.

Most of this I know from family members, because I don't clearly remember all these events. In fact, the year following The Accident—my kindergarten year—is mostly a blank. My memory picks up in first grade, which I almost failed because of bronchial pneumonia. Visits to the doctor, chest X-rays, and painful penicillin shots became part of my existence. Week after week, I stayed home in my pajamas. Grandma Louise read to me, and every day when Mom came home from her job at McDonald's, I asked when I could return to school.

Apart from being sick of feeling sick, I just wanted to go back to my favorite class with my animated teacher, Mrs. Foon, who called herself "The Purple People Eater." I vividly remember how she lit up my days with her magical presence. She read books out loud, enacting all the characters, and drew colorful chalk sketches of every kid in the class and posted them above the blackboards.

After a full month, healing arrived. Mrs. Foon said I could advance to second grade despite missing so much school. Bouts of bronchitis would come for me every winter until I was twenty years old. The onset of a sore throat and pained chest always scared and angered me. It meant a full week out of school. Trying to determine why I became sick so often, the doctor sent me to an allergist who poked my arms many times and then gave my parents a three-page list of all the foods and outdoor things I was allergic to. I began weekly trips to receive allergy shots that I have no reason to believe were helpful.

That summer, our family went on a field trip with Shirley Cash, who was famous in Oak Park. Her red neon sign, "Shirley Cash Realty," always lit up the front window of her office on Coolidge just south of Ten Mile. With a face decorated by heavy pancake makeup and a big blond hairdo, Shirley was always upbeat. She would have been equally at home selling houses in Dallas, Texas. She made house hunting fun, but I didn't realize that we were shopping for a new house for us.

"Honey, the key is to stay in Oak Park," Shirley told Dad, who was sitting in the front seat with her. "For the kids. For the schools."

We drove to a neighborhood a short distance away. The houses were made of the same tar shingles that were on the roof. Shirley parked in front of a small house that was at the end of a cul-de-sac. I don't know the pejorative of cul-de-sac, but the word is far too fancy for the geography of 33030 Redwood.

An English family lived there. The mother, a lady named Naomi Lippa, was sewing at a table in the living room when her husband welcomed us in. She had a very proper accent.

"Hello, young man, come here," Naomi said to me.

I approached her. She was sewing a dress.

"What's your name?" she said.

"Jeff," I said.

"Jeffrey," she said, "use your full name. It sounds better. I have a boy your age. Andrew?" A boy came out of a bedroom. "Show him to your room. See if he likes it."

She told my parents that they were getting ready to move to their dream house. Andrew took me down a short hallway to his room, which was a lot smaller than my old room. He seemed fun. I wondered if he could be my friend.

"Can you show me your basement?" I asked.

"There is no basement, honey," shouted Shirley from the living room. "But come look at the backyard. You'll love it."

She was right. The backyard had two sections—the area directly behind the house and another area to its left—the portion created by the curve in the cul-de-sac. There was a maple tree in the center, dividing the two halves. As we walked through the yard, I focused on the tree. I wanted to climb it.

"This yard is so big we'll build a pool," said Dad.

I loved that idea, and I believed him. I walked away from that house happy about the tall tree I would climb, and the swimming pool Dad promised. As I pushed the driver's seat forward so that I could get into the back seat of Shirley's gold Tempest, I heard her tell my parents how great this house was and how perfect it would be for us. I believed her, too.

On moving day, Dad drove a U-Haul with only half the furniture of our old house. I had a long dresser that was temporarily parked in the middle of the tiny new living room. I danced around it all afternoon, filled with the optimism of a kid who believed all change is good. The dresser never made it into my new room. It didn't fit.

We never built a pool, but our dog, Keelee, made the yard into her own racing track, carving a figure eight in the grass around the maple tree. I made friends with the tree. It was tall and robust and beautiful—the opposite of the house, and so much better than the neighborhood in which it grew. With two giant trunks for legs, strutting branches like arms, and thousands of hands made of green leaves each with five points like fingers, it danced in the sky. I would be Jack, the tree my beanstalk.

Chapter Two

ADVENTURELAND

IN JANUARY OF FOURTH GRADE, my Sunday school teacher announces that auditions for the annual Purim play are the following Saturday afternoon in the temple banquet hall. I have always loved watching the Purim play, which tells the Old Testament story of Esther, the young Jewish queen who saves her people from the murderous hands of the villain, Haman. With songs, dances, and new characters borrowed from popular movies and musicals of the day, it delights and ignites my imagination. I wonder, *How do the kids learn all these lines and songs?* I ask Dad if he'll drive me to the auditions.

"Get in the car," he says. He is as happy to take me where I want to go as he is to take me to the places he wants to go—like serving papers or playing pool at the Cush'n Cue Pool Hall. Going to Temple Israel in Palmer Park, one of the few remaining fancy neighborhoods in Detroit, is special.

A large building shaped like a round birthday cake made of gray limestone, Temple Israel is the Mount Sinai of Manderson Road. Tall stained-glass windows with scenes from the Bible rise from the ground to the roof. A sidewalk with a huge lawn covered in snow on either side leads to six gigantic wooden entrance doors. Dad drops me off and I walk up to the imposing ten-foot-high doors. I think about the gatekeeper in *The Wizard of Oz* telling Dorothy, "the Wizard says 'Go away!'" At the auditions, no one tells me to go back home, but no one welcomes me either. I sit by myself and fill out the contact form.

On one side of the banquet hall is a stage that has gold curtains and lights overhead. A teacher named Mrs. Glaser is in charge. She has black hair that's like cotton candy swirled on top of her head, dark eyes, red lipstick, and glasses hanging from a black cord. She doesn't tolerate noise. She talks about being "professional." This isn't just "fun," it is serious. Her sense of focus, of mission, grabs me.

When my name is called, I bound up to the stage. I've never recited lines in a play, but I love reading out loud in class and I say my speeches clearly and loudly. Some of the kids read the lines differently—with feelings. They get the main parts. I am cast as a sailor in the chorus. We sing and learn dances in this musical that blends the story of Queen Esther with the songs from the musical *South Pacific*. Thus, Queen Esther, expressing her frustrations about the king, sings, "I'm Gonna Wash That Man Right Outa My Hair." The sailors sing a song from the opera *HMS Pinafore*, "We Sail the Ocean Blue." Thus, my first musical is a mash-up of Rodgers and Hammerstein, Gilbert and Sullivan, and the Old Testament.

Going to rehearsal every Saturday and Sunday afternoon gives me a way to get out of the house. It's an introduction to a whole new world of creation. I learn stage directions—that upstage means the back of the stage, and downstage means the front of the stage, and right and left are from the perspective of the actor facing the audience. I love learning the sailor dance: "Step right, hop, hop. Step left, hop, hop." I love the warmth and color that emanate from the footlights on the edge of the stage. And I love the single performance we present on a Sunday morning in early March. Being in a play for the first time makes me happy. Wait. That's not good enough. Being in a play changes my life; I am filled with purpose for the first time.

The day after the triumphant performance, I decide to write a play. I think about the many times in which my best friends, Bruce and Jay (who is also my cousin and neighbor), and I have climbed on top of the shed in the backyard to play. It looks like a bombed-out dollhouse—with a center doorway but no door, octagonal window holes, but no glass, and a pitched roof of spotty gray shingles. The white paint is faded and peeling. It's our castle. After boredom takes hold, Bruce tears off pieces of shingles and whips them like Frisbees into the sky. We have contests to see who can throw the farthest. Bruce always wins.

Sitting at my desk in English class, I write the first scene:

Act 1, Scene 1; Time: morning; Place: Jeff's house; Characters: Jeff, Mom, Dad, Jay, Bruce

Mom: *Jeff, it's time for breakfast.*

Jeff: *Coming. Where's Dad?*

Mom: *He's tearing down the shed.*

Jeff: *I'm going outside (he crosses to the shed). Dad, how come you're cutting the shed down?*

Dad: *Because it's no good to us anymore.*

Jeff: *Well, don't tear it down.*

Dad: *Alright, but don't go on top of it because with any weight you'll fall right through. Now let's go eat breakfast.*

Act 1, Scene 2; Place: Kitchen

Jeff: *These are good pancakes, Mom.*

Mom: *Thank you. Oh, Jeff, please be good today because I have to go away.*

Jeff: *Ok, but Jay and Bruce are coming over.*

Dad: *Well, I have to go to work now, bye honey, bye Jeff.*

Mom: *Bye. Jeff, then please play outside. . . .*

(There is a knock on the door)

Jeff: *Coming. Mom, Jay and Bruce are here. Come on you guys, let's go play on the shed roof.*

Jay and Bruce: *Ok.*

(They go to the roof)

19

Bruce: *It feels funny up here. It feels as if we're gonna fall through.*
Jeff: *You're right.*
Jeff, Jay, Bruce: Help we're falling!!!!

We fall, not on the concrete floor of the shed, but through the sky, the stars, and the galaxies, landing on the moss-covered ground of a faraway land—Adventureland! There are giant redwood trees, open meadows, and shimmering lakes. It is beautiful but treacherous. Danger meets our every step. We encounter life-threatening villains: rabid lumberjacks with chain saws; murderous kidnappers with guns; and child-hating pirates like Captain Hook, who makes us walk the plank! Our saviors always come through in the clinch: Daniel Boone, Aquaman, and Peter Pan, who triumphantly flies us home in the last scene.

I start the play on Monday and finish on Friday. I call it *Adventureland* and share it with my teacher, Mrs. Novetsky, begging her to let me do it in school.

"I'm impressed," she says. "You can use the empty classroom across the hall."

I thank her. "Know what you are?" she says. "A theater kid."

I like that name. I recruit my sister, Laurie, to type the play on mimeograph paper to make copies, and my friends to act. I am playwright, director, actor, and producer. In a room with all the desks pushed to one side, we recite the scenes with scripts in hand. Then, I encourage all kinds of crazy action: The kids yell, jump, fight, and have a blast. Though we never perform it in front of an audience, this is my first effort to produce a show.

Chapter Three

CAMPING

AFTER WRITING AND WORKSHOPPING *ADVENTURELAND*, I'm home on the toilet after school trying to come up with my next play. It's the place I do my best brainstorming. I'm thinking about the maple tree in the yard and a new play about "Jack and the Beanstalk." I hear Dad's station wagon pull into the side drive. I jump a little when I hear the loud slam of his car door. Kind of like the recipients of his subpoenas and summons. He takes three big steps and opens the screen door.

"Hello?" he bellows. "Son, you there?"

"In the bathroom," I call out.

"I have a surprise for you, son."

Another pet, I assume. Dad loves bringing home stray animals. Snakes, raccoons, and rabbits have emerged from brown cardboard boxes in the wagon's rear, only to be returned by Mom's orders "before the Health Department fines us for sheltering all the goddamn animals from the Detroit Zoo." Once he came home with a large snapping turtle that almost bit off his thumb. And countless dogs, including Keelee, the Doberman pinscher we adopted three years before, when I was six.

Keelee is beautiful, small, and docile for her breed. She behaves more like a retriever than a guard dog. She is affectionate and eager to please, and her sweet gaze implies that she doesn't belong in her Doberman skin. She clings to me, perhaps because Mom and Dad used my underpants as dog diapers during her periods. Mom apologized for this inconvenience but explained that mine were the only underpants that would fit her. It might also be because she feels out of place in her Doberman body, and I feel out of place in my family home.

I complete my business, put my plans for Jack & the Beanstalk on hold, wash my hands, and go to the living room.

"Hey, Dad," I say.

"Come on out here, son," Dad says. He leads me out the front door to the back of the wagon, which he opens to reveal a huge load of camping equipment. There are a couple of tents, a Coleman stove, and a giant inflatable yellow raft with two wooden paddles. There are tin pots, plates, cups, Swiss Army knives in a couple of different sizes, and a giant red cooler for food.

I know we can't afford this stuff. "Where'd you get this?" I ask. I am a secret accountant for the family, constantly monitoring our financial health. Mom has recently taken a job as a clerk at a local drugstore chain. The pay is only four dollars per hour, but she receives health insurance for the whole family.

"A man was evicted from his house near Ten Mile and Greenfield," he says. "I had to serve him the notice. He left all this stuff out on the front lawn and told me to take it."

The equipment looks new. There are two sleeping bags, one big, one little. This stuff belonged to a man and his son before being passed on to this man and his son.

"We're going to go on a camping trip. You and me. We'll set up camp, we'll cook out, we'll take this raft down the Au Sable River."

I don't say anything. I am afraid to go camping with Dad. He hasn't been camping since he was a kid and I have no reason to believe he can find a campsite, set up a tent, or negotiate the current of a river.

"We'll bring Bruce and Larry along with us. Maybe Jay too. This is going to be great, son."

Bruce will be into it. His father, Larry, is more coordinated than Dad. And it will give us something else to do this summer.

I'm relieved when Mom returns home from work. While Dad is unpredictable, Mom is consistent. She walks in the house still wearing her blue smock from Cunningham's Drugs. Mom is tall, a little bit overweight, but not wide. She has short, threadlike brown hair, combed to the side, that exposes a little bit of her scalp. Her oily skin is weathered, and she doesn't wear makeup. Her brown eyes reveal a tinge of woe, but her presence is still comforting.

After Laurie shows up, Dad tells the story again about the man who was evicted from his home. Laurie listens but doesn't say much. A big girl, burdened by a bulbous nose, big bones, and dull brown hair and eyes, she has few interests. She is a poor student about to finish seventh grade, who disappears into herself and her few friends. I used to love playing on the jungle gym with Laurie, watching *The Brady Bunch*, sitting at the dinner table, and spitting out Mom's liver. But we don't have fun anymore.

Making dinner is one activity in which Mom and Dad work well together, exchanging jokes instead of sarcasm. She broils a cheap flank steak in the electric oven, and he makes a salad of iceberg lettuce, tomatoes, cucumbers, and peppers, with his own special salad dressing— olive oil and lemon. We all sit down at the orange Formica rectangular table in the living room. The light over our heads is a crooked white globe. Dad purchased it at Sears but couldn't get the installation right, so it hangs from its white cord with a cockeyed head.

Everyone in the family excels at eating except me. But I like to talk and, once in a while, Laurie will join.

"So what are you going to do on a camping trip, Jeff?" asks Laurie. "I don't see you 'roughing it.'"

"I was in the Cub Scouts," I say. Truth was, I hated the Cub Scouts and quit not long after the annual box car race, which was a sham because every boy's father built his car for him and mine had no ability to do so.

23

"This is going to be fantastic," says Dad. "I did this with the Scouts at Beth El."

"Sounds great," Laurie says, rolling her eyes.

"You don't have to be sarcastic," says Mom. "It's a nice idea."

A squeak emanates from Dad's seat. The first one is little. The next one is bigger. Dad can't control his gas; he's a prisoner to his bowels. On the third, still louder fart, Dad jumps up from the table and runs to the bathroom as fast as he can.

"Excuse me, folks," he says as he exits. "Sorry about that."

"Where's the spray?" asks Mom. Laurie gets up to find the Lysol to try to tamp down the sulfurous gas that just interrupted our dinner.

We pretend not to hear from down the hall as Dad, a giant squatter in a tiny bathroom, expels rivers of yellow and brown liquefied shit into a darkening white porcelain bowl. He shits as much as most guys pee, a result of his intestinal bypass operation. By removing a huge portion of his large intestine in 1966, doctors promised that he'd lose a hundred pounds from his then 350-pound frame, never gain another ounce, and eat whatever and whenever he liked. He was a pioneer, one of the first people to use surgery to lose weight. The only trade-off was that he would have diarrhea for the rest of his life.

And the only thing worse than the diarrhea? The farting. His days are filled with eating and farting and shitting. Eggs and toast in the morning. Buttermilk from Guernsey Farms, which he always finds time to visit even though it is fifteen miles away. He has no problem finishing off a half gallon straight out of the container. A Coney Island dog with "the works"—chili, onions, and mustard—for lunch. French fries to go along with it. Another helping of eggs for a midafternoon snack, this time in the form of his famous sandwich: toast with a layer of oozy scrambled eggs, smothered by a layer of blue cheese, topped by a generous sprinkle of hot red pepper flakes, and then all broiled in the toaster oven once more. The only thing smellier than the cooked sandwich is the fusillade of farts, as if from a cannon, that follow ingestion by about thirty minutes. There is nowhere to hide from the onslaught. Our only weapons to blunt the force of the stench are the cans of "spray" scattered throughout the house.

ON A FRIDAY IN JULY, with the station wagon filled with our new camping equipment, we head to the grocery store with our weekend campers: Bruce; his father, Larry; Jay; Dad; and me.

"We're gonna do some good eating on this trip," says Dad as we barrel into the local Farmer Jack to stock up for the weekend in the woods.

Five men tear up and down the aisles of a suburban grocery store, pulling food off the shelves like bears rummaging through a Boy Scout campsite. We buy steaks and potatoes, bacon and sausage, three dozen eggs, and a couple gallons of milk. We buy Ball Park franks and hamburger meat, ketchup and mustard, bread and buns. For dessert, marshmallows, Hershey bars, and graham crackers. Ham, turkey, salami, and bologna are also thrown into the cart, along with several packs of cheese, which fills me with dread. Dad's copious consumption of cheese will be followed by furious farts.

Bruce and his dad, Larry, are excited to join the trip and have their own ideas of activities they want to do. Specifically, target practice. Bruce is obsessed with Larry's pistol—the brand, the size, and where Larry stores it. Dad is so excited about this camping trip that he doesn't even comment on Larry's pistol, even though he's anti-gun. He declares it will be the "trip of the century."

Bruce and I became friends two years ago. He initiated our friendship when we were assigned seats next to each other in the last row of Mrs. Cook's third grade math class. Maybe he didn't remember that on my first day of school one year earlier, he said I looked like a girl because my hair was long. Maybe he knew that I was someone he could talk to. And he had a lot to talk about. After sports, there were cars—another topic in which I had no interest—and after cars, there were his plans to "go around" with pretty girls from the neighborhood. He had big dreams about the games he would win, the girls he would score, and the cars he would own. I was his sounding board, counselor, and confidant. He was my protector, my first friend who wasn't a girl or a cousin. He made me feel like I was his brother. No one called me a "girl" when I was with Bruce. And we shared lots of fun activities: riding bikes around the neighborhood, swimming at the Oak Park Pool, and—our favorite adventure—climbing the six-foot cinderblock wall that separated Cardboard Village from the fancier apartment complex next door, walking atop it as if on a tightrope, and then playing Ding Dong Ditch at the apartments.

Bruce is a strong boy—fast, coordinated, and talented with balls: baseballs, basketballs, anything round. He is the best third baseman in Little League. Jay is unlike any of the other boys in our neighborhood: He doesn't care what anyone thinks of him. He is a strong, athletic, good-looking kid who everyone loves—boys and girls. And yet, he is also a bit of a loner, as happy to hang out with the group as he is to be by himself. When he isn't playing sports, he is practicing his drums in his bedroom. Though we've played together since we were babies, our friendship deepened when I moved around the block from his house and started attending the same school.

After the Coleman cooler is packed, we pile into the back seat to start our trek north. As Dad drives, Larry, a good-looking, wiry man of thirty-five, does most of the talking while smoking a cigarette. In a Brooklyn accent that sounds like something from the movies, he tells stories about growing up in Canarsie and all the hot girls he dated as a teenager. He is cool in a way that my dad is not. But he and Dad have a camaraderie based on their common teenage experiences—they were both Jewish guys who grew up driving fast cars, having fun, and paying no attention to books.

We drive four hours up I-75, an expressway that's not as pretty as the photos of the beautiful Great Lake State that are featured in AAA magazine ads. Our destination: Oscoda, Michigan, a small town at the mouth of the Au Sable River along Lake Huron. It was the place Dad had gone camping with his Temple Beth El youth group when he was young. If Michigan is shaped like a mitten, then Oscoda is two-thirds up the first finger.

After exiting I-75, we travel east on a highway with scattered gas stations and fishing tackle stores. We pass John W. Putz Hardware in Bay City, Michigan. "Can you believe this?" says Larry. "Fuckin' Putz's Hardware. They wouldn't believe me back in Brooklyn if I showed 'em a picture."

"What's a putz?" I ask.

"You don't know what a putz is? Come on. A shmendrik, a dimwit?" says Larry.

"You mean, like an idiot?"

"You got it, kid. Don't forget it. Or else people'll be calling you a putz."

The woods take over where the businesses end. On either side of the highway are tall spruce, oaks, and maples, with lots of underbrush. It's a wall of green. "It don't look like Brooklyn," Larry continues. "I'll tell you that much, Mark."

"It looks exactly the same as when I came here when I was fourteen," says Dad.

"Except for the Edison signs," I say.

Every few hundred feet there are white signs attached to the trees with big black letters that say, "Private Property, Detroit Edison. NO TRESPASSING." It concerns me.

"Don't sweat it," says Dad.

"It looks like we're not allowed," I say.

"No one's gonna bother us here."

"Don't worry," says Bruce, "Larry's got his gun." I flinch. "It's a joke. Loosen up, Smeller, there's nothing to worry about."

Smeller. The nickname Bruce coined for me. Smeller Seller is a cute rhyme, unless your dad is the Abominable Fart Man. I try to ignore the signs and hope we won't see any more.

Dad turns onto a dirt road. We travel through a flat forest bed with trees, scrub, and bushes on either side. There are a few forks in the road, and he always veers left. Will Dad be able to find his way out of this forest maze? Is anyone keeping track?

We discover a swell campsite—a sandy area that slopes down to a small beach on the river. It is large enough for two tents and a camp-fire. The dirt is dry. It will be great for swimming, sleeping, and cook-ing out.

As Dad and Larry set up the makeshift kitchen area, the boys and I go off in search of firewood. We spread out on a huge open field looking for deadwood that we can carry.

We make a huge bonfire the first night, cook delicious burgers, and then roast marshmallows. Our tent is comfortable. I'm cozy in my sleep-ing bag. Sleeping under the stars feels like a flight into infinity. Morning is cold and getting out of the sleeping bag is like losing a layer of skin. But the sun rises, making it warm in no time.

Lunch on this warm day is hot dogs and beans. The sun beats down; the bugs are out for blood. Not just mosquitoes, but the big flies that bite. The first layer on top of our skin is sweat. And then a layer of suntan lo-tion. And then a layer of OFF! bug spray. My skin is choking, but the sun and the bugs stay out. Jumping in the river is the only release. And jump we do, with the pots and pans from our last couple of meals. Though our job is to use the silt to clean the pots, Bruce is more interested in a mud fight. He lobs a big glob of mud that hits me in the behind.

"Looky, Smeller, you got doody dripping down your leg. Shit your pants?"

"You got it," I say. "I'm cleaning the pot with it." I scoop the mud off my leg, wipe it into the pot and then fling it like a javelin back toward Bruce. "Here, try some doody soap. It's good for the skin."

"Gross," says Jay. Bruce sneaks up behind him with a pot of mud.

"Look out Herballs!" I shout. Jay's nickname. The prepubescent it-eration of his last name, Hurwitz. As mud descends on Jay's head, he jumps on Bruce and dunks him. Water fights ensue and we all swim deeper into the river with the joy that accompanies freedom and escape.

Dad extinguishes the campfire with Larry. "I need to go into town, take care of some business," he says.

He needs to go to the bathroom. He needs a toilet. Though he em-braces the term "roughing it" for sleeping outside, taking a shit is the

one activity in which he depends on civilization. His chronic diarrhea makes shitting in the woods too dirty. Perhaps he is preserving the woods. Larry knows what he is talking about.

"Cheddar cheese and beans that fast?" he says.

"Big time," says Dad. He yells toward me. "I'm takin' a drive into town. Wanna join me, son?"

"What?" I say. I pretend not to hear the question.

"Come on into town with me, son. Keep me company."

I look back at my two friends. "Don't kill each other," I say. "I'll be back." I walk over to Dad. "Where we going?"

"I gotta do my thing."

"Oh."

On this beautiful Saturday in the woods I get in the car with my father to accompany him on his bathroom break.

"Now we can finally spend some time together," he says, climbing into the car.

"We've been together the whole trip," I say.

"I mean alone. Without the other guys."

"Oh."

Driving over the lumpy dirt road, he reaches the first fork and blurts, "Which way do you think we go?"

"We did all lefts to get in, so maybe we do all rights to get out."

"You're a genius, son."

I look out my window and wonder again about the signs that say "NO TRESPASSING."

"That was a first-class lunch, son."

"Thanks."

"Lafayette Coney Island couldn't compare with those dogs you grilled."

"They were pretty good," I say.

"You know, I can remember the great times me and my buddies had camping in these woods when we were Scouts," he said. "In winter too."

I nod. We come to the paved highway and turn south.

"You boys having a good time?" he asks.

"Sure." A weird question, since he just pulled me out of the river where I was swimming and laughing with my friends.

"That's it?"

"Oh, I mean, yeah, we're having a great time."

I keep my eyes peeled to the roadside until I spot a station. "There's a Marathon over there on the left."

We pull in.

"I'll be back in a minute." He gets out of the car, lets out a fart, and goes into the office where he gets a key from the attendant. Then he disappears behind the building and reappears an instant later.

"That was fast," I say.

"No toilet paper."

"Oh."

The hunt continues. Dad shifts his weight around, trying to contain his growing discomfort. We drive in silence for about five minutes.

"Whatcha thinkin' 'bout?" Dad asks.

I hate that question. "What?" I reply.

"You're awfully quiet. I asked what you're thinking about?" He enunciates the words *thinking* and *about.*

"Nothing."

"You can't be thinking about nothing. Something's gotta be going through your mind."

"Just resting," I say.

"Can't think of anything to share with your father?"

"Not right at this very moment, I guess."

"You know, I sure wish I could figure out what goes on in that head of yours."

"Why is it that anytime I don't have something to say, you think there's something going on inside my head?"

"What's wrong with you?" he says.

"Nothing," I reply, defensive.

"You know what I don't get? I don't get why, when you're with your

31

friends or your mother you never shut up, but when you're with me, you can't think of anything to say."

"I don't think that's true." I am hiding. What I am afraid to say is, *It's no fun talking to you. You won't remember it tomorrow. You'll just ask me the same question over and over.*

Dad steps on the gas.

"You know, son, I don't know what's going on, but I don't like your attitude."

"Dad. I'm fine. There's nothing wrong with me."

"Don't tell me what you are and what you aren't. It's written all over your face," he says.

I don't respond.

"I am so fucking sick of your attitude. Your tone of voice. I mean, you're with your father, we finally have some time together, and you've got that bored, disgusted look on your face."

He starts to seethe, while my face starts to burn with fear; I need to try to cool down his rising fury.

"Dad, I'm not bored or disgusted. I'm just looking for a gas station. What's wrong with that?"

"You had better get rid of that tone of voice and wipe that look off your face."

I look at the speedometer. The needle is moving past the sixties into the seventies.

"Look at me." Dad is turning red; his eyes are watering. "Do you hear me?"

"Yes."

"I said, do you hear me?"

"Yes."

"You're not going to ruin this trip for me and for everyone else on it." He is crying.

"I don't think I am."

I am all the way up against the passenger side door when he raises his right arm and hits me across the face with the back of his hand. I freeze—scared, shocked, paralyzed. Then he clutches my shoulder, engulfing my tiny arm, and squeezes it as he shakes me.

Tears dripping down his reddened face, he is driving eighty miles an hour on the two-lane highway as he screams, "You're not going to talk to me that way, do you hear me? You're not going to talk to me this way and you're not going to treat me this way. Do you understand me?"

"Yes," I say. Tears burst through my eyes. My heart races. The skin where he hit me burns.

"I am your father, do you hear me? You're going to treat me better than that."

He is riding a wave of anger over which he has no control. I am trapped in the moving station wagon, desperately hoping this tantrum, which I cannot escape, will pass. I want to slip into the space between the seat and the door. I've witnessed annoyance, hurt, and spontaneous verbal combustion. This is the first time he's hit me.

A gas station turns up on the right. Dad pulls in. I am safe.

He is finally able to use the toilet. He returns with two wads of toilet paper in his hand.

"I'm sorry, son. Here, wipe your eyes." He hands one to me. "I just want to have a good time. That's what we came for, right? Now are we gonna have some good times?"

I try to smile. It's how I ensure this storm has passed. I'm relieved but I'm also enraged—only I can't show it. What's really going through my mind is that I hate my fat, smelly, shit-infested, process-serving, brain-damaged father.

We return to the campsite to blow up a giant yellow raft and paddle down the Au Sable River. Gliding down the bends of the river under the hot sun brings quiet over our band of fathers and sons. Exhaling, I feel my jitters subside. After an hour, we take a break on the shore of a sandy beach.

"Who wants to cool off?" says Dad. Without waiting for a reply, he bounds into the river.

He swims outward, and strokes right left, right left, while holding his head above water.

As we splash around, Bruce looks up and yells, "Oh shit!"

I look out. Dad is in the middle of the river, caught by the current. He breathes in hoarse breaths and coughs up jugs of water.

"Dad, Mark is stuck," Bruce calls out to Larry.

"Fuck," says Larry. "Mark, don't fight it. Don't fight the current. Try to ease your body to the left."

Dad chokes on water as the current carries him forward. His arm movements are sporadic. I freeze. Bruce yells, "Mark, veer left. It'll be OK."

"He's drinking the whole fucking river," says Larry.

I stand there, frozen. Blood is rushing to my head. I look up at the sky. I look down at the dirt. My heart beats fast. My ears burn.

An asphyxiating, choking sound emanates from the mouth of this human grizzly bear as his head bobs up and down. When he comes up, he spits. Huge rasps roar from his throat, and he inhales whatever air he can. No one is big enough or strong enough to help him.

Everyone yells but me. "Mark, move left! It's gonna be alright. Mark, relax, you'll get out."

We stand on the bank of the river, helpless. Am I scared that my father is going to drown? Or do I hope that the Au Sable River swallows him up once and for all? Is it possible to feel both?

After another moment he yanks himself free and treads water back to the shore. He coughs violently.

"You OK, big guy?" asks Larry. "I was afraid that current was gonna take you away."

"No sweat," says Dad. Pink as a balloon, burned from head to toe, and unshaken by his near drowning, he says, "This is the best camping trip ever."

Chapter Four

MOM AND DAD

M OM'S FATHER, ARTHUR, who was over fifty when she was born, was a Wayne County court clerk—the person who asks you to raise your right hand and swear over a Bible. Though he was a secular Christian, his puritanical demeanor was frightful. Tall, thin, bald, and cold, Arthur married a short, heavy, warm Jewess, twenty years his junior. He wore a suit to work every day and sat down for dinner each night in the same shirt and tie. He looked like the farmer from *American Gothic* minus the pitchfork and overalls. He was intolerant of childish behavior and frequently slapped my mother across her face for the smallest infractions. Mom's mother, Grandma Marian, was a full-time secretary for the Navy. Both parents earned steady government incomes and provided my mother a middle-class life. It was austere but stable and stayed that way after Arthur died of a heart attack when she was thirteen years old.

Dad's father, Jacob, emigrated with his large family from Lithuania to Montreal when he was eleven years old. A young man with hustle, he packed his few belongings and hitchhiked to Detroit when he was fifteen years old. He never became a legal citizen and never went back to Montreal. His first group of friends was the Purple Gang, a band of Jewish immigrants who were small-time bootleggers and bookies. Their hangout was the Schvitz, where they would make deals in the steam room, jump in the pool filled with cold water from the Detroit River, and then head upstairs to the restaurant for a T-bone steak.

After many financial ups and downs, Jacob gained a foothold in the scrap metal business, a thriving industry in the auto capital of the world. He landed a contract with the Pontiac GM factory, which sold him all its scrap. By the time my father was a teenager—the middle child between an older sister and a younger brother—the family lived in a large two-story home with a housekeeper and multiple refrigerators and freezers for the huge amounts of food that everyone consumed. Jacob hated banks and didn't trust the government. He saved his money in shoeboxes in the basement food pantry—the heart of the house. He gave my father his own car at age sixteen—an Oldsmobile 98 convertible in periwinkle blue. And he handed my father twenty-dollar bills (it was 1955!) any time he asked.

Dad was nicknamed Chip as in "chip off the old block." Though he was accepted to Cass Tech, the premier public high school in Detroit, he failed out when his father forced him to study chemistry instead of his passion, drawing. He stumbled through Cooley High by doing the least amount of work possible. He was not on a college track. His dad worked all the time and his mother, Louise, usually stayed in her bedroom or asleep on the couch. She suffered from migraine headaches. She was also addicted to barbiturates and was often stoned on the opioids of the '50s.

When my mom, Caroline, was a freshman at Mumford High, she spotted Dad and his gang, the Jokers, driving around town in his convertible. They were cool and exciting; she wanted to get to know this group of teenagers. Chip was the most gregarious and generous of the group—he was always the first to pick up the check—and he invited her to his senior prom. When he took her to the fancy Kingsley Inn restaurant beforehand, he told her to "order anything on the menu." But her mother had warned her, "If you're interested in a boy, and he takes you to dinner, do not order the most expensive thing on the menu." She chose the meat loaf and Dad became the first and the last boy she ever dated.

Mom was also an unremarkable student who hung out in her own little club with her two best girlfriends, Penny and Sheila. They often stayed at school through third period, when attendance was taken, and then fled in Sheila's car up to Cass Lake for a couple of hours to smoke cigarettes and talk about boys. These non-college-bound Jewish kids were like the characters from *Grease.*

By the time Mom started dating Dad at age fifteen, she was the only child of a widowed mother who worked full time. Chip introduced Caroline to a world full of camaraderie, fun, and love. Jacob adored her and called her "my princess." She was a welcome guest at the Seller house, which felt like a mansion compared to her own.

Before long, she was pregnant. Chip had just graduated high school and she was a senior about to turn seventeen. Dad asked her to marry him, and she agreed. Though Mom lost the baby early in the pregnancy, she still went through with the marriage. Her mom, Marian, had to accompany the teenage couple to City Hall and sign the marriage certificate because Mom was a minor. Her mother loved Chip as much as Jacob loved Caroline. Chip was lovable.

The first years of their marriage were exhilarating. They spent their honeymoon at the Hotel Edison in New York City. On another trip they saw Barbra Streisand in *Funny Girl* at the Winter Garden Theatre. They went out to dinner every night. Laurie was born and Jacob died, passing one of his two companies on to Chip. Poucher Gage and Tool, a specialized tool manufacturer, was a thriving business that grew exponentially when a US embargo on copper from China made its products even more essential. Chip took flying lessons and bought a four-seat plane. He rationalized that he could use the plane to visit his clients. He made Mom's greatest dream come true: owning a horse of her own. The horse's name was Cricket. Mom's favorite activity was to drive a half hour outside Detroit to ride Cricket in the beauty of the farm country.

But the horse didn't last. Neither did the plane, or the trips to New York. After he took over his father's business, Chip's spending exploded. Poucher was bankrupt months before The Accident left him brain-

damaged and temporarily paralyzed. Diminished physically and men-
tally, barely able to work, Dad was unpredictable—angry one moment,
a teddy bear the next, shut down at times, or enraged by the smallest
slight. Thrust into a life with no money, two small children, and a con-
valescent cheating husband, Mom did what she could to hold the family
together. Her glue came at a cost: She often seethed inside, expressing a
roiling sarcasm tinged with self-righteousness that her body could barely
contain. She could be warm and loving one day, cold and mean the next,
and cry uncontrollably from the emotional pain that each day delivered.

On a gentle summer evening a couple months before The Accident,
Mom borrowed her best friend Penny's red '68 Mustang convertible.
We went for a drive on Northwestern Highway to look at the horses at a
stable in West Bloomfield—Mom's favorite activity. Dad drove. Laurie,
who was seven, sat behind him in the back. I sat behind Mom. I was four
years old.

"Your mother had the most beautiful horse I've ever seen," said Dad.
"Her name was Cricket."

"God, did I love that horse," Mom said. "More than anything else in
the world."

"Where did you get him?" I asked.

"Her," said Mom. "We bought her from a breeder in Macomb
County."

"What's a breeder?" Laurie asked.

"A breeder is a person who helps animals to make babies."

"Did I come from a breeder?" asked Laurie.

Mom and Dad both laughed a little. "Of course, not," said Mom.
"You came from my tummy."

"Really?" said Laurie.

"Babies grow in their mommies' tummies," said Mom. "And after
about nine months, they come out into the world."

"Did I come from your tummy?" I asked.

Mom looked at Dad. And then she said, "You came from another
woman's tummy."

"Why's that?" I said.

"Because you were adopted."

"What's adopted?"

"Adopted is when you get to be chosen. You are the chosen child."

"The chosen child" was their answer to any question about adoption. Their goal was to make being adopted "the same." They said there is no difference between being adopted and being "biological" because "the love is the same." Mom barely acknowledged the existence of my birth mother. "I have loved you like my own since the day we brought you home. I'm your mother," she said with an emphasis on *I'm*. And I believed her—at first. I tried to think of my adoption as an objective fact—no different than having blue eyes. It was just part of what made me, me.

But as I grew older my feelings changed. When people learned that I was adopted, they reacted as if it was a rare phenomenon to be studied in psychology class. They asked if I knew my "real" parents—meaning biological parents—and "real" siblings, as if my actual parents and sibling were fake. They asked how it "felt" being adopted with no regard for how their insensitive questions were making me "feel," which was like a lesser being. This is what I did not say to their questions: "I don't know who or where I come from, and it makes me sad when I read the book *Are You My Mother?* because the bird finds its mother. But I don't."

All I knew was that, after my birth on October 16, 1964, I went to foster care. My parents brought me home at the end of January 1965, which meant that I was with someone else—I have no idea whom—for the first three months of my life. Some call this transitional period, along with the severing of the bond with the birth mother, "the trauma of adoption."

Forget trauma! Mom and Dad were throwing a party! My bris, the Jewish custom of circumcising newborn boys at a family gathering, was like a mini–bar mitzvah. Though purely ceremonial and, thankfully, not a reprise of the actual circumcision performed in the hospital, it was a huge celebration. "The Bris, starring Jeffrey Bruce Seller" was the title of their home movie that featured many family members and friends sporting the most up-to-date hairdos and colorful fashions of 1965. I brought joy and light into the Seller family. I slept peacefully and plentifully, smiled constantly, and inspired everyone with whom I came in contact to smile back. Therein lay the dichotomy of this adopted child: I glowed on the outside, but on the inside, faint feelings of isolation and loss that I could neither define nor voice lay dormant, waiting to express themselves in the future.

Chapter Five

MISS SHIVELY

THE SHORTCUT TO FROST MIDDLE SCHOOL requires hopping the chain-link fence behind our house and walking through the neighbor's yard. Then I walk two blocks to reach the busy road, Nine Mile, where there's a traffic light, installed after our neighbor Deena Cohen was hit by a car two years before. Just across Nine Mile is the school's back entrance, tennis courts, and ball field. I hate that field. During morning gym class, shoes wet from the melting fall frost, I dread running after a soccer ball I will never kick.

Between the building and the tennis courts there is a small parking lot for teachers. If the gold Pinto is in the lot, then I know Miss Shively is in her music room and it will be a great day.

I have loved Miss Shively since the first day of music class in sixth grade. She is pretty but not in an intimidating way. Her long, straight, dirty blond hair flows over her shoulders. She is thin and wears simple dresses. She never screams or loses her temper. She is a young teacher, under thirty, and is devoted to music, theater, and her students.

Miss Shively's popularity is strong enough to summon twenty boys to a 7:30 a.m. Boys Ensemble practice every Tuesday and Thursday. I join Bruce for baseball and flag football, and he joins me for Boys Ensemble. Composed of hockey players and baseball players, prepubescent sixth graders and randy eighth graders, our boys' ensemble learns songs from the Beatles to *My Fair Lady*.

The Winter Pops concert is a huge show every January. The school choirs and band perform, as well as a handful of student acts chosen by Miss Shively and the other music teachers. When audition slots open in December, I sign up and recruit Bruce to join me. We decide to perform a song called "Together (Wherever We Go)" from my favorite episode of *The Brady Bunch*.

To help students prepare for auditions, Miss Shively stays after school and gives coaching sessions. We sign up for as many sessions with Miss Shively as possible, which means that on Tuesdays that December, I see her three times a day, which means Tuesdays are my favorite day of the week. During one session we run overtime and she suddenly jumps up and says that she has to go get ready for a show that night. My interest piqued, I ask her what show she is doing. She explains that she is playing the Flower Seller in a production of *Oliver!* at a theater called Stagecrafters. I know that musical—we just did the song "You've Got to Pick a Pocket or Two" in Boys Ensemble.

"What's Stagecrafters?" I ask.

"It's a theater that does plays and musicals. I think this production is the biggest they've ever done because there are a lot of kids in it as well as adults."

"How old is the boy who plays Oliver?" I ask.

"He's the same age as you."

"That's amazing," I say, wondering what I need to do to be in a play at Stagecrafters.

BRUCE AND I PRACTICE "Together (Wherever We Go)" until Christmas vacation. The Winter Pops concert auditions are on the Friday right after the break and, when we enter the choir room, it's clear Miss Shively is no longer our coach, but the judge. She sits behind a table taking notes with two other teachers. She behaves with a formality that is different from our coaching sessions. Bruce and I launch into our routine, which instantly changes the environment. All three teachers start smiling. This buoys my confidence, and our performance grows as the number progresses.

We arrive at school on the Monday morning after the audition and the list of seven chosen acts is taped to the wall outside the choir room. Bruce and I are sixth graders, the low men on the middle school totem pole. We know that the eighth graders will be favored. I walk toward the list, my heart thumping in my chest. Our names and song are number six. We're in!

The concert is in the cafeteria, where there is a stage on one side of the large high-ceiling room and a couple hundred chairs. When our moment arrives, the curtains open and I am immediately blinded by the spotlight. It actually helps me concentrate; I feel like I am in a bubble. We perform the song flawlessly and receive hearty applause. It's the most fun I've ever had.

In the spring, Miss Shively directs *The Wizard of Oz* for the eighth graders. She recruits sixth graders to play the Munchkins. I am excited to be a Munchkin because it means I can spend more time with Miss Shively. I help build the yellow brick road after school and as I paint, we talk about theater.

"Do you know what? I want to do a production of *Oliver!* here next year," says Miss Shively. I'm thrilled by this news.

"I could finally play Oliver," I say.

"The Artful Dodger is the better part," she says. "That's where I see you. He has a lot of spunk and street smarts."

"If you say The Artful Dodger, then I say The Artful Dodger," I say.

"So, where do you get your talent—from your mother or your father?"

"Actually, neither," I say. "I'm adopted."

"I didn't know that."

"It's no big deal," I say.

"Your parents are very lucky."

I like the way Miss Shively talks about adoption. I like everything about Miss Shively—her direction of Boys Ensemble, the way she helped Bruce and me choreograph our number for the Pops concert, and, most of all, the conversations we have after school. Miss Shively isn't warm and fuzzy; she's consistent, reliable, and gently encouraging. Sometimes when painting bricks, we're both quiet. Yet, when I'm with her, I feel safe, understood. I like how she knows I would enjoy playing The Artful Dodger more than playing Oliver. She "gets" me better than anyone else. I wonder if my birth mother is like her.

That night, Mom and I wash the dishes together after dinner. I like washing dishes. It gives me a sense of accomplishment. It makes me feel as if everything is in its place. I'm happy to be home with Mom. It means that she and Dad won't wind up in an argument over something he did, or money he spent, or some withering look she made that angered him. I wash, Mom dries, and we both put them away.

"Have you finished all your tests? I can't believe you're almost done with sixth grade," she says.

"One more to go. The easiest one, I guess. Health. We just finished the last unit on human reproduction. Which is pretty absurd, considering that there isn't a kid in the sixth grade who doesn't know about sex and babies."

Mom nods and lets out a little "huh."

"We had this big discussion about abortion today and the Supreme Court decision that made it a woman's constitutional right."

"What do you think about that?" she asks.

"Well I definitely think that the government has no right to tell a woman what to do with her body."

"Damn right," she says.

"And I don't believe that life begins at conception either," I say.

"Yes."

"But it's weird, because I also know that I wouldn't be here today if my birth mother had had an abortion."

Mom looks at me and her eyes fill with tears.

"Son, you're the only good thing that's ever happened to me."

"Don't say that. What about Laurie? What about Dad?"

"Don't get me started on your father," she says.

I SPEND THE SUMMER looking forward to *Oliver!* I mow the back lawn and alternate sneezing with practicing lyrics to "Consider Yourself." I can't wait to see Miss Shively in September.

On a night in August, Laurie is babysitting for our neighbor while Dad is out serving papers, which means I'm lucky to be home again with just Mom. As we talk about the day, I feel her getting nervous. She has something she needs to tell me but is having a hard time saying it. I'm afraid she's going to tell me she and Dad are getting divorced. Finally, she just comes out with it:

"I'm pregnant, son."

"What?" I hear her, but I can't comprehend the sentence.

"I'm pregnant," she repeats.

This makes no sense. I was adopted because Mom couldn't have another child. This news makes me feel as if I'm falling backward, which happens every time I'm overwhelmed.

I know my mother loves me, maybe more than she loves anyone else. I know she loves Laurie. And I also know that my father is a source of frustration and pain interspersed with affection and fun. But Mom is not a touchy-feely, enthusiastic parent. Taking care of children doesn't fill her with joy. I am almost twelve, studying for my bar mitzvah; my sister is almost fifteen. It seems inconceivable that Mom would have another child with diapers and feedings in the middle of the night. She is already suffering from a form of female pattern baldness. She seems too old to have another child. Who will take care of this baby? Mom has been working at Cunningham's Drugs for a couple of years and we rely on her job for health insurance and extra income.

"Are you going to have it?" I ask.

"I thought about having an abortion," she says. "Your father and I had a big fight. 'I'll raise any child that comes into this world,' he said. 'Easy for you to say,' I told him. 'You're never around.' You know you can't talk to your father when he's made up his mind about something. He said he'd leave me if I had an abortion."

"I see," I say.

"But that's not what made me decide to keep it. When I thought about what you said about how you came into this world and how, if your birth mother had had an abortion, you wouldn't be here, I decided I had to have this baby."

"Well, then that's the answer."

Chapter Six

SPEAKING OF MURDER

THE GOLD PINTO ISN'T in the school parking lot on my first day of seventh grade. When I show up for music class, a new teacher named Miss Palme occupies the room. Miss Shively is gone. She left without saying goodbye. The new teacher says that she moved to Arizona.

I feel like a best friend has just disappeared. Or died. I am crestfallen. I need to talk to Miss Shively. I need to learn more about doing plays.

I remember that Miss Shively did shows at a theater called Stagecrafters. On a Saturday afternoon in late September, I find the phone number in the White Pages. With my heart beating so fast I have to breathe in deeply to steady my voice, I call the number. I'm hoping I can sign up for a play. A woman answers.

"Stagecrafters," she says in an accent that lands somewhere between Ohio and Kentucky. She sounds old-fashioned, as if she works in a five-and-dime.

"Hello," I say. "I'm calling to see if you have any, um, tryouts coming up."

"How old are you?"

"Eleven."

"You a girl or a boy?"

"Boy." I hate when people confuse me for a girl.

"We have a youth theater troupe called the Rag-A-Muffins but they just had their auditions for the fall play. I think the next play starts in February."

"Oh." That will be impossible because Mom is due to have the baby in March.

"But the adults are having auditions for the fall play this Monday and they need two children."

"Would it be possible, um, for me to try out?"

"You're not a member but hang on." She puts the phone down. I hear her yell for someone and then ask if auditions are open or closed. She returns to the phone. "If you come at seven p.m. on Monday then you can audition."

"Thank you," I say. "Oh, what's the name of the play?"

"*Speaking of Murder.*" Click.

After she hangs up, my heartbeat doesn't slow down but its quality changes. The quick, panicked fear of asking for something I want becomes the breathless excitement of doing something I want.

Mom works until ten p.m. on Mondays and Dad and I usually order pizza from Primo's and watch *The Rookies* and *S.W.A.T.* I ask him to take me to the auditions instead.

"Get in the car," he says without hesitation.

The theater is seven miles away, in a neighborhood of prewar houses. We find Bowers, a tiny street just off Main, and a green wooden clapboard church building with a painted sign of comedy-tragedy masks above the word *Stagecrafters.*

With rain threatening to come down any minute, we hustle up the front steps. I open the solid double door and enter a real theater. There is a sign-up sheet in the small foyer, which is separated from the auditorium by a few more steps and a black curtain. After placing my name on the list, I open the curtain to discover a small auditorium with real theater seats. This is the place where Miss Shively sang in *Oliver!* Though she is gone, I am standing in her theater.

A couple dozen people are scattered throughout the seats. I look around and scout three other boys: the competition. On the stage is the set of another show and two women reading a scene in which they are talking politely through gritted teeth. A long horizontal metal pole, four feet above their heads, spans the stage. It's not for curtains, it's to hold up the two walls of this theater converted from an old wooden church. When they finish reading, a man from the audience thanks them. No one applauds. He must be the director. This operation, with sets and a director and adults auditioning for a play, seems very professional despite the pole running across the stage. I will learn that theater people always find a way to work with obstacles.

A man calls out a name and a boy about my age—also with blond hair—walks to the stage. The woman in front of me leans into the woman sitting next to her to say that he was wonderful as Oliver last year. I am up against Oliver! He reads a scene with a tall man who is playing his father, and who is accusing him of shredding his stepmother's green dress. The boy denies it and becomes more upset as the scene progresses. He's pretty good, which only makes me more nervous.

The man sitting next to Don, the director, calls out, "Jeff Seller?"

"Here."

"Please read on page sixteen with Jim."

I rise from my seat, climb over my father, and join the man who read with Oliver. He is a big guy, almost as big as my father—like a giant looking down on me. He starts the scene and I look up at his eyes, which seem to be getting angrier by the second. I feel like I am in trouble. He accuses me of ripping up the dress. I become defensive and then angry. As his own impatience and incredulity expand, my outrage and fear explode and as I start crying, I hit him repeatedly on his chest with the script still in hand and wail, "I didn't do it. I didn't do it."

The scene ends. A few people applaud. I exhale a big breath and walk back to my seat. I know I've done a good job. I know I was better than the kid who played Oliver. I don't look at Dad. I wonder if he knows that while I was reading with the actor, I was thinking about the time that he hit me in the car during that camping trip. He doesn't say anything, but puts his large hand on my thigh and gives it a gentle squeeze.

An hour after we get home, the phone rings. It's the assistant director, Dave, saying that they'd like me to play Ricky, the son. I feel as if Miss Shively opened the door and I walked through it. He asks to speak to my dad, who talks to him for a moment about the schedule and driving. Dave lives nearby and offers to drive me to rehearsals, but he goes directly to work at a hospital after, so he can't drive me home. My father assures him that he or my mother will pick me up the three nights a week that we rehearse.

"Congratulations, son," he says after he hangs up. "I'm proud of you."

I smile. "Thank you."

"You don't need to thank me. You did it."

"No. For taking me to the audition."

"Anytime, son."

ON THE NIGHT OF the first rehearsal, I sit on my couch next to the front door and look out the window waiting for my ride. I'm delighted by the idea that I'm in an "adult play," which to me means practically professional. I anxiously look down at my watch, waiting for it to be 6:30 p.m. At 6:32 p.m., I start panicking: What if Dave forgot to come get me? Finally, a dirty, beige compact car pulls up in front of the house and I see him in the front seat. I bound out of the house with such force that I could run all the way to rehearsal.

"Hello," I say as I open the door and sit down in the passenger seat.

"Are you ready to get started?"

"Like you wouldn't believe," I say.

The first thing I learn when we arrive at the theater is that we don't rehearse on a stage. We rehearse in a basement room that they call "the green room" because a) it is painted a light lime green, and b) it is a theatrical tradition to call the space for congregating the green room. Dave gets busy applying masking tape to the floor to designate where the stage begins and ends. The director, Don, has a low, stentorian voice, dark and silver hair combed over his head, and a dark goatee.

Don places some ratty old furniture around the playing space and, once he is satisfied that it is in the right place, he calls me to come up and sit in the chair. I grab my script and jump to the chair.

"Where's your pencil?" Don asks.

"Sorry, I didn't know I needed one," I say.

"How are you going to write down your blocking? Dave, get this boy a pencil, please."

I don't know what blocking is, but I'm too embarrassed to ask. He might fire me and get the kid who played Oliver if I don't know. I grip the pencil in my hand as we start rehearsal.

I learn that blocking is physical movement—where and when the director tells you to move during the scene. I am the only actor on stage when the play begins, which means that I have all the blocking for the first hour of rehearsal.

"Wait, why aren't you writing down what I'm telling you?" asks Don.

"I can remember," I say.

Don rolls his eyes and proceeds.

My first scene is with the actress playing my stepmother. I enjoy doing the scene with an adult who is old enough to be my actual stepmother. I like making eye contact. I like that she treats me as her fellow actor and not as an eleven-year-old child.

When I come home from rehearsal that night, the first thing I do is count my lines: 168. It seems like a lot; I'm happy that my part is big. My role is pivotal to the plot: In this drawing room melodrama, a widower with two children has recently remarried. His children's nanny is secretly in love with him. Her mission is to kill the new wife by locking her in a safe that no one uses anymore and to frame the boy as the perpetrator so that she and her employer can live happily ever after.

Whether at school or at home, I'm constantly thinking about rehearsals. I love bringing the play to life. I'm also intrigued by every aspect of the process, and I closely watch Don block the scenes I'm not in, wondering how he knows where the actors should walk or cross or sit down. How does he make these decisions? Compared to the plays I did before, I prefer being in a play with adults instead of children. I learn that I enjoy expressing emotion, making eye contact, and watching other people's scenes.

I learn my lines by reciting each one five times in a row while standing up, which cements the whole speech in my head. The next challenge is to memorize my cues—the lines that the other actors say before mine. The key is to know the last sentence of each speech that precedes mine. This whole process is like playing a game of Concentration.

Don blocks the show over the first two weeks of rehearsal and then we go back to the beginning and start working on scenes without our scripts. While Don never tells me how to feel in a scene, he sometimes tells me to talk louder or softer, or to change where I'm standing a little bit. I don't receive many criticisms or compliments from Don. The freedom of running the scenes without scripts is like dropping the training wheels on a bike.

I am eager to move our rehearsals from the green room to the stage, which the set builders are transforming into a fancy home library that becomes more lifelike every day. Cases are filled with books. The carpet is real, as is the plush couch and sitting chairs. I am amazed by the enormity of this undertaking and my responsibility to begin the show alone on stage. I like spending time in this library of a fancy home, and dream that someday maybe I'll live in a home as nice.

Tech rehearsals—the incorporation of sets, costumes, and lights—are scheduled all day on a Saturday and Sunday. Dad is supposed to come home from work to drive me at noon. When he's twenty minutes late, and I'm about to be late for rehearsal, I call Mom at work. She is angry.

"See, that's why I didn't think this was a good idea," she says.

"That doesn't help me right now," I reply.

"Well, there's nothing I can do, Jeff. I can't leave work to take you."

"I get it. I'll talk to you later," I say. I'm panicked. Everyone at the theater is counting on me for this rehearsal. They can't start the show without me. I call Dave, the assistant director, who is already at the theater. "I'll be there in twenty minutes," he says, saving the day.

When Dad pulls into the side drive later that night, I'm both relieved that he wasn't shot while serving papers, and angry. He apologizes and says he forgot. After a big day at tech, I go to sleep early with my bedroom door open only to be awoken when Mom arrives at 10:30 p.m. and starts berating Dad for not driving me to rehearsal.

"See, this is exactly what I said would happen. You said you'd take care of it."

"Won't happen again," he says.

"Fat chance," she says. "You don't take care of anything but you."

"Here we go again," he replies.

"If you're out serving papers morning, noon, and night, then tell me why I'm trying to figure out how to pay all the bills?"

"Will you stop it? Your face is like a peach pit," he says.

"I'm working on my feet all day while carrying your baby. Fuck you."

"Caroline, your inability to be happy for one minute is sickening."

I quietly get out of my bed to shut the door so that the sound is muffled enough for me to sleep. This fight, which I caused, feels like a volcano getting ready to erupt. I pray the mountain cools off.

Eight performances are scheduled over three weekends. Both the Purim play and the school music concerts were one performance, so I am excited for the chance to perform this show multiple times. Each night, the stage manager calls "places," and I walk to my position on stage. When the lights come up, I feel a little bit of heat on my skin, and I step into my character with confidence. I cry, stomp my feet, bang on my father's chest, and enjoy going on the ride of the play, which concludes with my father slamming shut the safe door one last time (and this time, the nanny is locked inside, hoisted by her own petard) and saying, "Let's keep this damn door locked."

On the final weekend of the play, I sit in the men's dressing room looking into a mirror surrounded by light bulbs. A volunteer applies pancake makeup to my skin and a little bit of rouge to my lips. My blue eyes are illuminated by the bright lights. I observe their blue-green perimeter that outlines a lighter shade of blue within. They are luminescent and powerful. I understand why sometimes I'm mistaken for a girl. I've had family members tell me I'm handsome and aunts call me gorgeous. But I don't usually feel handsome or gorgeous. At school, people reserve those adjectives for more athletic boys like my friends Bruce and Jay, not me.

However, in front of this dressing room mirror, I see me. I see my bright eyes and my dirty blond hair and my smooth skin. I am ready to go onstage and bring my character to life. I feel good-looking. I feel like a winner.

Chapter Seven

A BABY AND A
BAR MITZVAH

THE MOUNT SINAI NATAL waiting room has a beige tile floor that is clean but looks dirty, as if forty years of expectant fathers' pacing has rubbed dirt from the bottom of their shoes into the wax that will never come out. The room is made chipper with curved plastic seats that alternate red with white. Outside the windows, ice slowly melts to reveal the beginnings of buds on the trees. It is the first day of spring.

Our whole family is there. Dad is like his twenty-four-year-old self, excited for the birth of another child whom he never expected and already loves. I am with Laurie, who is fifteen and a sophomore in a high school she hates. What do you talk about when you're at the hospital waiting for a new sibling to be born?

"You know you were born here, too?" Dad says to Laurie.

"I know," she says.

Am I happy to be here? Sort of. How awful not to say that I am giddy. I am concerned for the future—for the days and months and years ahead, after the euphoria of the birth of a baby boy recedes.

Over the past six months, I have subscribed to the hope that a new baby will bring joy to our family. I was happy when my mom announced, after the amniocentesis, that the baby was a healthy boy. We are unified, in a way we never have been, by this extraordinary year: a baby for Dad, a bar mitzvah for me, and a sweet sixteen for Laurie. Mom plans to take a couple months off work to care for the baby and then we will all take turns. Laurie promises to babysit. Dad will do the night shift. I am relieved that I will still have my own room where I can hide, escape, and dream.

During a planned C-section, Mom delivers Aaron at the exact time the doctors scheduled. His name begins with an "A" in memory of her late father, Arthur. When the doctor arrives to relay the good news, Dad is euphoric. Mom is less euphoric as they wheel her out of the delivery room. Her thin, oily hair shows the bald spots on her head. She looks spent on the rolling bed, as if she has just survived something grueling. She doesn't glow. This real-life scene doesn't match what I've seen on hospital shows on TV.

Two days later, baby Aaron is coming home in cute striped red and white pajamas that make him look like a candy cane. As Dad walks to the parking lot to get the car, Mom sits in a wheelchair with Aaron in her lap. Laurie and I are thrilled to be bringing home a newborn baby. Can a baby make parents more loving toward one another? Can a baby make two siblings kinder to each other? Life seems so much happier that I wonder if Aaron is channeling baby Jesus. I become an expert diaper changer and bottle feeder. I elicit the most satisfying burps. I call his little legs "chicken legs." Big brother is a new role I embrace.

ON OCTOBER 15, 1977, the day of my bar mitzvah, I enter the marble lobby of the great Temple Israel to see the rabbi speaking quietly in Mom's ear with concern on his face. Rabbi Syme is a towering figure in the community—respected, beloved, and feared—who delivers inspired sermons in a powerful baritone that sounds like the voice of God. He gently takes hold of Mom's elbow and turns her one step away from Dad, Laurie, and me. We have just finished taking bar mitzvah photos in the sanctuary and guests will be arriving soon.

"The ladies in the kitchen just told me that there's very little for the kiddush," says the rabbi quietly to Mom.

The kiddush is the celebration that follows the Saturday morning religious service that includes punch, wine, and copious amounts of pastries. The expectation is that the family of the bar mitzvah boy provides a huge "spread." The big party is a dinner dance on Saturday night.

"I did exactly what was asked," she says. "I provided what it said on the sheet," she says. My mother looks like a girl in trouble.

"Are you sure there aren't any more trays in the trunk of the car?" he says.

"We brought everything in," she says.

"The ladies don't think there's enough for the Saturday school students."

My heart thumps. I am standing five feet away, turning red.

"The instructions said we could order cookies to go with the punch for the students and that the adults would eat the other pastries," says Mom.

"I see. That's just not how it's usually done," he says.

The rabbi pauses. He is thinking about what to say next. He looks over at me and sees the concern on my face.

"OK. I'll explain it to them," he says. "It will all work out, I'm sure."

My bar mitzvah is in forty-five minutes. My Torah portion, or Bible story, Noah, is ready. I am not nervous about singing prayers or reading from the Torah in a giant sanctuary in front of a couple hundred people. I'm more worried that we don't have enough food for the congregation and that it will reflect poorly on me.

Temple Israel has given me an enormous gift and a painful burden. It gave me my first experience in the theater, the Purim play, for which I have always been grateful. But, in many other instances, this wealthy temple that caters to its many affluent members has underscored my shame at being poor and my feeling that I am less than the other kids and families who attend.

I trudged to Hebrew school twice a week since fourth grade to master its unique hieroglyphs. When Hebrew class ended at 5:30 p.m. and the other kids ran to their parents' cars, I hung back and tried to disappear.

Mom wouldn't arrive for another twenty minutes because she got off work at 5:30 p.m. On the coldest days of winter, I would hang out in a vestibule or the boys' bathroom before a janitor would kick me out. My goal was to keep moving so that no one would stop and ask me where my parents were, or worse, insist on giving me a ride home—to Cardboard Village.

The previous year, I had a teacher who was explaining the history of the Warsaw Ghetto. During the lesson, he said, "The Jews lived in very poor conditions. They lived in tiny houses or apartments and weren't allowed to leave the walls of the ghetto. Oftentimes many family members shared one or two small rooms. There was no medicine. They went days or weeks with little or no food. Potatoes, rice, whatever root vegetables they could scrounge up. Can you think of any modern-day equivalents to the Warsaw Ghetto?"

A girl spoke up. "I don't think that exists. We don't have those kinds of poor people anymore."

"Can you think of anywhere in America today that might be similar?"

No one spoke up.

"Let me give you an example. There's a neighborhood in Oak Park, only a couple miles from here. It's behind the A&P on Nine Mile Road."

My skin started burning.

"All the houses are small, and they're made without bricks. They don't have basements. And instead of garages, they have something called carports. They are what you might call the lower class."

The way he said the word "they" meant that "they" were inferior to everyone in this classroom of the comfortable.

"Would you call that a ghetto?"

"Maybe," said the girl.

"There's a colloquial name for it. They call it Cardboard Village."

"Kind of like 'The Ghetto,'" said the girl.

"In a modern sense, yes," said the teacher.

I stayed still and silent, holding my breath, trying to resist the formation of tears behind my eyes, hoping that this discussion would pass, hoping I would not be discovered. How I hated this place.

Mom planned the details of my bar mitzvah, and I knew it was a huge undertaking. I asked if we could have the big party at The Raleigh House on Telegraph, the location of the best bar mitzvah I attended. Mom and Dad said yes even though they couldn't afford it. We chose the least expensive meal: chicken. Mom loved shrimp, so she added an hors d'oeuvre table with a gigantic bowl of shrimp cocktail. Even though it wasn't kosher, Dad said it was "fine" because we were Reform Jews.

Between the dessert table, flowers, photographer, live band, and kiddush, the budget has exceeded anything my parents can afford. So I'm not surprised Mom chose the least expensive option for the kiddush and I'm sure the ladies in the kitchen at the wealthiest temple in Detroit were not used to that.

Despite the rabbi's words ringing in my head, I focus on my recitation of Noah, delivering the story of the deluge and God's chosen survivor as if it were a play. It feels like a successful stage performance.

We have a wonderful party that night. The gigantic bowl of jumbo shrimp never runs out. The band, called The People's Choice, sounds great. I am lifted in a chair during "Hava Nagila." The winners of the dance contest receive a copy of Fleetwood Mac's album *Rumours*. Standing before the crowd, getting ready to give my thank-you speech, I open the jacket of my three-piece brown suit and pull out a bunch of envelopes—many cards with checks inside.

"It's nice to be Jewish," I say. Laughter from the crowd. I thank my parents and the guests from out of town. I thank everyone for showing up and supporting me. I feel comfortable for the first time today. I've done a fine job, and I know it. Mom and Dad have done a great job. I am proud of them, maybe for the first time.

Unfortunately, my parents resume their war of attrition right after my bar mitzvah. Dad spends money on food and clandestine trips to the pool hall and stays out serving papers at all times of the day and night. Yet his time away does not translate into more dollars for the family. Mom speaks to him with scorn and makes snide comments that only heighten the conflict. I try not to pay attention.

My Hanukkah gift is a bout of pneumonia, which I contracted right after singing with the children's chorus of Michigan Opera Theatre in a production of *Carmen* at the Music Hall. Sitting on the couch on December 26, watching the five o'clock news, I'm drinking water, trying to calm my violent phlegm-saturated coughs. It's getting dark outside. The snow is piled a foot high outside the window. Aaron bounces in his baby seat on the floor. Mom is doing some dishes at the kitchen sink. Dad is at the dining room table eating a sandwich and reading the *Detroit News*. A conversation I've been tuning out starts to pick up speed and volume. I feel the temperature rise. The tone turns dark.

"I'm asking you a question. Did you pick up the mail?" Mom asks Dad.

"I suppose so," he replies.

"Were there checks?"

"I don't remember," he says. It is impossible to know if he is being flippant, condescending, or genuinely forgetful. All three are possible.

"Did you cash them? Where's the money?"

He doesn't respond.

"Hello?" she says.

"I'm not talking about this with you," he says.

"The car payment was due two weeks ago," she says.

"Not my problem."

"It's your fucking car," she says. "And the mortgage is due the first week of January."

"You always do this."

"Do what?"

"Harping on me. Stop treating me like a child. You never stop," he says.

"You know what? You're full of shit. And I'm sick of dealing with it every fucking day of my life. I've been putting up with your shit for over twenty years, and I'm the asshole who takes care of the kids and goes to work every day so our son who's sitting right in front of you can go to the doctor."

I watch my father's skin turn from pink to red. Water starts to fill his eyes. When the dam of his bruised feelings bursts, there is no stopping the rage that will ensue: the helpless screaming; the lumbering frame losing all control. He is a one-man stampede in a house that is too small to absorb his unruly movements.

He lurches out of the chair and strides toward Mom at the kitchen sink. I jump from the couch and run to the kitchen doorway. I know he is about to hit her.

"Stop it!" I shout. "Don't you touch her."

He jerks his head in my direction and stops. He pauses for a beat and then bounds by, pushing me out of his way. "I'll do whatever the fuck I want," he says. He blasts through the living room, opens the front door, letting in a cold wind, and then realizes he isn't wearing his coat. He turns back, rips his coat from the dining room table, toppling the chair. Then he storms out the front door.

Mom walks to the door and closes it. She sits down at the table and lights a cigarette. "I'm sorry, son," she says. "I'm sorry this year has to end like this."

Aaron starts crying. I return and rock him in his bouncy seat. I read him *One Fish, Two Fish, Red Fish, Blue Fish*. I focus on his pain to try to forget my own.

When I get in bed that night, I look out the window. Icicles drip from the roof and snowflakes whip through the bare branches of the maple tree. Wheezing from pneumonia, trying to calm my burning chest, spitting up bits and bulks of phlegm that feel like the nodules of my lungs, I can see.

I can see that my sister will suffer and meet trouble; that my brother will be caught up in a war of bitterness against which he has no defense and no means of escape; that my mother and father will continue to yell and scream at each other and that sometimes my father will threaten her physically; that I will continue to wheeze under the cloud of Pall Mall smoke that is essential to my mother's ability to get through the day; that my father will come home in a few hours, make up with my mother, eat until oblivion, and then lose his temper the next day or the day after that for the smallest slights, infractions, and hurts; that he will never provide for the groceries, or doctor's visits, or car fixes, or mortgage payments on which we all rely; that we will be stuck in Cardboard Village for years to come.

But I also see that I will get out. That I will climb to the top of that maple tree and fly away.

Chapter Eight

PLAYS, MUSICALS, AND A TALK WITH DAD

O N A FREEZING AFTERNOON in January 1978 I trudge home from school wrapped in a navy blue down jacket, mittens, and a wool ski cap. Red and white moon boots shield my feet from the snow and ice. At Nine Mile Road I hit the button for the traffic light, then cross the street and walk toward the house with the backyard opposing ours. I walk up the empty driveway, then climb over the chain-link fence—right foot into one hole, left foot up a foot higher. At the top of the fence I jump into our yard. The ground is dirty—gray and yellow snow, strewn with mud and poop from Keelee, her figure eight still carved into the muddy ice.

Jumping that fence marks the moment I pass from one world to the next. It separates the world in which I'm a thirteen-year-old from the world in which I'm a virtual parent.

I enter the back door into the tiny utility area, then remove my boots, coat, hat, and mittens.

"Hello," I say, a little loud so Mom can hear me wherever she may be.

"Hi, son," comes the answer. It's a warm salutation, but not a happy one—laced with love but also worry and drain.

Mom is in the living room with ten-month-old baby Aaron. She kisses me hello, puts out her cigarette, takes one more sip of her Maxwell House

Instant Coffee, rinses her cup in the kitchen sink, and then puts on her coat to leave for work. Her shift at Cunningham's Drugs is from four to ten p.m.: six hours for four days a week plus eight hours on Saturdays get her over the thirty-hour threshold to maintain our health and dental insurance. Her pay is now five dollars per hour, which means that her six-hundred-dollar monthly income pays for the mortgage, her car payment, and food for a couple of weeks regardless of what Dad earns.

My job is to babysit Aaron until Mom comes home at 10:30 p.m. or Dad shows up. I take this responsibility seriously. I read to him, feed him dinner in the high chair, and bathe him after. I am expert at diapers— fast and efficient. I make funny faces that elicit squeals of laughter. Aaron has soft light brown hair, blue eyes, and a delightful smile. He manifests the best physical qualities of Mom and Dad. Taking care of this cute new member of the family makes him happy and gives me a sense of order. But it also makes me feel isolated. Because Mom leaves immediately after I get home from school, I barely see her. And being with Dad makes me lonelier because, as much as he loves me, we can't build on a conversation without starting from the beginning. Caring for a baby brother every day is like being a single parent.

I hear Dad pull up in the driveway at 4:30 p.m. By the sound of his car door slamming, I can tell he's unhappy. I'm already tense as I watch him open the front door, frowning and oblivious to anyone or anything around him. Though I'm not in trouble, I'm wary of his dark mood. He goes to the kitchen where he makes his egg and cheese sandwich and sprawls out on the living room carpet reading the *Detroit Free Press.* An hour later, he gets up.

"I'm going out to serve a few papers, son. I'll be home in a couple hours." I'm relieved that he's leaving even though I keep wondering why, if he works so much, he earns so little.

My babysitting responsibilities also mean less time to spend with Bruce and the other kids who attended my bar mitzvah last fall. Plus, I am about to get busy with another play, which is more fun than hanging out with kids who goof around and smoke pot.

On Super Bowl Sunday I could care less if the Denver Broncos beat the Dallas Cowboys. All I care about is going to Stagecrafters, where the Rag-A-Muffins youth theater is holding tryouts for *The Adventures of Popcorn Pete*. I win the part of a clown named Jack-in-the-Box, which provides many opportunities to delight the audience with silliness and laughter. During our run of four shows, I pay attention to how each performance is going over with the audience and observe a few things. First, the play is not very good. Not much happens in its sixty minutes; there is not a strong conflict. Second, the title is silly. Who wants to see a show called "Popcorn Pete"? And finally, we never play to more than half the house. Maybe it's winter; maybe there's a lot of snow on the ground. Or maybe the lousy script with the infantile title was not a good choice.

"Who picks the play?" I ask Mrs. Janney, the mother who oversees the Rag-a-Muffins.

"The Play Reading Committee," she says. "They read plays all year and then make recommendations to the board."

"And who's on the board?" I ask.

"Kids like you who like to read the plays and lead the group. I'm just here to help. You kids do all the work."

I know what I need to do next: 1. Get on the Play Reading Committee; and 2. Get on the board.

Beyond taking on more responsibility at Stagecrafters, this is the winter in which I experience a whole new world of theater: touring Broadway musicals. It starts when Mrs. Finn, the free-spirited fifty-year-old middle school librarian, tells me that there is a Broadway show I need to see at the Fisher Theatre called *Shenandoah*. It's a musical about the American Civil War and how it challenges a large family in Virginia. I ask my parents if we can see it. They want me to go, but they can't afford four tickets.

"Take your son," Mom says to Dad. "You'll have a nice time."

Dad and I go to the Ticketron counter at Hudson's, which is the beginning of remote box offices, and buy two tickets in the mezzanine for ten dollars each, for a Tuesday in January. At home for dinner the night of the show, Mom prepares a shrimp salad that has the pungent aroma of boiled crustacean enveloped by tangy, lemony Miracle Whip and celery. I eat quickly while watching the clock, making sure that we are out the door by 7:15 p.m. to drive to downtown Detroit for the eight o'clock curtain.

This is my first trip to the Fisher Theatre. *Fiddler on the Roof* played its first out-of-town tryout here, and the Jewish community felt a sense of ownership over the success of the show. The theater is a mid-century modern auditorium with gold seats and warm oak-paneled walls; it is ensconced in the limestone Art Deco skyscraper the Fisher Building. Walking through the marble lobby of the building, which I learn is called an arcade, and then into the theater, I am struck by the sense of occasion. Something special is happening here. Something people care enough to buy tickets in advance for, to drive downtown on a Tuesday night in cold January and then line up to take their seats in a warm, golden auditorium.

The first scene, which takes place in a church, makes me lean forward in my seat. I love the set and the lighting—its ability to project ethereal light, sunlight, or moonlight, the way it changes during big dance numbers. When the father, played by a musical theater star named John Raitt, steps forward and sings a song called "I've Heard It All Before," declaring that he wants nothing to do with the war, I am riveted by his purpose, his passion, his love for his family. He sings as if he's talking directly to me. Act Two leads off with a number called "Freedom" sung by the daughter-in-law and a young enslaved boy about my age. It's the best song in the show and receives the biggest audience response. I love it.

And then I feel a tingle in my stomach. The kind of tingle in the base of the belly that sends a tickle to the back of the throat. Then a cramp followed by a painful rumble that pays no attention to the events transpiring on the stage. My eyes are happy. My ears are happy. But tragedy is befalling my stomach. A deep, dark force of something—shrimp and Miracle Whip—is rising up. I stand in the dark theater and excuse myself as I slide my way into the aisle then sprint to the bathroom.

I reach a stall, pull up the seat, and throw up. My stomach constricts and sends up copious amounts of shrimp and celery. It's loud, it's painful, and it's ugly. After a pause, I sit on the floor trying to calm my body. I'm shaking a little and I have the chills. But I'm determined to watch the rest of the show. I go to the sink, wash my hands, and rinse my mouth. I wince in the mirror a little and then return to the auditorium where the usher nods and lets me back in.

The next month, Dad takes me to see *Pippin*, recommended by one of the lawyers he works for, but we know nothing about it. The musical opens on a dark stage. As the eerie music begins with a soft drum and the echo of voices, many pairs of hands are illuminated. Unattached to bodies, they dance in the dark space. A narrator emerges from the darkness and leads us through a number that includes hands, hips, and magic tricks by an ensemble dressed in vivid, sexy costumes. It changes my idea of what theater can be.

Though the show takes place in the Middle Ages, there is nothing old-fashioned about it. The set is a series of backdrops made of rope, like strands of muscle. The music, which is nothing like *South Pacific*, gives me goose bumps. It sounds a little like songs that play on the radio when I'm in the car with Mom—James Taylor or Carly Simon. When the character Pippin sings "Corner of the Sky," I feel like I'm him. He's singing about concerns I'm wrestling with at age thirteen: "So many men seem destined to settle for something small, but I won't rest until I know I'll have it all." The story of a young prince who rejects his royal family to run away and find his purpose in life feels like mine—minus the royal part.

Dad and I sit in the mezzanine again and I have no stomach trouble, but about halfway through I need to go to the bathroom—except there's no intermission. The show is dazzling, and I can't leave my seat. At the end of the play, after Pippin rejects the narrator's offer of fame and glory by going up in flames, the narrator takes away all the sets and lights. All that is left is the back wall of the theater. Pippin is on an empty stage with his new wife and child. He embraces love and family over grandiosity. The last words of the show are "Ta-da." I'm exhilarated at the curtain call and run to the bathroom following the performance.

A month later, Dad takes me to *A Chorus Line*, the musical that the directing staff of *Popcorn Pete* talked about nonstop. Once again, I'm amazed that this show is so different from the others. There are no sets and costumes. The dancers, who are *playing* dancers, wear leotards, T-shirts, shorts, and tights. And yet, through music, movement, and lighting, they make beautiful shapes and patterns on the stage while revealing intimate secrets about themselves through contemporary songs. What is so compelling is that the musical takes place today. It's about real people with real problems. They talk a lot about childhood, puberty, and sex, and several of the men are gay. I notice that they are funnier than the other characters, but also more pained. I'm in love with theater more than ever. I save my weekly allowance to buy the albums to *Pippin* and *A Chorus Line* and listen to them over and over again.

On the first Sunday night in June, Mom, Dad, and I are watching an episode of *60 Minutes* about Russians who live to be a hundred years old. Dad rubs Mom's feet in an act of love that makes me feel happy. After it ends, an award show for Broadway comes on. It's the Tony Awards and it takes place in a Broadway theater. The first number is about a fancy, sleek train called the 20th Century, which looks amazing on stage. Then I watch a song by a bunch of teenagers, some my age, from a show called *Runaways*. I'm amazed that a Broadway show is populated by all kids. Then a small group of Black performers sing a medley of songs by a jazz musician named Fats Waller. The group is led by a woman whose voice is so bright, so hot, it could sear a steak. Her name is Nell Carter and she emanates the power of the sun. I'm mesmerized.

ON THE LAST DAY OF EIGHTH GRADE, Joanne Cooper, who is in my year, has a party at her house to celebrate the end of middle school. Her dad is a Michigan state senator, which gives him a level of prominence and achievement far above any of our parents. He is also absent, recently separated from Joanne's mother, who also doesn't appear to be home during the party. Kids occupy the family room, living room, and kitchen, where large plastic bottles of Mountain Dew and open bags of Lay's and Doritos sit on the kitchen counter. The soundtrack to *Saturday Night Fever* plays on the stereo—wall-to-wall Bee Gees with a little Yvonne Elliman thrown in.

Bruce is with his girlfriend, Lori Resnick. I've never had a girlfriend. I fantasized all year about asking Paula McCreary, a small, pretty girl with an adorable tiny nose, to "go around," which is the lingo kids in Oak Park use for being a couple, but I never worked up the courage. I was sure she would reject me—too skinny, too short, insufficiently masculine.

My first kiss was last fall with Marcy Cohn, two weeks before my bar mitzvah. It happened at a party in the basement of Mark Seuries's house during a game of Truth or Dare. Marcy and I had one trait in common: We were both prepubescent. It was my first time Frenching, and I liked touching our tongues, even though our teeth bumped while we were kissing.

In Joanne's family room, I'm making out with Debbie Edmonds, who played Dorothy to my Scarecrow in the fifth grade. When I open my eyes, all I see are limbs, teenage legs hanging like entangled linguine off the long sectional gray couch. Most of these legs are clad in blue jeans—Levi's or Lees, with Keds or Pumas or Stan Smith Adidas covering the many feet of the boys and girls who are marathon necking. If I look sideways, I see T-shirts, halter tops, or long-sleeved Qiana prints ripped off from John Travolta in *Saturday Night Fever*. It's the second time I've kissed a girl and the last time I will kiss anyone for the next six years. I like the feeling of being entangled with Debbie's body. Her lips and tongue are enveloping and playful.

These parties are complicated. Doing stuff with the girls makes me nervous. The conversations are stupid. But being included is better than watching *Donny & Marie* alone at home on a Friday night. At the end of the party, Bruce, Jay, Lori Resnick, Lisa Cutler, and I go to our friend Harvey's house.

"So let's go around the circle and everyone has to say something about everyone else," says Lori. "Say something that bothers you about each person and something that you like." After a few rounds of kids teasing each other, Lori turns to me.

"Jeff, I've wanted to say this for a while," says Lori.

"What?" I say, nervous.

"No offense, and I want you to know it's OK, but I want you to know that you're gay."

"What?"

"I think you're gay."

I freeze. My heart thumps and jumps. I feel as if pins are pricking my face. I blink my eyes to make sure tears don't leak out.

"No, I'm not," I say.

"It's OK, but I think you are."

"I don't know what you're talking about."

"There's nothing wrong with it," Lori assures me.

"I've never even thought about it before."

"So, thank me," she says.

"No. I'm not," I say again.

"I'm just saying." Lori shrugs.

No one says anything. No one comes to my defense, but no one teases me either.

It's true that I have never thought about it before. Outside of kissing two girls, one of whom was two hours ago, I haven't thought about sex.

Jay and the girls go home. Bruce and I camp out on the floor of Harvey's room. Bruce always likes to talk in the dark at the end of these summer days. "I think I'm going to go all the way with Lori this summer," he says. "I mean, if my dad lost his virginity at fifteen, I've got to lose mine before. I've got four months to go."

"Uh-huh," I respond.

"Just so you know, I don't care about what she said."

"I still don't know what she was talking about."

"It doesn't matter," says Bruce.

BY AUGUST, summer is getting old. I'm sick of hanging out and doing nothing with my friends. It is too hot, but we finally have air conditioning thanks to Grandma Marian, who gave Mom and Dad money for new furniture, carpet, and cooling.

After making my favorite Hamburger Helper with beef and tomato sauce for dinner and then putting Aaron to sleep, I sit on the front porch in an aluminum lawn chair with fraying webbing to continue reading *Harvest Home*, a novel I found buried in the small linen closet that houses the few books and records from Mom's collection. I am drawn to this story of a family from New York who move to a small, idyllic country village in Connecticut. As their first year progresses, they slowly get consumed by pagan assemblies led by the women of the village. Men, it turns out, are the human sacrifices of the rituals.

Mom and Dad pull up as the sun goes down. They are returning from a five-day vacation to Las Vegas, a reward they've given themselves after Laurie's sweet sixteen, my bar mitzvah, and Aaron's first birthday. They get out of the car smiling.

It is the first time since I was a baby that they have taken a trip together. It feels like a sign that our family has taken a big step forward—to be happy, to do fun things together, to be like other normal families. Maybe we are doing better.

The feeling doesn't last.

One week after they return home, I am in the living room with Aaron when I hear an argument emanating from their bedroom. I can't hear much. All I can make out is Mom saying, "Will you ever fucking stop?" Stop what? I'm not sure. What is clear is the angry tone, the hurt, the rising volume, and the tension of waiting for the explosion—a chair flying, a body flinging into a wall. But this time, the eruption emanates from Mom. The door bolts open; she runs down the hall screaming, "I never want to see your fucking face again!"

I freeze. Dad comes bounding out of the bedroom. He is red. His step is unsteady. He does not look at me or Aaron or Mom. His direction is the front door.

"Get the fuck out of this house!" she yells.

He heads out the door. Mom walks over and slams it shut.

"Your father and I are getting a divorce."

The blood drains from my head when she says these words. It feels like being shocked by a light socket. It doesn't matter that Dad is unpredictable, combustible, and unable to remember what has taken place yesterday. It doesn't matter that Mom is often sullen, angry, and sarcastic. It doesn't matter that we live in Cardboard Village. What matters is that we are still a family. A family who enjoys eating dinner together during the school year and barbecuing at the park in the summer. A family who watches *60 Minutes* together on Sunday nights.

Mom goes into the kitchen, lights up a cigarette, and then sits down at the dining room table. Dad isn't home when I go to bed that night, but he is at the table reading the paper when I wake up the next morning. The storm has passed. The next day is normal. And the days after that. I finish reading my novel about women who gather in the woods at their annual Harvest Home ritual to slit men's throats, cut out their tongues, and then fertilize the field with their blood.

A couple of weeks later, Dad is home with Aaron and me. It's the evening and Mom is working her four-to-ten p.m. shift at Cunningham's. I bake Empire Kosher chicken breasts with soy sauce for dinner. After, we are sitting on the couch as the evening light falls through the shutters onto the carpet. Keelee is lying on the floor next to me.

"First-class dinner, son."

"Thanks."

"I owe you an apology, son, for what happened between your mother and I last week."

I am surprised. He usually doesn't remember their fights.

"Thanks," I say.

"I didn't adopt you to leave," he says.

"OK."

"Because I'm not going anywhere."

"OK."

"I'm going to see someone to try to help me. I'm, um, going to a psychiatrist," he says.

"Oh." I pause, unsure what I'm supposed to say. "What made you decide to go?"

Dad pauses. "I was, um," he lets out a little blubber explosion from his lips. "I've been what you might call a playboy, son."

"I don't know what that means," I say.

"I was involved with another woman."

I become dizzy. Though I am sitting on the couch, I feel like I am falling backward. Overwhelmed again.

"I thought you knew, son."

I didn't know anything. "Um, no."

"I thought you knew that it was Daryl's mom."

"Daryl from the camping trip?" I say.

"Yep," he says.

For the previous summer's camping trip, Dad arranged to bring along another boy named Daryl whom I didn't know. I was twelve, Bruce was thirteen, and this boy—tall, lanky, and introverted—was sixteen. Larry tried to loosen him up with jokes and made up a nickname for him: Radar, a reference to the character from the TV series *M*A*S*H* who was nerdy but industrious, with lots of equipment attached to his belt. I didn't understand why my father brought him on this trip. I was annoyed he was interfering with something that was ours—Bruce's and mine—but I thought he was doing a good deed by helping this young man.

"His father was in my graduation class. Your mother and I met them again at my twentieth reunion last year."

As soon as he says it, I remember going with him to the Westland mall, where we went to the department store's ladies' clothing section. He talked to a woman who was working behind a glass counter. He told me she was the wife of his high school buddy.

"Oh."

"I thought you already knew," he says. "I thought that's why you didn't like Daryl."

"I didn't not like Daryl. I didn't know Daryl."

"Oh," he says.

We sit silently for a while.

"I'm glad you're going to a psychiatrist," I say.

"Thanks, son."

I believed Mom when she told me that intercourse, or "making love," was the purest expression of love between a man and a woman. I assumed she and Dad lived by those values. We occasionally witnessed them getting ready for bed or taking a nap in the afternoon. They had a phrase they used for spooning: they called it "making a chooch," like a choo-choo train. I was a little grossed out by the idea of my parents having sex. But I was also comforted by their affection and intimacy. If Mom and Dad were making a chooch, we were going to be OK.

I thought I knew everything there was to know about my dad—from teenage Joker to wooer of my mother, to bankrupt businessman, to wandering process server. His love helped make his impulsiveness and temper tolerable. But I never thought he was a liar. After this conversation, I can never see him the same way. I try to forget it. To erase it. I don't succeed.

AS HIGH SCHOOL BEGINS, all my relationships are changing. I avoid spending time with Dad and, when we're together, fail to hide my anger, which seeps out in withering faces and condescending words. When he perceives my disgust, he blows up at me. I'm no longer friends with Bruce and the kids who attended my bar mitzvah because we no longer have anything in common. And I still haven't started puberty, which makes changing in the locker room before swimming class embarrassing.

I don't have one friend who is a boy, but I do make one new friend in the fall of sophomore year, a tall, heavy senior named Miriam Sherbin. We sit near each other in the Mixed Choir and have fun conversations about art and pop culture. She loves Woody Allen movies and smart dramas. We go see *Kramer vs. Kramer* together at the Americana Theatre. After, we go to a restaurant in Birmingham at 220 Merrill Street, which is in a handsome redbrick building with a slate tile roof and mullions in the windows. We nickname it 220 Meryl Streep. It feels sophisticated, like the life I want to inhabit when I escape from Cardboard Village. We order cheesecake and hot chocolate for dessert. I pay for these ventures with money I earn babysitting on Saturday nights for a young couple who live nearby.

In late January 1980, I'm in my bedroom after dinner studying for finals. I type my final paper for composition class on my Smith Corona typewriter and begin studying for the dreaded biology test, where I'll be lucky to eke out a C. I can't memorize the strange words and functions that make up the inner workings of cells. Lying on my stomach, trying to memorize the differences between a membrane and cytoplasm, I start rubbing my pelvis against the bed. I have never done that before. My penis starts to get hard. It feels good. I continue pushing my pelvis into the bed. Then I get the idea to put a pillow under my pelvis. It feels a little softer to mash my pelvis and penis into the pillow. I undo the top button of my Levi's and unzip the front. Now my underwear is rubbing against the pillow and my penis is becoming even harder. I continue rubbing. Then an eruption happens that I've never experienced before. It starts in my penis and balls and spreads through my whole body. I get dizzy for a second. My underpants are wet. The front is spotted with an opaque white liquid that has a strong smell—almost like chlorine but not that strong, a little sweeter. I zip my pants up and get a tissue from the bathroom.

Now I know. At age fifteen, I've finally discovered what it means to "jerk off." I like it.

The next day I come home from school, and before anyone else is home, I do the same thing again. It feels good. The next day, same thing.

In my tiny closet there's a blanket that Mom stored after Grandma Marian died. It's a pale blue comforter made of a silk-like material, soft and smooth. I pull it out and place two pillows next to one another the long way. I place the blanket on top of the pillows and create a crack in between the two pillows. I place my hard penis in between them and start moving my pelvis back and forth. I'm fucking the space in between the pillows and it's the best feeling ever.

My sessions become a daily event, in the hours right after school before my parents return home. I imagine that I'm fucking a girl from American government class named Abby. She's skinny and, with her big blond hair that swirls around her face, looks a little bit feline. I like the fantasy of putting my penis into her vagina.

One night, as I start to gently pump my penis, a boy from my swimming class, Adam Wasserman, pops into my head. I start to imagine that I'm pumping his penis. And it feels even better. I want to touch his hard penis and pump it until it explodes. Then I imagine touching his chest, sculpted a little bit from swimming. I feel his hard curves and touch his nipples. All of this electrifies me. My explosions are bigger, more exciting, and more pleasurable. *I am not gay*, I think to myself. I still love fucking a homemade vagina.

This goes on all spring. I find the book *The Happy Hooker* by Xaviera Hollander buried in a closet and start jerking off to her many stories of having sex. I fantasize about her interaction with men's bodies as opposed to their interaction with her body, and I justify it by reminding myself that this book is about heterosexuals.

My literary choices expand in other directions as well: I read *Death of a Salesman*, *The Great Gatsby*, and *The Glass Menagerie*; I watch Bob Fosse's movie *All That Jazz* over and over, which becomes my favorite movie for its funny, sexy, compelling depiction of what it's like to make a Broadway musical in New York City amid the constant presence of death.

My world is opening. I'm going to fancy restaurants with large women who like to hang around sensitive young men and talk about movies, theater, and the meaning of life. I'm discovering my body and what makes me feel good. And I'm also frustrated that I'm too short, too skinny, insufficiently masculine. My wrists are so thin that I can encircle them with my thumb and forefinger. I want muscles like Adam Wasserman's because I think being more muscular will make me more masculine. Mom says that I'm fine the way I am. What I am, though, is a boy who yearns to touch another boy, or another girl—another somebody. But I'm afraid to try.

Chapter Nine

"GOWER CHAMPION DIED TODAY"

O N THE SECOND SUNDAY IN JUNE 1980, I turn on the Tony
Awards. This is my third time watching the awards. It's an escape
into another world, and I love everything transpiring on that stage.
Sandy Duncan is flying as Peter Pan, the Sharks and Jets are facing off at
the high school dance in *West Side Story*, and P. T. Barnum is declaring
"there's a sucker born every minute" while walking a tightrope. Each
number is more thrilling than the last.

And then they start performing a song from a new musical, *Evita*.
The scene starts with a woman and man in fancy bathrobes singing to
each other while getting ready for bed. He's a politician competing for
power and she's his wife. He has doubts about the upcoming election
and she does not. Her first line, "It doesn't matter what those morons
say," draws me in immediately. While it's clear he's the candidate, she's
the powerhouse who's leading the charge. It's an intimate duet that starts
in the bedroom but soon expands: Union workers with flags, torches,
and placards fill the stage, all rallying for this man, Juan Perón, and his
wife, Eva. She sells her husband to the crowd, singing a musical stanza
unlike anything I've heard before. It's singing and screaming—belting is
the word—using the power of her voice to declare her quest to obtain
power. With a voice like that, you know she can't lose. There's yet an-

other voice on stage, a narrator, who is also powerful and provides vocal balance to Eva's belting. I learn that the actress playing Eva is named Patti LuPone and the narrator is Mandy Patinkin.

I'm astounded by this new show. I go to the Oak Park Public Library and flip through the Broadway cast albums. I find the *Evita* original Broadway cast double album. I take it home and put it on Laurie's stereo. It's the most compelling music I've ever heard. It pricks my ears in wholly new ways—it's orchestral and rock, it employs violins and an electric guitar, recitatives, and soaring songs. I'm transfixed by the opening chorus of a funeral for Evita, which transforms into a rock 'n' roll rant by the narrator, Che. I love how the different groups—the military and the upper-class snobs—each have their own musical themes. The sound of the show rings through my ears with colors I've never imagined in a musical before. It's aurally different than *A Chorus Line*, or *Pippin*, or *Annie*, or *Fiddler on the Roof*. I buy my own copy of the double album, embossed with the logo on the jacket. I memorize every word.

As July starts, I'm home sick with bronchitis for three weeks, which really sucks because I had to drop out of the summer musical, *Yankee Doodle*, at Stagecrafters and the only thing to watch on TV is the Republican National Convention, where they are nominating a former actor named Ronald Reagan. After my recovery, the only activity to fill the summer is working my first real job: busboy at Katz's Delicatessen on Nine Mile Road, which bears no relationship to the famous Katz's in New York City.

Katz's is known for having the best corned beef because they cook it on-site. The meat simmers in its fat, salt, and juices all day in a steel vat that is half as big as me and sits in the small kitchen in the back. Every evening, I empty the vat and scrub it, removing all the leftover fat that's lying on the bottom or clinging to the sides. It's brown and sticky, like clouds of gelatinous goo. Once that mission is accomplished, I head to the dingy dining room. I place the dirty dishes into a large rectangular plastic tub filled with half eaten sandwiches, cold French fries smothered in ketchup, hardened matzoh balls, and cigarette ashes. I keep this area tidy during business hours and then, upon closing, move all the tables and chairs to one side to sweep and mop the entire floor. But it's not my most unpleasant activity of the night. That is reserved for scrubbing the floor behind the deli counter where the deli boys make sandwiches and drop waste between the rubber grates on which they stand. The space is narrow, and the grates have gouged big indentations into the linoleum tiled floor over many years. These indents are filled with filth. I must sweep in small three-foot motions from side to side to release the filth, and then pull it sixty feet down the narrow aisle to the back of the room before mopping and drying the floor, then returning the rubber grates to their place. When I walk out at 10:30 p.m., smelling of corned beef and Clorox, I've earned thirteen bucks plus an additional buck from the waitresses who complain about "how slow it is." There is nothing fun about working at Katz's. But I stick it out three nights a week, which pays for me to go to nicer places like 220 Merrill for dessert.

One night after arriving home from work, I get in the shower to scrub myself of Katz's grime and when I emerge, Mom and Dad are watching Channel 7 Action News. After they cover sports (the Tigers lost) and weather (it will be another hot and humid day tomorrow), anchorman Bill Bonds says, "Diana has the breaking news from the opening night of the new musical, *42nd Street*."

"That's right, Bill. The eagerly awaited musical, based on the famous movie from 1933, had a triumphant performance at the Winter Garden Theatre tonight. But when legendary producer David Merrick took the stage during the curtain call the world was in for a shock. Here is the footage we just received from our New York affiliate."

On the television, a line of Broadway actors is holding hands, smiling, and taking repeated bows as the audience cheers and fans throw flowers onto the stage. Then a man with black hair and a mustache, wearing a tuxedo, enters from the wings. The cheers grow even louder. But he's not smiling. He looks pained. He looks down at the stage. The audience keeps applauding and he raises his hands to signal them to stop.

He says, "It's a tragic moment." The audience roars in laughter. He shakes his head no. "I am sorry to report that Gower Champion died today."

Then he turns toward the cast and hugs the leading lady, who sobs. The leading man looks offstage and yells to a stagehand to bring down the curtain. "Bring it in."

"One of the most emotional, historic moments in the history of the theater," says Diana. "Director-choreographer Gower Champion dies the day of the opening of his triumphant new musical."

"That's terrible," says Mom.

"Gower Champion used to dance with his wife. What was her name?" asks Dad.

"Marge," Mom replies.

"I loved them," says Dad.

"This is unbelievable," I say.

When I get in bed that night, I replay that scene in the theater over and over in my head. I wonder what it was like to be in the audience. I wonder how the cast felt. And I wonder about the family and how they must have been both sad to lose their loved one but happy that he made one more show.

The next day, I go to the Little Professor Book Shop looking for any article I can find about *42nd Street*. I stand in the aisle reading *Variety*. "You can't get tickets to this smash hit for a year!" one article reads. I learn the meaning of the gross—how many dollars an individual show earns in ticket sales in one week. Merrick's opening night announcement put the show on every TV in America. He made it a national news story. This savvy producer made it a show everyone must see.

I think nonstop about shows and this producer, David Merrick, as I get ready to present to the board of the Rag-A-Muffins options for the upcoming season. I'm chairman of the Play Reading Committee, which consists of me reading many plays and making recommendations to the board. I think about plays while daydreaming on my bed, mowing the lawn, sitting on the toilet, or taking a shower. I ask myself, *How do you make someone want to see a show? What will make them buy tickets?* We need to pick two shows for the season, and I have two big ideas.

"So, tonight I get to share with you what I've been up to," I say to the board at our big meeting. "I've read a lot of plays. And I've thought a lot about our theater, our audience, and our troupe. And I think that our biggest challenge is that we haven't been doing shows that people care about. I loved being in *Popcorn Pete* but the audience couldn't care less about it. People know *Punch and Judy* as an old puppet show, not a play. I think part of our job is to do plays or books or stories that people love right now. I'm recommending two plays. The first is *The Hobbit*. It's one of the most popular kids' books of all time, it's an adventure with twenty-nine parts, which will be good for participation and selling tickets."

"He's got a point," says Mrs. Janney, one of our adult supervisors.

"It's a good idea," says Carrie, a board member. "What's the other one?"

"I found this fun musical called *Cheaper by the Dozen*, which is based on the famous old movie with Clifton Webb. It's a touching story and it has lots of parts for kids. I also think the show will attract a bigger and wider audience because it's more substantial than the shows we usually do and because the title is recognizable."

"Who do we get to play the adults?" Carrie asks.

"We can ask the adult troupe to audition for the father and mother."

"We've never done that before," says Carrie.

"All the more reason to try," I reply.

"You're a good salesman, Mr. Seller," she says.

They approve both shows for the new year.

Chapter Ten

OLD MEN AND CLOWNS

BACK AT SCHOOL IN the fall of senior year, I'm cast as one of the fathers in the high school production of *The Fantasticks*. I'm playing another old man. Last summer I played Sir Percival Smoothely-Smoothe at the Northwestern High School theater camp, the previous year I played Old Man Hasler in *The Pajama Game*, and the year before that I played the Professor in *Punch and Judy*. I have leapt from playing a nine-year-old boy in *Speaking of Murder* to playing a variety of geriatric men while still in high school.

Old men are safe. They are nonsexual. They don't require me to confront what it means to be a teenage boy who doesn't feel "manly" enough. I feel so uncomfortable in my body that I don't trust my body to tell a story. I have learned the tool of caricature to hide my true self. I use my voice and facial expressions to make people laugh—kind of like a clown. I have become expert at the double take. At Northwestern theater camp, the movement teacher, Lynn Baber, told me I act from "the neck up." It doesn't help that I am slightly afraid of men. I have no male close friends; I feel less than a man because I fantasize at night about touching other men. Playing old men as clowns makes me feel comfortable because I am not judged by my masculinity, or my lack of physical prowess. On stage, I've jumped to the phase of life when our manhood has receded with our hairlines.

But I'm not the only actor depicting old men and clowns. Another clown rises this year from our little house in Cardboard Village. In my seventeen years, I've witnessed many events and predicted many outcomes. None prepares me for this conversation with Dad.

"Son, I'm gonna be a clown," he says one day in September.

"Wait. What?" I reply.

"In the Shriners."

"Aren't they professionals?" I ask.

"Nope. All volunteer."

"What about work?"

"You know how much I love little kids."

Hardly an answer to my question. But no matter. Nothing can stop him.

Dad has always been in search of new diversions beyond serving papers and creating new names for his business, the latest of which is Attorney Action Associates, which replaced Sudden Service Associates, which replaced Search and Serve. In fact, Elmore Leonard, the famed crime novelist, used this name for a process server's business in his book, *Unknown Man #89*, after hanging out with Dad for a couple of days. Dad has no hobbies. He can't play sports, doesn't exercise, and hasn't had any real friends since his accident. With little short-term memory, it's impossible to maintain connections. But when he joins the Masonic Brotherhood as an apprentice in clowning, he becomes obsessed.

If the only bathroom at 33030 Redwood isn't cramped, cracked, or moldy enough, it now receives a new layer of soil: talcum powder. Dad's transformation requires an hour in the bathroom putting on his clown makeup. He covers his face in white base, and then paints a big, smiling red mouth around his lips. Another red spot on the tip of his nose, and two more big red arches to represent eyebrows. After making sure white covers all his skin, he shakes the talcum powder all over his face and neck, covering the bathroom in a spotted layer of white that drives Mom crazy.

After painting his face, he adds his fluffy orange wig that is its own burning bush. Next, he puts on the costume that he designed himself,

having hired a seamstress at the local cleaners to sew a giant jumpsuit for a six foot three, 250-pound clown. Under a red tunic is a baggy suit with an alternating pattern of red and white diamonds—his own version of the Harlequin. Three black pom-poms line the front like buttons. It has two large red pockets, each embroidered with CHIP in bold black letters. He is "Chip Chip the Clown," a throwback to his childhood nickname.

He starts his avocation slowly: making appearances at local hospitals to provide cheer to children. He becomes an excellent balloon twister. With his powerful chest and lungs, he blows up the balloons to make dogs, bunnies, cats, and an occasional horse, which requires more than one balloon.

Before long, it becomes a part-time job. Once a week turns into twice a week, and then thrice. All the appearances are preparation for the ultimate activity: the three-ring circus that will open in spring at the Michigan State Fairgrounds in Detroit. The Shrine Circus, produced by the Masonic Brotherhood, is the real thing: trapeze acts, tightrope walkers, elephants, and tigers. I remember being a small kid and walking with Dad into the five-thousand-seat Coliseum and enjoying the sweet and glorious smell of cotton candy from inside the chilly auditorium with curved steel girders holding up the arched roof.

One day in early March, he comes home with a box full of posters: A colorful illustration shows tigers, elephants, and clowns falling out of a red felt fez above the dates March 19–April 4, 1982. I peek at his calendar and see he has volunteered for thirty shows over the fifteen days, which means he will be at the circus for most of the day for more than two and a half weeks. It's going to be a full-time job.

When the circus starts, he basically lives at the state fairgrounds. I only see him early in the morning and when he comes home late at night, his eyes bloodshot from wearing the white paint all day. The good part is that he is out of the house most of the time, which means less tension, less anxiety, fewer blowups.

The second week of the circus, Mom, Aaron, and I are all home eating dinner when Chip Chip the Clown opens the front door and enters. He has just returned from the afternoon circus, still wearing his costume, but with another identical costume in a cleaners' plastic wrap draped over his right arm.

"Good evening, folks," he says as he enters the house.

"Hey Dad," I say. "How was the circus today?"

"Fantastic," he says. "I had a great afternoon. I've gotta shower." He sets the hanger with the clown suit down on the couch and then walks to his and Mom's bedroom.

Mom gets up from the table and walks over to examine the clown costume that is in the plastic wrap. She looks at the sales slip. From my seat, I turn and look at the slip as well. It has a total at the bottom of $105.00. He has paid the seamstress at the cleaners to make him a second costume. She shuts her eyes and looks like she is about to explode. Then she crosses to the side table where her cigarettes are sitting, lights one, and inhales deeply. After a couple puffs, she walks to their bedroom. She opens the door as Dad is taking off his costume. She forgets to close it.

"What is that costume sitting on the couch?" she says.

I hear everything coming out of her mouth. The bedroom is about twenty-five feet away and the walls are so thin you might say they are made of cardboard.

"I need a spare, so I have a clean one to wear every day."

"You just went out and spent over a hundred dollars for a second costume?" she says. "That's more money than I spend on an entire wardrobe."

"I can't wear a dirty costume tomorrow. I'm around kids all day."

"Mark, you're making me crazy."

"You're making yourself crazy," he says.

"No. Crazy is spending over two hundred dollars on clown suits when we can barely make the car payments. How am I supposed to put food on the table when you keep spending all our money on clown stuff?"

"Don't give me more of your negative attitude. The next checks will pay for the car."

"What next checks?" she screams. "You haven't served a paper for weeks. There are no checks because you're running off to the circus every day while I work for five dollars an hour so we can have health insurance and make the mortgage payments."

"You should see yourself," he responds. "You're a sad case." And with that, he moves past her, goes into the bathroom, and shuts the door.

"And one more thing, Chip Chip the Clown," she says, "clean up your own damn powder."

Mom returns to the table. We eat in silence.

He never invites us to see him at the circus, and Mom does not express any interest in going. She wants nothing to do with it. But I am curious to see what kind of a circus clown he can be. One day, after finishing my shift at Arby's—my step up from Katz's Deli—where salty roast beef has replaced fatty corned beef, and making French fries and milkshakes is more fun than mopping a disgusting floor of gristle, I walk up to the Ticketron counter at Hudson's and buy a single ticket for a Saturday afternoon performance toward the end of the run.

I drive east on Nine Mile Road—past the Dairy Queen, past the Fotomat, toward Woodward. I am going to see my dad in a show. I park at the fairgrounds and approach the Coliseum. The smell of cotton candy fills the air and familiar green sawdust covers the floor, reminding me of when Dad took me to the circus as an eight-year-old.

I take my seat halfway up the rafters. I scan the arena trying to spot my father. When the first act concludes, he's still nowhere in sight. I wonder if this spying trip is justified or moral. Am I just being sneaky? And then I see Chip Chip—a tall, large, red and white clown giant. Across the floor, on the opposite side of the ring, he is greeting a family in the handicapped zone. He makes a balloon animal for a young blond girl in a wheelchair. I see him twisting the purple balloon into dog legs and ears. I see the little girl looking at him with wonder. I see my father hand the balloon animal to the little girl with a sense of gentility and generosity that shows him in his best form. He makes that little girl's day.

Now I understand.

When I go home, I collect all the photos I can find of Dad as Chip Chip. I go to the art supply store the next day and buy a big white poster board, a glue stick, and Magic Markers. Over the next few weeks, I pull them out after school and create a big photo collage with the words "Chip Chip the Clown" in the center. There are many photos of Dad smiling at, holding, and enjoying the presence of little kids. Under a big photo of Dad with his arms around four kids, I write, "Shrine Circus, March, 1982." I frame the poster and give it to him. He looks at it as if he is discovering treasure. He examines each photo of Chip Chip as if the clown in the photo is a different man, one he doesn't know but whom he likes very much.

His participation in the Shrine Circus is a perfect encapsulation of his behavior: kind, generous, and deeply childish and irresponsible. But it doesn't last. The Shriners reject his application to advance from apprentice to full member of the clown unit. His first Shrine Circus is also his last.

Chapter Eleven

GO BLUE!

I APPLY TO THREE COLLEGES: Northwestern, my dream; the University of Michigan in Ann Arbor, which I loved visiting in the fifth grade, and which is the "go-to" school for the smart kids in the state; and Wayne State University, which is the commuter school located in downtown Detroit and my backup if I don't get into the other two.

I am hopeful about Northwestern because I studied at their high school theater conservatory for rising seniors, I wrote a strong essay, I had a good interview, and my theater experience is more extensive than that of most teenagers. My main worry is that I haven't earned straight A's in high school. My GPA is barely a B+ and I was a washout on the SATs. I am rejected from Northwestern.

Plan B: I'll go to U of M. The theater program is unremarkable, but the school is one of the best public universities in the country. The application is straightforward. The school puts me on hold pending my first semester senior grades, which will come out in late January. I earn straight A's, including for Honors Composition, International Relations, and Advanced Journalism, where I'm the editor-in-chief of the yearbook.

I receive no news through the month of February. In early March, I call the admissions office and make an appointment to see an admissions officer, whom I am confident I can win over in a meeting that demonstrates my serious intent and verbal skills in a way that the SAT did not. On the day of my meeting, I drive the forty-five minutes from Oak Park to Ann Arbor. I park behind the postwar, 1950s glazed orange brick LSA (Literature, Science, and the Arts) administration building on State Street and check in at the Admissions Office. It's a stark workplace, with several officers seated at desks in one long room with windows facing out onto the late winter gray.

A man in his forties, dressed in brown slacks, a blue shirt, and a loose tie with no jacket or belt, walks to the reception area. His brown hair is turning the color of metal. He wears wire-rimmed glasses.

"Jeffrey Seller?" he says.

"Yes, sir."

"Come with me, please."

He does not shake my hand. He turns around and walks, with a slight limp, down a hallway of desks and sits behind the last one. I sit in the chair opposite his desk.

"What can I do you for you, Mr. Seller?" he says as he leans back in his chair, angling away from me.

"I wanted to come here to talk to you about my application."

He looks at me and nods. He doesn't say anything but springs back to an upright position. He picks up a pile of manila folders that are to his left and finds one with my name on it. He opens it, pulls out my transcript, and examines it as if he's never seen it before. He squints. He frowns. He doesn't say anything. He doesn't look at my essay or my list of extracurricular activities.

"Hm," he says. One syllable. One short beat. Something between a hum and a grunt.

I feel like I need to say something.

"When I was put on hold pending seventh semester grades, I knew I had to prove myself. And I worked really hard last semester. I'm the editor-in-chief of the yearbook. So, when I received straight A's, including for Honors Comp., I felt like I had met my end of the bargain."

He takes another look at the transcript. And then he lets go of it so that it glides back onto the desk. "Two years of math, no chemistry, no physics, no language at all. You've basically fulfilled two-fifths of the college requirements. Why should we admit you?"

I don't have an answer maybe for the first time. "I'm sorry, I just thought . . . thank you for your time," I say.

"Good luck, Mr. Seller."

I feel like a loser. My grandiose protestations to anyone who listened that I didn't need math or science were wrong. I've made a big mistake, and I can't go back and change it. I'm infuriated with my parents for not telling me what I needed to do even though they didn't know.

My only remaining option is Wayne State in Detroit, which means staying home.

I am not going to get out. I am stuck. I am not going to climb the maple tree in the backyard and fly over the clouds. I am not going to start a new life in a new city. I am going to stay in Cardboard Village. The dreams I've concocted while sitting on the toilet, while standing in the shower, while lying on my bed, are crushed by my lopsided high school grades and my bad decision to drop math and science. I am glum all spring. I come home from school every day and watch Luke and Laura on *General Hospital*. It doesn't make me feel better.

One afternoon, I feel so lethargic that I put on shorts, a T-shirt, and gym shoes, drive to the park, and start running. I've never run in my life. It feels like the only way to release the tension, anxiety, and fear that's swirling inside me. One circle equals one mile. After a half mile, I'm out of breath and cramping in my side. I walk a little, start again, and complete one mile. I try again the next day. About three weeks later I can run three miles with no stops. While my legs move my body forward, my brain asks, *Where am I going?* Should I just study at Wayne State, become an English teacher, get married with kids, and live in a nice house in the nicer part of Oak Park? This cannot be my fate. Where does that leave me? While I don't reach any conclusions, my body feels a little bit freer after a three-mile run.

At school, Concert Choir starts every morning at eight a.m. We are rehearsing an oratorio, the Poulenc "Gloria," which we will perform with the Oak Park Orchestra on a Sunday afternoon in late May. On a Monday morning at 8:45 a.m., as we're hard at work in choir practice singing, "Gloria, in excelsis Deo," the school secretary rushes into the choir room. Our teacher, the intrepid Miss Powell, doesn't stop playing and conducting. The secretary goes to her piano and whispers in her ear.

"Jeff, your mother is here to see you," says Miss Powell.

That scares me. Something must be wrong. She has never done that before. As Miss Powell gives notes to the sopranos, Mom charges into the choir room, crying. I jump out of my chair.

"What's wrong?" I say.

"You got in, son, you got in!" she screams. "You're going to Michigan!"

I am stunned. "Oh my God."

"With financial aid. I'm so proud of you."

The whole class claps and cheers for me. I hug Mom.

"Go, take a few minutes with your mom," says Miss Powell. "Oh, and Jeff, congratulations. You deserve it."

Mom and Dad make our favorite dinner at home that night: flank steak—medium rare—with Dad's famous homemade French fries and salad. After, we make Sanders Hot Fudge Sundaes, my favorite dessert in the whole wide world.

"You're a first-class act, son," says Dad. "You're going to be the best freshman Michigan has ever seen."

I feel as if I've just received a "Get Out of Jail Free" card. Only I don't know why. And I don't ask. Perhaps my trip to see the stern admissions officer was more productive than I thought. Bottom line, I'm moving to Ann Arbor!

Chapter Twelve

"AND I AM TELLING YOU I'M NOT GOING"

WHEN I WAS TWELVE, just after the three-week run of *Speaking of Murder* at Stagecrafters, I told my parents that I wanted an agent to help me get auditions for professional theater and commercials. Everyone in our extended family knew that "Jeff wanted an agent." My cousin Marty, thirteen years my senior, and a PhD student at Vanderbilt University in Nashville, sent me a brown nine-by-twelve-inch envelope with a book inside. I opened it and found a traditional black-and-white spotted composition book with a note on the inside cover.

With all the success you're having in the entertainment industry, I expect you to fill this book with your next play or screenplay. As always, Marty. P.S. I couldn't fit the agent into the package.

Marty was a role model, the most intellectually gifted member of the family and the first to pursue a PhD. He was the first family member to "leave" for things greater than Detroit. Though I didn't see him often, he always kept up on what I was doing.

When I graduate high school in 1982, he and his wife, Andrea, are living in a suburb of New York. For my graduation present, he sends me two tickets: a plane ticket to visit him and Andrea in New York, and a theater ticket to see *Dreamgirls* on Broadway.

OK, stop right there. Yes. I am going to see *Dreamgirls* four weeks after Jennifer Holliday won the Tony Award for Best Actress in a Musical; four weeks after watching one of the most exciting Tony Awards in history—the night in which Jennifer Holliday received a standing ovation for "And I Am Telling You I'm Not Going"; the night in which *Nine* and *Dreamgirls* battled it out for the Tony Award for Best Musical; the night in which Tommy Tune beat Michael Bennett for Best Director; but Michael Bennett beat Tommy Tune for Best Choreographer; the night in which our hearts broke when *Dreamgirls* lost to *Nine* and I didn't think their number, "Be Italian," was that great. There was one more memorable moment of that telecast: a Shakespeare play, *Othello*, won for Best Revival. Starring Christopher Plummer and James Earl Jones, it was produced by a husband/wife team named Barry and Fran Weissler, who were larger-than-life when they appeared onstage to accept the award. Their ebullience, charisma, and flashiness stuck in my head. If I were to do a play about Broadway, I would cast them as the producers.

After I fly into Newark and stay the night at Andrea and Marty's house, he and I drive to the city. We park on the roof of the Port Authority Bus Terminal. Eighth Avenue and Forty-second Street is my first step onto the New York pavement. We walk north and turn right on Forty-sixth Street, which I don't yet know will become integral to my future. We reach the nexus of Broadway and Seventh Avenue: Times Square.

I see the famous neon Coke sign to my left, as well as a huge blue Panasonic sign that covers the side of an entire building. I wonder what they do with the windows. A billboard for *Annie* is being painted over. Behind me is Howard Johnson's and a flickering neon sign that says "Gaiety Theatre." I wonder what goes on there. Across the street is a Calvin Klein ad—four stories tall—of a ripped man sunbathing on a phallic white stone. I can't stop looking at this Adonis in white underpants. Across the avenue is a shimmering black-and-silver billboard for *Evita*. More signs for Japanese electronics: Sony, Aiwa, and Casio watches. *E.T.* is playing at a movie theater across the street from the Palace, which advertises Lauren Bacall in *Woman of the Year*. The street is grungy, as if nothing has been cleaned in a long time. The brightest part of the square is the TKTS booth, which is a trailer clad in red-and-white plastic flags.

We continue walking east and reach the new Citicorp building, which is remarkable because the whole building is standing on three legs. There is a plaza where the "fourth leg" should be. We eat lunch at a salad market inside, and then walk back to the theater district, where Marty drops me off in front of the Imperial Theatre, the home of *Dreamgirls*. I have never been to a show by myself. I take my seat in the center of the front row of the mezzanine. It is the first time I am sitting in a Broadway theater, and what Mom told me is true: The theaters are much smaller than the Fisher Theatre. The first row of the mezzanine is very close to the stage.

I am mesmerized the moment the music starts. The set consists of six towers with lights inside that move all over the stage. They create different playing spaces, shifting and dancing with the music, which is a propulsive amalgamation of Motown, soul, and pop. The actors never stop moving, like all the people walking through Times Square. There are not traditional "dances," but the whole show is like choreographed life. When Jennifer Holliday begins her song, "And I Am Telling You," I start bawling from her pain, passion, and ferocity. The entire audience stands up and cheers at the end of her number. This is the most thrilling experience I have ever had in my life and it is only intermission.

The music pulses through my body. The moving machinery of the set captivates my eyes. The story inspires and saddens me. I love the people it portrays—a family of artists who love each other, fight for each other, and rise together, but end up breaking up because of ego, ambition, and resentment. It is especially satisfying to see Jennifer Holliday's character, Effie, who is unjustly fired, receive justice at the end. *Dreamgirls* shows that success comes with a price and asks us to question its cost. I am exhilarated. Marty picks me up in front of the theater and we meet Andrea at a restaurant called Joe Allen, which Marty says is the best theater restaurant in New York. He is right, both in 1982 and forty years later.

After three days in the suburbs with Marty and Andrea, I take a train back into NYC where Stephen Gutwillig, a friend from theater camp at Northwestern, meets me at Penn Station. He is hosting me for three more days. Stephen lives on East Ninety-sixth Street between Park Avenue and Madison with his sister and mother. His existence seems to be one out of a TV show: A senior in high school, he lives with total independence on the Upper East Side in an old-fashioned apartment building. In fact, his mother is out of town. It's as if the occupants of that apartment are roommates, not family members.

Stephen knows everything about New York. On our first day, we walk down Fifth Avenue to the Metropolitan Museum and then on to the Delacorte Theater, where we meet up with one of his friends. I am amazed by the way he easily gets us around the city. It's as if Central Park is his backyard. I want to see *The Fantasticks* in its original off-Broadway home, the Sullivan Street Playhouse, and that evening, we get in a taxi from East Ninety-sixth Street, pick up his friend in front of her fancy contemporary apartment building on Park Avenue and Seventy-ninth Street, and then drive downtown to the West Village.

When we arrive at the Sullivan Street Playhouse, we file into a tiny theater that's the shape of an oval. It's smaller than the Little Theatre at Oak Park High School. One hundred seats are arrayed like a fan around the small stage. The walls are black and the old seats creak. It uses one piano, just like we did, and the same simple props, with only a small white curtain strung up between two poles with the title painted across it.

The Fantasticks makes something out of nothing. It's the opposite of *Dreamgirls*. Seven actors and one piano on a tiny stage, versus thirty actors, a huge orchestra, and a huge production in a large theater. *Dreamgirls* is like witnessing a theatrical tsunami. *The Fantasticks* is like witnessing a superb card magician—everything happens in the palm of his hand.

After the show, we go for dinner at a small restaurant on Bleecker and Sullivan Street, a place that feels as if Bob Dylan or Allen Ginsberg might walk in. When we're done, we begin our trek north, working our way through Washington Square Park, where folks are playing chess, selling pot, and skipping through the fountain; Union Square, which seems like a campsite for homeless people; and Rockefeller Center, where we take a break at the fountain of the gold Prometheus sculpture, hanging out with the god who gave us fire, heat, and light.

The next night Stephen takes me to a play I've never heard of. It just opened at the Little Theatre on Broadway. The title, *Torch Song Trilogy*, is foreign to me. Though I know it will have three parts, I don't know what a torch song is. The show starts early, at seven p.m. We sit down on the right side of the orchestra, not far from the stage. The lights go down and a woman on a platform stage left starts singing a slow song about love and the man who left her. OK, now I get it: torch song.

The lights shift to a man standing downstage center, by himself, smoking a cigarette. He talks in a low growl that is effeminate in tone and rhythm, baritone in pitch. His name is Arnold, and he is wickedly hilarious as he describes his screwed-up love life. As the monologue progresses, he expresses surprise, discomfort, and pleasure in his face and body; he makes sounds of groaning. It slowly occurs to me that he is being fucked from behind. This scene is outrageous. He makes the act of getting fucked by a stranger in a back room funny and, sort of, normal. I'm transfixed by his courage to say things I've never heard anyone say before. He's the kind of man I have been afraid of, like the guys in *A Chorus Line* or the gay hairdressers the ladies at home talk about with both affection and condescension. But this time I like him because he's funny and sad and smart.

Each scene is punctuated by the woman singing a torch song. The narrative follows Arnold's on-again, off-again relationship with a bisexual man. In the third act, which takes place a couple years later in his downtown apartment, he and his lover are raising an adopted son who is also gay. Two men raising a child is a family I've never imagined. They are visited by Arnold's mother, who doesn't approve of his homosexuality or his parenthood. A war between mother and son ensues with results that are messy and real, funny and heartbreaking. I love Arnold, I love Harvey Fierstein, the author and star, and I love this play.

Stephen and I aren't close. We don't talk about personal stuff, but he is a fountain of knowledge about New York and theater. He is generous. On the final day I'm down to my last ten-dollar bill and need to get to JFK for my flight home. As he brings me down to East Ninety-sixth Street to hail a cab, he puts twenty dollars in my hand to pay for the taxi. He has shown me New York through the eyes and experiences of a seventeen-year-old kid. I'll appreciate it forever.

I come home, work at Arby's, and get ready for school. But the summer is tempered by another family setback. Cunningham's Drugs, where Mom has worked for eight years, and which provides our health and dental insurance, is sold. All its employees are fired. The store is renamed Arbor Drugs and employs only non-union labor at minimum wage with no benefits. The Reagan era has officially begun. Mom works the picket line and worries about what happens next. Her unemployment will have negative consequences. Having no health insurance makes me even more scared of getting sick. But my education is safe. The U of M financial aid office formulates a package to pay for all my schooling costs with grants, loans, and work study. I realize something: I am becoming an independent adult who takes care of himself and is separate from them. And I'm ready to go.

Chapter Thirteen

FRESHMAN FABLES

BRUCE LEE SCOWLS AT me when I open the door to my dorm room. Not the actual Bruce Lee, but a life-size poster. Arms extended over his head, holding nunchucks, Bruce Lee is the hero my roommate, Rich, a bony-brained bodybuilder from Mount Clemens, places over his bed. Patti LuPone, arms extended over her head, posing as Evita, is my hero, and she goes on the opposite wall. Who are you going to bet on?! This is not a relationship destined for success and Rich moves out after three weeks.

My second roommate, Eli Cohen, seems like a better fit. He is tall, gangly, hyper-intellectual, and shares my interest in political science. Mr. Lee is replaced by multiple maps of the world. Eli lays on his bed during free time memorizing every country and capital. It would be helpful if he spent a little more of his free time washing his stinky socks or taking a shower.

I love my World Politics class, taught by a heavily accented European Jew, Professor A. F. K. Organski, whose lectures about the nature of "power" are half Italian aria, half oration on the causes of war and peace. I make a few new friends—all girls—and enjoy living on my own away from Cardboard Village.

That fall, I meet my friend Adrienne for dinner one night at her dorm, and she tells me about a rare new disease that seems to only affect gay men in New York and San Francisco. It's called AIDS. I try to act disinterested, but my heart starts to accelerate with fear. I have never had sex with anyone. The last time I kissed anyone was Debbie Edmonds in the eighth grade. The truth is, I masturbate to fantasies of touching men's chests, abs, and penises, but I also dream about getting married, having children, and forming a family of my own.

"Is there a cure for it?" I ask.

"No," she says. "What makes it so scary is that everyone who gets it dies."

I lose my appetite.

In the spring, I apply to be a drama director for the summer at Camp Tamarack in Ortonville, Michigan. There's a program for rising ninth graders, the oldest campers, called Specialty, in which the campers choose an activity—sports, swimming, drama, or arts and crafts—to practice for half of each day. At the interview, the shy, short program director of the camp, Elliot Sorkin, looks at me with doubt. He glances down as I talk. There's a little bit of sadness in his eyes. There are long pauses after I talk.

"I'm not sure you're, um, old enough to be the head of Specialty Drama," Elliot says. "We think it's better if older students are their counselors and teachers."

I listen and resist saying, *Then why the hell are we sitting here?*

"I've been doing theater since fourth grade," I say. "I've done community theater and high school theater. I've competed in thespian theater festivals. I studied theater at Northwestern in the summer of 1981. This year I took acting, theater tech, and theater history."

"I'm just afraid that you're too young. You're only nineteen."

"Actually, eighteen. I turn nineteen in October."

"What kind of play would you do?" he asks.

"At my youth theater we used a publishing company called Anchorage Press that specializes in plays performed by kids. I'd choose one of their musicals."

"That's a good idea. We'll see what happens."

Elliot doesn't have any other candidates, so I get the gig.

My mission this summer is to direct and produce my first show since *Adventureland*. I am also set designer, lighting designer, and touring supervisor, which means overseeing several trips out of camp. The pay is eight hundred dollars. I'm thrilled.

I arrive at camp in late June, one week ahead of the campers. The mosquitoes are my welcoming committee, and I'm covered in bites within the first two hours. Camp Tamarack is huge. It sits on a square mile of woods populated by oak, maple, and evergreen trees in northern Oakland County. A mile-long road snakes from the top to the bottom of the camp and there are eight separate villages spaced equidistantly just off the road. Each village has its own housing and lodge in which campers congregate, sleep, and eat their meals. At the center of camp sits the amphitheater that will become my primary workplace.

Specialty Village, where I work and live, is the only coed village in the camp. My bunk, which I share with two other counselors, is a small wood-framed cabin with no electricity, water, or bathroom. Two masculine and handsome roommates treat me with respect. Steve Stein, a laid-back med student at U of M who wears a lot of green scrubs, and Mitch Rosenwasser, who is a gung-ho camp fanatic. There's another resident of our village, Joel Colman. Ten years older, a camp veteran, Joel used to be the drama director. He's over six feet tall, heavy, with a brown head of unkempt hair and a full beard. He's a teddy bear, our camp Tevye, and the guy who leads our village in song after meals. Joel treats me like a younger brother and regales me with stories, like the production of *Jesus Christ Superstar* he did at Michigan (even though he was a student at Central Michigan) in which he played Caiaphas.

On a Sunday morning after breakfast, the counselors and I head to the camp entrance with our "SPECIALTY" sign to greet the arriving campers. The green buses roll in, and an assortment of teens burst through the doors. Fully equipped with Walkmen, boom boxes, Ocean Pacific T-shirts, and K-Swiss gym shoes, they are suburban cool.

Our first theater session is after lunch. I've chosen a musical that was a big hit for my youth theater: *Aesop's Falables*, a kid-friendly musical adaptation of *Aesop's Fables*. At 2:30 p.m. we round up nineteen girls and two boys and walk to the amphitheater. I'm nervous because I need to instill respect.

We do some physical warm-ups and theater exercises like throwing an imaginary ball around the circle. After a few minutes, I invite everyone to sit down.

"OK, so here's what we're gonna do. Tell us your name, where you're from, and maybe a little bit about your interest in the theater. I'll start. My name is Jeff, I'm from Oak Park and I go to U of M, and I've been doing theater since fourth grade."

Seated to my right are two sisters, identical twins Julie and Lisa Stein, adorable and springy in their blue jeans, bright socks, and wavy hair in different shades of auburn.

"I'm going to explain to you how to tell us apart and how we got our hair this way," says Julie. "And no one should ever ask to hear it again. My sister Lisa . . ."

"That's me," interjects Lisa.

". . . and I were cast as the twins in *The King and I* at Andover. You know, it takes place in the Far East . . ."

"Burma," Lisa adds.

"Yeah, Burma, and they wanted us to do our hair and makeup, so we'd look Asian . . ."

"So, we decided to dye our hair with a rinse-out black dye."

"It had to be temporary because our bat mitzvahs were the week after the show," Julie continues.

"But our mom totally screwed it up," says Lisa. "She bought a dye, not a rinse, and we both wound up with shiny black hair . . ."

"A week before our bat mitzvahs!"

"So, we ran to the beauty parlor the day after the show ended and they dyed it as close to our original color as they could."

"But I went back a second time," says Julie.

"And that's how you can tell us apart," says Lisa.

"Because my hair is more auburn," Julie concludes.

I'm sold. They are born storytellers and performers, cute and compact with their dyed hair and effervescent personalities. We move on to one of the two boys present.

Eddie Cohen, age fifteen and also from Oak Park, is an operator. Two years older than the other campers and only three years younger than me, he treats me like his peer as opposed to his director, which is annoying. Tall and skinny, he's a wily talker, always working an angle to get something—attention, candy, special treatment.

After all the kids introduce themselves, we try some games from my handbook, *Improvisation for the Theater*. The kids practice scenes in which they create objectives from simple verbs and use spontaneity to explore different emotions. They show spunk and enthusiasm. Elliot Sorkin, the program director who hired me, stops by to watch, and takes a seat halfway up the bleachers.

At the end of the period, I bring everyone back into the circle. "This is an excellent start," I say. "Tomorrow we'll start work on our musical. It's called *Aesop's Falables*. It's a new take on the fables we all grew up with—but this time, the sheep are chasing the wolf, not the wolf chasing the sheep."

"That sounds fun," says Lisa.

"Who's playing the Wolf?" asks Eddie.

"Tomorrow you'll all sing and read from the play so I can figure out who's going to play what part."

"So, it's an audition?" says one of the kids.

"Kind of. We gotta figure out who's the best fit for each part. We're going to perform the play at the end of the session at the JCC for your parents, and then for the younger campers over at Brighton, and then we'll do it here for the entire camp."

"So, we'll be, like, touring it," says Lisa.

"That sounds cool," says Eddie.

"The *Aesop's Falables* bus and trailer," I joke. "OK, kids, go have fun at the beach!"

I bound up the bleachers to greet Elliot. "Hello, sir, how's the day? Do I have a piano player yet? We start tomorrow."

"I know. I'm sorry. It's been hard," he says. "Could you make use of a trumpet player?"

"Are you kidding me?"

"He's a good trumpet player," he says.

"Elliot, you can't sing to a trumpet."

"I'm doing the best I can."

I have no other options. The trumpet player makes me a cassette in which he plays all the melody lines from the songs.

The next morning the kids read the different roles. There is ample energy and talent to populate this show. After the morning session, Eddie runs up as I walk to the village for lunch.

"Jeff, can I talk to you about something?"

"Sure, Eddie. What's up?"

"I'm really hoping you'll cast me as the Wolf." Eddie knows the Wolf is the lead.

"Eddie, I'm going to cast you in the role I think best suits you."

"I just wanted you to know because, I think I'd be a great Wolf, I'm kind of like him already."

"Thanks for the advice," I say. His chutzpah is either impressive or outrageous. His reading was neither.

I decide to cast a camper named Jackie Frank as Wilfred M. Wolf. A mature, natural leader, Jackie exudes easy confidence. All the girls go to her for advice and guidance. She behaves older than her fourteen years. And it doesn't hurt that she's tall.

As for Eddie, with his lithe frame and cocky attitude, I cast him as the Hare, who is arrogant and narcissistic, and loses the big race to the humble Tortoise.

After assigning the rest of the parts, I explain that they are playing animals but that they should rely on their human qualities, while imbuing their characters with a semblance of their animal traits.

Falables moves quickly, like a TV variety show, with many antics. A panoply of animals—a hare and tortoise, crows, mice, eagles, sheep, and, of course, a wolf, play out their tales on an open stage with two boxes, a large ladder, and a load of props. Employing knowledge I've acquired watching directors and seeing musicals, I begin blocking the show. I invite the kids to suggest how they want to behave and move in each scene. They pick up my energy and thrust the drama forward.

Dreamgirls was staged from back to front. There wasn't a lot of dancing but there was constant movement. The actors usually entered upstage and crossed downstage in diagonals. It seemed as if they were coming down two slides from the back of the stage. I try to emulate what I remember to make the action fast and energetic. I love bringing these scenes to life.

Aesop's characters start to emerge. Jackie is consistent as the Wolf but does not blossom. Eddie is as lazy and overconfident as his character, the Hare. He'll be fine.

When I'm not rehearsing with the kids in the morning, I'm reviewing the cassettes from the trumpet player in the afternoon. I must learn the songs first so that I can teach them to the kids the next day. Tired all the time, I can't figure out how to ration my energy. After three hours of rehearsal each morning, my voice is spent. And I still have multiple responsibilities for the rest of the day and night.

"Every day at camp is like three days in the real world," says Fran, the camp social worker. She's not wrong.

We need an escape. Steve Stein, my bunkmate, takes our Specialty staff out to the local bar where we eat doughy breadsticks, drink beer and wine (I only drink Coke), and feed the jukebox, which plays David Bowie's new hit, "Let's Dance." I'm happy and relieved to be part of the "in-group." I dance with my codirector, Karen, whose humor and warmth remind me of Bette Midler.

One morning we're staging a scene in which the Jack-in-the-Box is taunting the Wolf, who is having no success stealing the delicious red grapes he wants to eat. I've cast both the twins to play Jack-in-the-Box, the ubiquitous clown who narrates and provides comic commentary. It will surprise and delight the audience if one Jack pops out of the box on the left side of the stage and then the other pops up a second later somewhere else.

"Lisa, for this next scene, I want you to pop out of the box, say your lines, then go back in. Julie, can you quietly exit out the back of the stage, run to the back of the amphitheater and then appear from the audience on the next line?"

"I love it," says Julie.

"This is going to be a great bit," I say.

We try it. Julie runs out the back of the theater. When the time comes for her speech, she's a little late and out of breath.

"Can you leave a little earlier?" I ask.

We do it again. Julie makes it this time. She's still out of breath. The kids holler their support. I reassign a couple of speeches so she has a longer window, with no need to sprint. We run it one more time—success! The bit is timed perfectly, and I can see how the audience will delight in this sleight of hand.

Monday morning. We start with our exercises. With the sun climbing in the sky and the heat rising, the kids are distracted.

As Jackie launches into her first big monologue, she goes up on her lines, and then runs off stage crying. "I'm sorry, I can't do this."

"Yes, you can," I say.

"It's OK if you want to get somebody else to do it."

"Come on, let's do it again. If you can't remember your line, don't freak out, just call, 'line.'"

Jackie is stuck. She's burdened by a heavier issue. Her best friend's dad died unexpectedly a week ago. The mother of the friend decided to place her daughter in camp to be near Jackie, who is her primary source of comfort. Jackie is overwhelmed.

On our first break, I'm sitting on a bench when I hear screaming from the stage.

"I can't take her anymore," yells Julie. "She's ruining my life."

"Oh, please," says her sister, Lisa.

"That's what I'm talking about. She's constantly undercutting me. Everything I do. 'Precious, perfect Lisa.' And it's not just about us. It's everyone around us: 'You're so cute, you're so adorable. You should do everything together.'"

"Shut up, Julie," says Lisa. "Nobody wants to hear your complaining."

"I've been listening to you tell me what to do my entire life," says Julie. "Leave me alone. I don't want anything to do with you."

So much for the disciplined twins. They annoy each other, they drive each other crazy, and yet they can't exist without each other. The cast members split into support groups, one for each twin. I'm suddenly in the land of the Jets and Sharks.

These emotional outbursts are like a virus. The whole cast seems to be breaking down. In the middle of a scene, a clutch of girls surrounds crying Dayna Shapiro, who plays Clarissa the Crow. With a mop of brown wavy hair, braces, and a tan of which I am deeply jealous, Dayna is a hardworking performer in rehearsal and capable of driving everyone nuts outside. Her parents recently separated, and she received a letter that morning from her mother, telling her that her dad is selling their house.

"Their divorce is going through today," says Dayna. "I'm afraid they're going to send me to California to live with my grandparents."

"Hey, everybody, come on over here," I call out to the cast. "Let's all sit down and relax for a few minutes." I need to figure out how to reset this rehearsal, quickly. I feel for these kids dealing with death and divorce. I think about moving from our house on Northview. I remember how many times my parents said they were getting divorced, which always panicked me that our family was falling apart.

"I know this isn't easy. But the last couple days we've lost focus. It feels like everything that's going on outside is finding its way inside. And it's hurting our work. I know many of you have a lot going on. Stuff with your parents, your friends, or even your siblings. But when we start rehearsal every morning, your job is to dive into your character and what's going on in the world of Aesop. I want—no, I *need* for you to leave everything else outside this theater. And, if you do, I promise, you'll have more fun, and we'll make a better show."

Back to work. With a week and a half to go, we still have no piano player. I can't take one more rehearsal singing songs to the tape of a trumpet player. We still need to stage two dances, and the physical production isn't close to complete. I need more time for rehearsal but there is an "All Camp Sports Competition" coming up that will subtract a full day. I persuade Elliot to let the Drama kids skip it and rehearse. My fellow counselors revolt.

"This whole show is taking over everything," says Lydia, a British law student who talks and looks as if she's Margaret Thatcher. "The kids are working too hard. Camp life is now second to the show. It's hurting the cohesion of the village. It's infringing on the experience of the campers."

"I think their camp experience is made better by this," I say. "Do you think in twenty years the kids in waterfront are going to remember what the fuck they did?"

"You don't have to get so angry, Jeff, we're just talking," says Ron, the Specialty Supervisor.

I'm trying not to burst. I feel like crying.

"I'll tell you one thing," I say. "Twenty years from now, these kids are going to remember when they made this play."

I'm outnumbered. I relent. I walk out of the lodge and go sit at a picnic table.

Joel comes over. "Here, I have a gift for you."

"You don't need to do that," I say.

He hands me an old, ruffled copy of a book, *Act One*, a theater memoir by Moss Hart. "Here, read this," he says.

"What is it?" I ask.

"It's the best book about the theater ever written."

"Who's Moss Hart?"

"One of the most successful playwrights of all time. And he directed *My Fair Lady* and *Camelot*. You know how he got his start? He directed theater at summer camp."

"Ha!"

"It wasn't easy for him. And it isn't easy for you."

"You can say that again."

"Just keep going. That's what we do," says Joel.

"Thanks."

"Let me know what you think of the book."

While the campers scream and shout and lose their voices at All Camp Sports Day, I sit at a picnic table outside the lodge and read *Act One*. I immediately connect with this ambitious young man whose experiences growing up poor and ashamed in the Bronx in 1915 feel so much like mine today. Reading *Act One* makes me feel less alone. It ends with the triumphant Broadway opening of the thirty-year-old author's play, after which he rescues his family from poverty. If Moss Hart can do it, can I?

One week out, Elliot finds a music teacher and pianist named Judy who rescues us from trumpets on tape. Finally, the show starts to click. The pace is swift, each scene has its own dramatic arc, and each character is specific and endearing. The kids are passionate. They paint the muslin *Aesop's Falables* sign and spend their afternoons gathering costume pieces and props.

The next morning, we get ready to hit the road—to the JCC for the parents' show, to Brighton for the younger campers tomorrow. The kids are putting the finishing touches on the *Aesop's Falables* sign when a news crew from Channel 2 Eyewitness News arrives to do a story on summer camp. Anchor Ronnie Clemmens takes one look at what's going on at our amphitheater and decides to videotape our rehearsal and interview me. We run the opening number. As they perform, I stand on the benches watching as a cameraman shoots over my shoulder.

At the end, Ronnie claps. "Kids, this is unbelievable. Can you show me some more?" The kids do two more numbers and then Ronnie and I sit for an interview, after which Joel and I drive to the JCC to set up the lights and sound.

With a friendly audience of parents, family, and friends, the kids do their first full run-through with every element of the production. They are energetic and flexible. They help each other and bring a sense of joy to the whole endeavor. Their families love it.

"Good show tonight," says Joel.

"Thanks."

"How's the book?" he asks.

"Talk about a tough childhood," I say. "And his camp experience makes this look easy."

"Keep going," he says. "It gets even better."

The next afternoon is the performance at Brighton, which is forty miles away and has more than a hundred campers between the ages of eight and ten. This performance is a different challenge for the actors because the stage is smaller, the crowd is younger, and the show is outdoors in the afternoon. The kids have more confidence but new problems creep up: Eddie, a little nervous, skips four pages of the script. Another kid makes an entrance from the wrong location. They learn to solve problems on their feet.

On the final night, the sky is dark blue, and the air is cool. Three hundred and fifty campers fill the wooden benches along with a hundred staff. Older folks from the senior citizens' camp on the other side of the lake are bused to the amphitheater with their lawn chairs to sit in the space between the first row and the stage. This enthusiastic crowd, the biggest I've ever seen assembled at camp, is ready to see our musical.

The music director sits at the piano, the stage lights shine, and Julie as Jack springs from her Box. The kids from Specialty applaud. Her opening speech is exuberant and winning. She disappears and Lisa pops out of the Prop Box. Magic. I look at the audience. They're wondering how we did that trick. Wilfred M. Wolf arrives and makes his case with the charm of a movie star. The audience laughs. Jackie has grown over these past three performances. She's let go of everything else going on in her life and is enjoying her character.

The crowd howls at the silly sheep; they go nuts when the magical Jack in the Box makes her entrance at the back of the amphitheater seconds after she has just disappeared from the stage. When we reach the big race, Hare and Tortoise are on the starting line, Clarissa the Crow blows the whistle and then, as they start moving in slow motion, the theme from *Chariots of Fire* plays. The audience squeals with delight and applauds as the characters move to the rhythm of this beloved movie theme song.

I'm happy. This show reflects my values, my sensibility, my imagination. The kids and I made a new thing. Everything I've done before has led to this moment. When I arrive home for the weekend break, I turn on the six o'clock news to find Ronnie Clemmens interviewing me on TV.

"Jeff, I understand you've been working with these kids all summer," says Ronnie. "What makes theater so special?"

"It gives them a chance to make something. It's not easy, it demands creativity and commitment."

"What do they get from this?"

"It forces them to work together. They discover they can achieve more together than they ever could by themselves."

"I hear it's part of a village called Specialty," he says. "What makes your program special?"

"It aims higher. I'm constantly asking, 'Can we do better?'" The segment cuts back to the news desk where Ronnie says, "I think these theater kids are going places."

The question "Can we do better?" gets implanted in my brain.

I'm starting to feel like I was meant for this adventure—picking plays, producing, and directing, working with kids to make something in which the whole is greater than the sum of its parts. I'm ready to do it again.

Chapter Fourteen

SCENES FROM A SOPHOMORE YEAR

AT THE BEGINNING OF sophomore year at U of M, Dad drops me off at the dorm where I have a new roommate: Andrew Lippa. Yes, the boy I met at age six—when he showed me his bedroom that became my bedroom and his family sold my family their house in Cardboard Village. In the years since, we've been friendly as performers in the high school choir and plays. He's a stupendous singer and a great piano player. He played El Gallo in our high school production of *The Fantasticks*. One year behind me at Michigan, he will study piano, voice, and music education. We share a love for theater and a passion for the original Broadway cast albums of *Evita* and *Sweeney Todd*. I asked him to be my roommate with some trepidation because he was more popular than me, but he replied with an enthusiastic yes. I haven't had a close friend who is a boy since eighth grade, so I'm hopeful for this new friendship.

Soon it's October 16, 1983: my nineteenth birthday. A rainy Sunday keeps me in the dorm room. I'm looking forward to the arrival of Mom, Dad, and Aaron, who's now an adorable six-year-old. They're coming up to take me to dinner at the Whiffletree, one of my favorite restaurants. At 5:45 p.m., there's a gentle knock on the door. I open it to my mom standing alone.

"Sorry, we're a little late," she says. She gives me a perfunctory hug and kiss.

"Where's Dad and Aaron?"

"They're sleeping in the car," she says. "I didn't want to wake them."

"Oh."

"I didn't bring a present," she says. "I had no time, worked for the last two weeks." She couldn't at least get me a card? "Happy birthday, son."

"Thanks," I say.

We walk to the car. Dad is startled when I open the door. Aaron wakes up and greets me with a "Happy Birthday" sticker. "Here, brother, this is for you." I stick it to my sweater.

When we make it to the restaurant and sit down at the table, there's an awkward tension in the air. I'm getting the sense that something is wrong. We all order prime rib, the specialty. We make small talk, which consists of them asking about my classes and me asking why we still don't have health insurance even though it's been a year since Mom lost her job and union benefits.

"What do you expect me to do, Jeff? We have no money. I haven't even been able to buy myself a fall coat," Mom says.

"Maybe we shouldn't be eating at this restaurant," I say with sarcasm laced with bitterness.

Dad stays silent throughout this conversation, as if it doesn't concern him or he plays no role in its causation.

"What if I could lend you the money to get the plan?" I ask.

"You wouldn't even be covered because you're over eighteen." Everything is impossible to my mother. Our conversation is all contention, no joy. We sputter into another argument about her new, low-paying job at another pharmacy. These are scabs I can't stop picking.

"I'm sorry if asking you up for my birthday inconvenienced you," I say.

"Why would you say that?"

"This hasn't exactly been a very happy dinner."

We go through the motions of eating dessert. They sing "Happy Birthday" over a piece of chocolate chip cheesecake. At least it tastes good.

I return to my room feeling as badly as Mom looked and open the door to Andrew waiting for me. "Welcome home," he says and joyously hands me a gift-wrapped book with a card taped to the back. I open it quickly, feeling gratitude that at least someone remembered to get me a birthday present. The card says, "Happy Birthday, Jeffrey. Thanks for being my roommate." The book is *The Current Crisis in American Politics*. Though half my classes are in theater, I've declared my major to be Political Science. It makes me feel good that Andrew sees me.

"Thank you, Andrew," I say. "This means more than you can imagine."

"Hey, wanna finish our board?"

"Love to," I say.

We pull out our Magic Markers and pens; we work together on our customized memo board that we affix to the door outside our room. Andrew makes the frame, I draw bold bubble letters for our names, Andrew and Jeff, which we then color in. Both perfectionists, we work well together as a team.

"How was dinner with Aaron and your folks?" he says.

"Don't ask."

"Everything OK?"

"Not sure," I say. "This looks terrific." We glue the memo board to our door with a dry erase pen attached by a string.

"Best board on the fourth floor!" says Andrew.

I like making stuff with Andrew. Our conversation continues when we each get in our beds and get ready to go to sleep.

"I'm just glad my birthday is over."

"That's a terrible thing to say."

"I dread it. I'm always afraid no one will do anything for me. It feels like every year I'm hurt or disappointed."

"Well, guess what? This year someone did do something for you."

"I'm really glad you became my roommate."

"Me too," he says.

Mom calls me a few days later saying she needs to come up and talk.

She picks me up at my dorm room again, but this time she's alone. And she looks even more despondent than last week.

"Come on, let's go to McDonald's."

I never turn down a trip to McDonald's. As we walk from the car to the restaurant she starts talking. "The reason I came up is because your father and I are getting a divorce."

"Oh." So many divorces have been announced and called off, I'm a little bit sad, resigned, and tired of the ups and downs of their marriage.

"Your father isn't happy with his life and I'm certainly not happy with mine. Do you know what he did last week? I don't have enough money to get dental X-rays for your brother but he goes out and buys three frames for his clown photos. And I say, 'Do you really need three?' And he explains that one is for the kid in the photo and one is for us."

"And who's the third one for?"

"He's sending it to Ronald fucking Reagan. He didn't even vote for him."

Four days later Dad calls the divorce off. After impulsively setting it in motion, he realizes he won't find a better situation. What I don't understand is why Mom keeps going along with his decisions. He wants to divorce. Fine. He wants to stay married. Fine. What does she want? She will be tormented by his impulsive actions forever; she will sacrifice her happiness for him; she will allow him to come back over and over.

I MAY BE A blond-haired, blue-eyed, fair young man, but I'm cast as a Shark in the fall student production of *West Side Story*. Regardless, I'm just happy to be in a university production. The Sharks don't have names; the Jets are principals. But the Sharks perform "America," the "Tonight" quintet, "Somewhere," and the "Prologue" so I throw myself into the process. The director, Mary Kelly, is a rigorous and demanding Brit who treats everyone equally.

It's not a great production and Mary's concept of making it contemporary with "punk" costumes is met with disapproval by traditionalists, but it doesn't matter. What matters is learning *West Side Story* from the inside out. I find a book that puts the text of *West Side Story* and *Romeo and Juliet* side by side with scene-by-scene comparisons. The book concludes that the ending to *West Side Story* is superior because Anita chooses not to deliver the crucial message to Tony after she is assaulted by the Jets, which is more dramatic than the apothecary simply reaching Juliet too late.

After *West Side Story* closes, Andrew and I talk as we lie in our beds before going to sleep. This is where we have our best conversations. I wonder if it's because we are both looking at the ceiling right above our heads, not at each other.

"I'm not sure our production was great. But the musical is great," I say. "What did you think of the contemporary take?"

"I don't understand how you can do that music and say those lines and have it take place in 1983."

"Good point."

"I know she was trying to show how things are still the same," Andrew says. "The 'Tonight' quintet is still the best musical theater composition ever."

"You may be right," I say.

"What do you think is better, *West Side Story* or *Evita*?" he asks.

"Is that a trick question?" I reply.

"No. I'm just curious what you think after singing the Bernstein score."

"Well, *Evita* is still my favorite score. But I'd have to agree that *West Side* is a better show."

"Which is better, *West Side* or *Sweeney Todd*?"

"What do you think?" I ask.

"They're both unlike any other musicals. They're both tragedies," says Andrew.

"They're both modern," I say.

"What's amazing is how Sondheim starts his career as lyricist for *West Side* and then advances to *Sweeney* twenty years later."

"You like musicals, you play piano, why not write them?" I say to Andrew.

"I've never thought of that," he says.

"Let's write a musical. You'll write the music, I'll write the lyrics, you know, like Andrew Lloyd Webber and Tim Rice."

"That's a great idea," he says.

We go to the Oak Park Library during Christmas break and search through the children's section to find something that inspires us. Looking for a story that's dramatic and fun, I discover a book called *Jack the Giant Killer*, which is a series of English folk tales that includes *Jack and the Beanstalk*. It reminds me of the maple tree in my backyard that I wanted to climb to escape Cardboard Village. *This is fate*, I say to myself. We'll write an action-adventure musical that will be a swashbuckling blast!

Jack the Giant Killer gives me a new project during the Christmas break when being at home is more challenging than ever. There is barely any food in the refrigerator. Hanukkah presents are reserved for Aaron. Dad still lives under the delusion that he's a rich man. A "free agent" after being rejected by The Shriners, he performs four clown events at hospitals over the holiday. I write lyrics for an opening number in the town square that introduces Jack and his neighbors. I can't help borrowing the 3⁄4 waltz meter of "A Little Priest" from *Sweeney Todd*, the album I listen to almost as much as *Evita*. Is this stealing from the best?

Back at school in March, I receive another visit from home. I wake up early on a Saturday. Andrew is away for the weekend. I put on my Mozart *Greatest Hits* album and clean the room, hoping it will slow down my heart rate. Dad is coming to talk. Just me and him. He is coming to tell me that he and Mom are getting divorced—for real this time. When Mom told me this a few days ago, like she had so many times before, I called Dad and asked him to come up and talk to me.

Looking out of my fourth-floor window I see him pull into the circular driveway of the dorm in his blue Ford Escort. He's dressed in his daily uniform—polyester brown slacks, a tan terry cloth pullover shirt, gym shoes, and a green windbreaker. His "Chip Chip the Clown" base-ball hat covers his head.

Three firm knocks on the door. The type of knock only a six-foot-three, two-hundred-fifty-pound man can make. I open the door.

"Good morning, son," he says.

"Good morning," I warmly reply. I want to set an open tone for our conversation. He hugs me and leans down to kiss my cheek. I jerk my face away.

"Let's sit down."

Dad sits in the chair at my desk, and I sit in Andrew's chair facing him. The sun washes the window.

"You know, in all the times I've been told about you and Mom getting a divorce, it's always been from her," I say. "So, this time I wanted to hear it from you."

"I'm honored." This isn't sarcasm. His respect for me is steadfast. He perceives my need for an explanation as a reflection of my concern and love for him.

"Son, in all the years I've been married to your mother, I've never had a fulfilling love life. Your mother, because of her own screwed-up childhood, is completely incapable of love, of passion. In the almost thirty years I've been with your mother, son, I've never been in love with her."

It's hard to listen to him talk about Mom. It's hard to separate his feelings about her from his feelings about our family. The memory of all of us watching *60 Minutes* in the living room flashes through my mind: Dad is sitting next to Mom on the couch with her feet across his legs, gently caressing them after eight hours on her feet at the pharmacy.

"She's always brought me down. She's got her tight grip around me so strong it limits everything I do. Son, your mother is, in my estimation, not capable of being in a relationship."

He's not yelling, he's not red with anger. He's talking with a sense of equilibrium that makes this even harder to absorb. We sit in silence for a minute.

"Dad, I understand and respect your need to be in love. But what

I'm concerned about is your money situation. Things have been going downhill for so long. When you can't even afford to feed your family . . ."

"I know I've fucked up, son. Big time. I just got fed up with every-thing. With me free of your mother I really see myself making money again."

"That's what I've been begging you to focus on," I say.

"I know there's serious money to be made out there from insurance claim investigations, much more than in process serving."

"That's cool." I want so badly to believe him.

"Your mother has never been a happy person. Once I'm free of her, everything is going to get better."

"You've already said that. Twice."

Silence. He looks down at the floor and then up at me as if he just got caught stealing candy from the drugstore. With his legs spread on the chair, his elbows resting on his thighs, he turns his baseball cap to the side and lets out a long sigh.

"Your sister already knows this," he says. Another pause. My heart races. "There's another woman in my life, son."

I freeze.

"I intend on having a life with her."

"Who is she?"

"Do you remember that camping trip . . . ?"

"Yes," I say. My mind jumps back to our last camping trip, the sum-mer before eighth grade, when Dad brought along Daryl, the nerdy boy Bruce and I didn't know. "Daryl's mother?"

"Not that one," he replies.

I feel like I'm falling backward.

"Remember the camping trip where it rained and we stayed in Tawas?"

"Yes," I say. Of course I remember: The rain had driven us to take shelter in a motel. The question running through my mind is how this man with a short-term memory problem is having no problem remem-bering stuff.

122

"Do you remember the blond lady we met? With two sons?"

The blond lady in Tawas—she and her sons were the only other guests at the motel. This seems like a joke, all these affairs traceable to our camping trips. I'm nineteen years old and this affair started a year before Aaron was born. It's been happening for ten years. I feel trapped, dirty—as if I have marks on me that can't come off, like when an iron burns a shirt and there's nothing you can do to remove the burn. The last time he told me about another affair with another woman, when I was thirteen, I also felt like I was falling backward even though I was sitting on the couch. I was flummoxed. I tried to bury it, forget it. This new story makes me feel like my entire childhood was a lie. Our family wasn't real. I sit motionless and listen and try not to get angry. "She lives in Flint and owns a flower shop. She's been divorced for quite some time and her sons are now grown up and on their own. She has a beautiful house that would easily be worth two hundred thousand here. Please don't think there's any motive behind this. I really love her, son. Do you know what it's like to be in love for the first time in your life?"

My body feels like it's going to erupt. Darts ricochet around my guts and heart and stomach. I focus on Dad and say, "I'm glad you've found what you need to make you happy."

"I'm going to make things better. With Sue, I'm going to be happier. And everything else will flow from that happiness."

He stands up and gently takes my hand and pulls me out of my chair. He gives me a bear hug and whispers, "I love you, son. Please forgive me for everything I've done."

I stand in his arms for another moment and then pull away. I kind of believe him.

I watch him get in his Ford Escort and drive off. I put on my shoes and go running. It's the only way to relieve the pain.

IT'S HOT. NINETY DEGREES inside the house and out. I'm home for six weeks between school and my second summer at Camp Tamarack. We can't afford to run the air conditioner. We can barely afford to eat. Mom is working as hard as she can, making her own car insurance payment that Dad is supposed to make, and providing for all of Aaron's needs. Laurie is struggling to take care of her own daughter, born a year earlier. We barely talk.

This break might be pleasant if not for the heat and Dad's presence. The divorce was finalized a month ago, but he hasn't moved out. In between trips to Flint to see Sue, he loafs in the living room and sleeps on the couch. Mom stays in her bedroom.

I seek refuge in the backyard, sitting in one of our tattered lawn chairs. I read another book that helps me imagine my future: *Contradictions* by the producer and director Harold Prince. He describes his career from office boy and stage manager to producer and director, and every show he worked on from *The Pajama Game* to *Candide* in 1974. It comes to me in a flash: I want to do what Hal Prince does. But how?

One day as I'm sitting in the sun, the phone rings in the kitchen, interrupting the *Sunday in the Park with George* recording blaring from my cassette player. I stop the tape just as it aptly plays "It's Hot Up Here" and run to answer it.

"Hello?" I answer.

"Is Mr. Seller there?" a woman asks.

"No, he's not," I say. "May I take a message?"

"This is Ford Motor credit calling. Do you know when Mr. Seller will be home? He promised to be here in person today to make his car payment and it's five o'clock. If he's not here by noon tomorrow, we'll begin taking steps to repossess his car." She hangs up before saying goodbye.

Dad's situation is getting worse. He has no money and is barely working. The car he isn't making payments on has a broken driver's seat, a cracked windshield, and almost nonexistent brakes. Reclaiming it would be useless; it's worth nothing. I see a pile of opened mail on the kitchen shelf. There's a cancellation notice for his car insurance. His business phone was canceled for not paying an overdue balance of 150 dollars. Total Petroleum is sending a collection agency to re-claim the five hundred dollars he owes them. A court summons that is not for him to serve but that is *for him* demands that he show up in person regarding his latest traffic ticket. If he doesn't appear promptly, his driver's license will be revoked. As I'm reading the summons, he pulls into the driveway. I quickly put it back with the other letters.

"Hello?" he says as the screen door slams behind him.

"Hi," I say, stepping out of the kitchen and sitting down at the table.

"What's happening, son?" he says, striding to the refrigerator.

"Not much," I reply, watching him study its measly contents. "Ford credit just called. I guess you were supposed to see them today to make a payment or something?"

"Yep," he says, pulling two red apples from the fruit drawer.

"They said if you didn't show up by noon tomorrow, they're going to take back the car."

"Yep," he replies. He sprawls out on the living room floor with his two apples and the *Detroit News*. I wonder why a man so out of touch with his own life is interested in current events. I sit at the table watching him eat our food. My thighs are sticking to the cracked vinyl dining room chairs.

"I have a problem," I say. He turns his head to me. "Two months ago, I sat with you in my dorm room. You told me you were going to make a new start. How you were going to pull it all together and start your new life and get your shit together. Now the situation has worsened to the point that Mom had to go to Jewish Family Services for money for food for your son. And you're eating it."

He looks at me. He doesn't blink.

"It's not you that has a problem," he says. "It's me."

I stare at him. His eyes are glazed over with tears.

"I don't want any more explanations," I reply. "You are on your way to killing our relationship. I don't know how you live with yourself."

"Me neither," he says. He gets up off the floor, folds his newspaper, and starts out the door. "I'll talk to you later."

While this conversation gives me no relief, his absence is still preferable to his presence.

I yearn to see Andrew, but he's been busy singing in the chorus of *Anna Bolena* starring Dame Joan Sutherland at the Michigan Opera Theatre. I saw him briefly on opening night, and he seemed pleased, but also distant. He didn't want to go out for dessert after the performance. It's as if the last year of our friendship—talking every night before going to sleep, performing together in a production of *Hello, Dolly!*, working together on our musical—didn't happen. He has become my best friend and I miss him.

That's only partly true.

The truth that I've been avoiding, dodging, and trying to ignore is that I miss him because I'm in love with him.

A few days later he calls as if nothing is wrong. I'm happy to hear his voice and set my insecurity and new awareness aside.

The second week of June, I return to camp enthusiastic to start work with a new batch of theater kids.

A DAY AT CAMP begins at 7:30 a.m. when we wake up the campers and get ready for breakfast at eight. Today, for the July Fourth holiday, we all get to sleep in until 8:30 a.m. Hallelujah! When the alarm goes off, I hustle to the boys' bathhouse to wash my face and brush my teeth, then return to the chilly cabin. I put on my navy Adidas shorts, a white T-shirt, and a U of M sweatshirt, then walk down the dirt path that leads to the village lodge where we eat. Walking toward me from the other direction are my seven-year-old brother, Aaron, and Dad. I stop in my tracks, not knowing what to do. Visitors are not allowed in camp and are never allowed to enter the villages. Specialty is a full mile from the main gate. How did they get through? I'm worried I'll get in trouble if anyone finds out that they're here.

"Dad, what are you doing here?"

"I need to talk to you, son."

"Hi, brother," says Aaron, happy to see me.

"Hello, brother," I reply, trying to be cheerful for Aaron while wanting to kill my father. "Dad, you're not supposed to be here."

"I'm sorry, son. I just had to see you."

"Let's walk out to the car," I say, leading them toward the road where his dilapidated Escort is parked and hoping the supervisor of Specialty doesn't see us. "We can't talk here with the campers around."

"Son, I . . . I found a house. In Royal Oak." His words come out in bits and spurts, with tears welling up in his eyes. "I can move in immediately. I can finally get my life in order. I just need six hundred dollars to move in, son. Seven-fifty would be even better if you could afford to be that generous. I'll pay you back by September first, son."

I don't know what to say. "Dad, this is hardly the right time to be talking about this. I'm working."

"I know, son. I'm sorry to get in your way, but, but, but I'm just so excited about this, about getting a fresh start."

"We'll talk about it when I'm home the day after tomorrow."

"I don't mean to pressure you, but the banks close early on Saturday."

"Dad, we'll deal with this Friday night. Now, you have to leave. You have no idea what kind of trouble I'll be in if they catch you here."

"Thank you, son. You don't know how much this means to me."

This scene plays out in my head the whole day. I try to look at this request objectively: He's already up to his neck in debt and moving will only flood him with new expenses. He'll never pay me back by September. I can't give him three quarters of my summer salary. On the other hand, getting him out of the house would really help Mom. I would be doing this for her as much as for him. Most of all, though, I'm infuriated. I'm nineteen years old, putting myself through college. And my father is asking me for a loan. Has he no self-respect?

I come home for my day off Friday night. It's his birthday, July 7. Today, he's forty-seven years old. When I arrive, he's waiting for me.

"Are you ready to talk?"

"Why don't we go into the bedroom?" I say. My old bedroom is Aaron's bedroom, so we must retreat to Mom's bedroom. He sits on the edge of the bed. I sit down next to him.

"So, what do you think, son?"

"No," I say.

"What do you mean?"

"No."

"You won't lend me the money?" he says.

"I won't lend you the money."

He rises, trudges past me, opens the door, and takes his huge strides that catapult him to the front door in about four steps. He slams the screen door, gets in the car, and drives away.

I write him a letter.

July 12, 1984

Dad,

> *I only have disgust for you.*
>
> *You have failed as a father—to Laurie, to me and, most importantly, to Aaron. You obviously DO NOT really love us. You've said you do time and time again. Yet, in reality, all you show is your love for yourself. You live to please Mark Seller. A real father demonstrates his love by: A) Acting as a role model and living as a responsible human being. As a man without a job, without a car, and without a home, you are not a proper role model, and you are not a responsible member of our society. B) Providing the basic necessities to his offspring. No one has a right to be a parent unless he can care for his children. If any of us got really sick our lives would be in jeopardy. If Aaron woke up tomorrow in need of emergency surgery, or with a chronic illness like leukemia, you couldn't do anything to help him. If Aaron was in your care, he would have no clothes on his back. No shelter, no food, no health.*
>
> *Why has this all happened? Bad luck? No. You have failed as a professional. You put your needs like clowning, carrying on with mistresses and hanging out in pool halls ahead of your responsibili-*

ties. It is clear why your business went down the drain. You fucked it up. Your interest was not in making our lives better, but yours.

In the fifteen years since you bankrupted Poucher Tool you have learned nothing. My mother worked and strained and kept us afloat. Her earnings supported us. Your earnings supported you. You are as self-serving, self-centered, and selfish as you have always been.

You have failed as a husband. After putting your ex-wife through twenty-seven years of lies and selfishness, then reject- ing her, you expect her to let you sleep in her house. You expect her to support you. She is not your mother. She is the woman you threw away. Now, she only wants you out of her life so she can pick up the pieces. You won't even let her do that. No grown, capable man who lives off others deserves to live.

That sums it up. You're a loser. Leave us alone. You make me mad, sad, bitter, and hurt. I don't want to be near you. We're finished.

Jeffrey Bruce

I look over the letter before I put it in an envelope. I stop at the phrase "no grown, capable man who lives off others deserves to live." I realize I want him to die. I want him to drown in the Au Sable River or get shot by an angry summons recipient. Only his absence will make this pain go away. After I sign this letter, I leave it on the dining room table for him.

When I return home from camp for one week before school starts, I ignore him. I have one more important activity before going back to school: I need to get my wisdom teeth removed. Mom can't take me because she has a new job filling prescriptions at a private pharmacy that is paying her more money than she has ever made, and she works thirty hours per week. I ask Andrew to accompany me and bring me home after. He's happy to help. He takes care of me through the whole process—driving me to the clinic, sitting in the waiting room during the oral surgery, holding me up as we walk to the car after the removal of four impacted wisdom teeth. He is present and caring. I feel comforted and safe in his presence.

When we arrive home, my mouth filled with gauze, my body sagging from anesthesia, Dad is in the living room. I walk past him without acknowledging him. I seek refuge in Aaron's bedroom, where I stay during my short visit.

A few days later, Andrew returns to pick me up. We are about to drive to our new apartment, and I'm walking out the door when Dad abruptly asks me to stay for one more minute.

"Andrew, I'll be right out," I say. Andrew walks to the car after tentatively saying goodbye to my father. He doesn't want to disrespect him, but he doesn't want to be disloyal to me.

I stand by the door and look at Dad. He starts crying, huge tears emanating from his hazel eyes. He heaves.

"Let's see if I can get the words out," he says through his sobs. He can't catch his breath. "Your letter was shocking. Please know that I never consciously did anything that I thought would hurt you or your sister."

I pause to take in his words, which I know are heartfelt. I also know that his intentions and his actions are completely opposite, and I'm finished giving him another chance.

"I can't listen to your promises anymore," I say. "And I can't talk to you, I can't have anything to do with you until you restore your life. Get a job. Get an apartment. Give Mom the money she needs to raise your son. Then I'll talk to you. But not before."

I walk out the door. Andrew and I drive to Ann Arbor.

Chapter Fifteen

628 PACKARD STREET

WITH OUR FRIEND NANCY, Andrew and I move into our apartment on the top floor of 628 Packard on Saturday, September 1,
1984. It's at the corner of State Street, a few blocks south of the Student
Union and a few blocks north of the football stadium. It's in the middle
of everything.

I'm sitting on a mushy green couch that sits on top of a greenish-
yellowish worn carpet looking at our living room and kitchen. The drapes
have green floral patterns against a yellow background. I guess the landlord
likes green. A crossbeam spans the living room ceiling to demarcate the
kitchen and dining table from the living area. There's a wide-open study
area in the hallway between the bedrooms and kitchen that has two desks
and shelves. Andrew and I each get one. Nancy has her own bedroom,
while Andrew and I share the other with a bunk bed his father bought us.
I'll sleep on top. The bathroom has two sinks, like the bathroom the kids
share on *The Brady Bunch*. It's bigger than the bathroom at home.

Our lives are stacked up in boxes and plastic milk crates in the living
room. I smile, excited that this is my new home.

Living with Andrew in our own apartment is different from sharing
a room in the dorm. This is more private. Now, we're not just roommates living together out of convenience. It's no longer possible to avoid
the current of connection between us.

It starts with a sock. We are sitting in the living room, Andrew on the couch, me on the adjacent chair. My right foot, covered in a saggy, twisting tube sock with two red rings, is resting on the arm of the couch. Andrew gently leans over and straightens it. That one touch goes straight to my heart. We've known each other since we were six, been friends for three years, and best friends for one year. But this is the first time he touches me in a way that feels different. Intimate. Love is in that gesture. Desire is in that gesture. Then he adjusts the frayed right leg of my sweatpants. I touch his hand as it touches my leg. My touch is short but intentional. I don't linger.

The moment passes. We make dinner together and eat with Nancy. At bedtime, we both get into our bunk beds. I know that tonight will be different, tonight we won't go to sleep until we talk. I'm excited and afraid.

My heart is beating so fast I think I might have a heart attack and die right now, but I finally blurt out, "Andrew, you're my best friend in the whole wide world."

"I want to keep it that way," he says.

"But, um, I have more to say."

"OK."

"You know, um, when you were doing the opera last May, I knew you were busy and all that, and I didn't want to bother you."

"Singing behind Joan Sutherland was a dream come true."

"But when it was over, you still kind of ignored me, or stayed distant, or I don't know what. And, at first, I was angry. But what I really was, was hurt."

"I'm sorry," he replies. "I never meant to hurt you."

"And it's only because of, because I love you. And I missed you. And I needed you while my family stuff was so fucked up."

"I'm so sorry," he says. "I know I disappeared. I don't know how to say this except to just say it. I was keeping a secret. I didn't know what to do."

"You can tell me."

"There was this guy. His name was Tim. He's a couple years older. And he asked me out on a date."

"I see."

"And we went out. And then we came back to my house—my parents were away visiting my sister. We started making out and stuff and then he asked me if I was inviting him to spend the night. I wasn't sure what to say, so I said yes."

"Wow," I say.

"Weird, I know," says Andrew. "And I was so scared that you'd be angry at me or judge me or something. Because I don't want to do anything to harm what we have."

"I'm not angry at all."

"I think I'm going to throw up," he says.

"Please don't throw up," I say. "Not that it could possibly make our carpet any worse."

He laughs. And cries. "I've had such a long string of best friends. I wonder why you would pick me."

"I needed a stereo to listen to my *Dreamgirls* album."

He laughs again. "I love you very much," he says.

"I need to pee," I respond.

I go to the bathroom. I return and sit on the floor. I pull a sheet and blanket around me. Safe cover. I'm hugging my knees together. I can't get the words out.

"After everything I've said, you can't talk?" he prompts. "What's the holdup?"

"I don't know how to say this except to just say it," I start.

"What?"

"Ever since I was fifteen, soon after I first masturbated, I've had homosexual images in my head as well as heterosexual images."

"You're so clinical."

"I know, I get that from my mother," I say. "I've known since last year that I'm in love with you. I've never been in love with anyone in my life. I feel good when I'm around you. I love being with you. I love talking to you before we go to sleep every night. I miss you when you're gone. I want to spend my life with you. I've never felt this way about anyone before. And I guess I'll have to take the consequences. Because I can't not be with you.

"I knew you were gay when I asked you to be my roommate," I continue. "But I didn't care. Because I liked you. And I wanted to be roommates with you."

"I loved that you asked me to be your roommate," he says. "And I love you, too, Jeffrey Seller."

"So, what do we do now?" I ask.

"You tell me," he says.

I'm still scared. I climb to my bunk and lie down. Neither of us says anything for a couple of minutes.

"Can I come up there?" he asks with hesitation.

"Yeah."

At first, we hold each other, not just our bodies, which have never been this close, but our history, our friendship, our yearning. Then Andrew leans in and kisses me on the lips, which changes everything.

Making love with Andrew is a cascade of feeling. If we had lain in bed and just held each other and kissed it would have been the most sensuous, safe, rewarding physical intimacy I'd ever experienced. Taking off our clothes is another new experience, one that liberates me from years of solitude. The warmth and excitement of being with another man is like being reborn.

Do I think about AIDS that first night? No. Andrew had sex twice with one guy from the Detroit area. My only sex has been masturbating against a silky blue comforter left by my dead grandmother. Do we talk about AIDS? No. This rare disease has nothing to do with us. Andrew is my safe haven.

A week later, I'm at the laundromat with two loads in the wash, including the sheets. I've never had to manage this much laundry. Our talks every night are followed by lovemaking. I love kissing Andrew. I love his full lips. I love touching him. I love being touched by him. On Saturday mornings, I jump down from my top bunk and cuddle with him under the covers. It's our free morning, our chance to just "be." Eventually, our morning cuddle ends with me getting up and saying, "Gotta get the day goin'" and Andrew saying, "OK, Mr. Get the Day Goin'!"

I feel unburdened, lighter. Though I'm keeping a new secret, that will work itself out with time.

Our relationship continues to deepen when we're hired to direct and music direct *Grease* for the Soph Show, the annual fall musical sponsored by the University Activities Center. I've seen the movie many times but have never seen or read the play. I delve into the script and music. These lovable characters aren't the students who get straight A's and go to fancy colleges. They are the "greasers," the teenagers who screw around and graduate to working-class jobs. I know these kids. I know their stories. They are my parents. This is a musical about Mom and her friends Penny and Sheila; and Dad and his friends, "the Jokers." That connection makes me love these characters.

On the first night of auditions, Andrew and I, along with Larry Nye, the choreographer who just transferred to the school, sit behind a table to watch the auditionees. My first time behind a table, I think about how to behave. I must give each auditionee my full support and attention. The students sing their own songs and then learn a dance with Larry. They will read with each other at the callbacks. The turnout is big—sixty kids.

A guy comes in and introduces himself as Jamel. He has dark brown, almost black hair. Wearing a tattered T-shirt and Levi's, he's cool. He confesses that he's never been in a show before, but he loves *Grease*. He sings "It's Still Rock and Roll to Me." Crystal clear high notes fly out of his mouth. He is an amazing rock tenor. He's charming and masculine in an easygoing way. The fact that he's never been in a play before feels like a plus. I think, *We've got our Danny Zuko.*

A thin, beautiful Black woman with short hair comes in. She's soft-spoken, sweet, and a little bit shy. Then she opens her mouth. Andrew and I look at each other. It's as if Jennifer Holliday walked in the room. Her voice is too good to be true. She's a rousing gospel singer. I think we have found our Rizzo.

Another young woman performs "I Cain't Say No," from *Oklahoma!* She sings the song with just the right tang and flirtatiousness. She's cute. She doesn't perform as well at the callback the next night, but we decide to trust her first audition. She'll make a good Sandy.

After the callbacks, Andrew, Larry, and I, along with our two producers, Steve and Jamie, go up to the Soph Show office to make our decisions. It starts off easy. We agree on all the principals. Then we come to the issue of a chorus. There was no chorus in the original Broadway show. It was an ensemble with seventeen cast members. Larry wants to cast eight more people to pump up the dance numbers. I want to stay true to the original.

"Why would we change it? I want to do it the way they did it on Broadway," I say.

"We don't have to do it that way just because that's how they did it on Broadway," says Larry. "In summer stock we do whatever we want."

"The show is the longest-running show in Broadway history. Why are you messing with it?"

"Because it will make the big numbers better," Larry retorts.

"Oh, so you're going to be better than a Broadway show?"

"Why are you so obsessed with how it was done? This is now. And, by the way, nobody knows the show. Everyone knows the movie. And there's tons of people at the high school dance."

"Well, I guess the good thing is that we'll get to cast more people," says producer Steve.

"Isn't that the point?" demands Larry.

"The point is to make the best show possible," I say.

"Andrew, what do you think?" asks Steve.

I don't wait for Andrew's answer. "It's the longest-running show on Broadway," I say. "Why the fuck are we messing with it?"

Larry gets more and more frustrated. "This is the craziest conversation I've ever had," he says.

"Really?" I say. "The craziest?"

"My job is to make great dances. I can't do that if I don't have dancers."

"It's not about great dances. It's about making teenagers look like they're having fun."

"Oh, so now you're telling me how to be a choreographer?"

"You're a great choreographer. I love watching you. But I'm the director."

"You know what, I can't take this. I'm out." He leaves the room.

"Larry, don't go!" Steve, the producer, runs out after him.

The producers are bewildered by this conflict and beg me to agree to a chorus. I feel like it's me against the world. I can't afford to see Larry quit. I give in.

We recover but with a cost. I never apologize to Larry for my behavior. I can't admit to myself that I was a stubborn asshole. I made a discussion into a war. I wouldn't listen to any idea that wasn't mine. I was afraid that if I veered from my original plan, the whole endeavor would fail. I was beholden to the way it was done on Broadway. The wound from my conflict with Larry is deep. He always delivers great work, but we never get close.

The cast is exuberant from the first day of rehearsal. Andrew is a superb music director. Makes me think I'm watching a pro like Bob Fosse in *All That Jazz*. I love being in the room with the actors and use everything I've learned in acting class over the past year. I give them a basic structure—where to enter and exit, what part of the stage to occupy, and then encourage them to pursue their objectives and let that pursuit guide their movements. Then I edit or add a bit that might be funny or effective.

I feel more productive than ever this fall, making time for running twice a week, preparing for each rehearsal, researching a project on party identification for my American Political Parties class, and analyzing newspaper coverage of the 1984 US Senate race in Michigan for work-study at the Institute for Social Research.

Early in the process, our Rizzo, Judy, is out sick for several days. She calls to tell me she's having some tests for abdominal pain. Her description of what's going on is scary. The doctors are testing her for cancer. I assure her that it's going to be OK and that we will be waiting for her when she's able to return. This news rattles me and sparks my fear of getting sick without health insurance.

Thankfully, her tests come back negative. She's diagnosed with a small, treatable ulcer. She returns to rehearsal the following week. One night, while Larry works with the boys in one room, Andrew and I work with Judy on "There Are Worse Things I Could Do."

Andrew and Judy review the music and then we start playing with it on its feet. I sit on the floor against the wall. Judy starts tentatively. She feels her way through a first pass of the song.

"Let's talk about this," I say.

"Please."

"You know, on the surface, the lyrics are pretty straightforward."

"Right."

"But I think there's more going on underneath," I continue.

"Definitely," she responds.

"Tell me what's going on for you."

"Rizzo comes off as, you know, um, tough. She's kind of hard. She's got a thick skin. She's not afraid of anything."

"Yeah."

"But I think that she's also hiding a lot," says Judy.

"What do you mean?" I ask.

"She acts like she doesn't give a shit what anyone else thinks of her, but I think she actually does."

"Go on."

"It hurts when people think she's a slut," she says.

"Yes."

"And she doesn't think she's done anything so terrible that she deserves to be judged."

"You mean getting pregnant?" I say.

"Yes."

"Nice. Let's try the song."

"Judy, you know the notes," says Andrew. "Take your time, make your own tempo. I'm going to follow you."

She starts. Not much changes. I interrupt.

"Just start by speaking the lyrics," I say. "Just focus on the words and then let the music take over when it feels right."

She starts speaking to the music. It's soft, matter-of-fact. She slowly builds as if she's shifting into second gear.

"Can you let go musically?" asks Andrew.

"More?" she asks.

"I want you to imagine throwing paint at the wall," says Andrew. "How much paint can you splatter on that wall?"

"I'm going to add one more thing," I say. "I want you to think about how you were feeling a week ago, when you were waiting for your test results. When you didn't know what was going to happen to you. I want to see you express that feeling in the song."

"You told me you sang in your church," says Andrew. "Think of this as church."

Judy starts the song again. She plugs into her gospel roots. Her soulful voice brings a new dimension to the song. She builds intensity with each phrase and then lets it all go on the bridge: "I could stay home every night . . ." She lands on the word *night* and holds it for several beats. She splatters the wall with vivid colors and electricity shoots down my spine. She has transformed a simple ballad about dating guys and getting pregnant into a song about survival. It's our Jennifer Holliday moment.

Everyone is bowled over. The assistant director is in tears. Judy is in tears. The song is going to tear the roof off the Mendelssohn Theatre. Goodbye Stockard Channing. Hello Judy Creagh. "That was the most amazing coaching session I've ever had," says Judy.

"We're a good team," I say.

Walking home, Andrew says, "I loved working with you on that."

"Me too," I say. "What I love most about this whole process is being with you."

For the first time in my life, I don't feel lonely. I finally have someone to talk to about everything—my likes and dislikes, my internal conflicts and insecurities, my fantasies and apprehensions. We are both Type A, which presents its own challenges, but we resolve our conflicts on the spot—we fight it out and cry and hug and have sex. I'm the happiest I've ever been.

That night I have a dream about my father: He's choosing to give up and die because he has nothing to live for. I rush home to see him one more time where he's getting ready to lie down in a coffin. I wake up feeling guilty. I also feel a deep sense of loss and emptiness. The dream makes me question my letter and ceasing contact with him. It makes me realize that I miss him. I miss his big heart, his encouragement, his enthusiasm for my pursuits, even when he can't remember the details. I put this dream aside and get on with classes, the show, and my new relationship.

Judy is fantastic as Rizzo. Jamel is an endearing Danny Zuko, and the other boys are sweet and winning; I love the Pink Ladies. Trying to figure out how to best amplify the sound on a limited budget, we decide to use two cordless hand-mics for all the solos and duets. We find fun ways to reveal them and pass them off. The character Marty pulls one out from under her pillow right before she sings "Freddy, My Love."

A week before the show opens, Mom drives up to take me to her favorite lunch joint, Blimpy Burger. It's a small dive with a counter and a few tables—first come, first served—and no waiters. We give our order to the cook, with whom Mom is friendly after many visits, and then enjoy watching her fry our burgers on the grill and deep-fry the onion rings, which are crunchy and delicious. When the food is ready, we take our trays to a table in the corner. There are only two other people in the restaurant on this cold Saturday in early December.

"So how are you, son? I came up because we haven't talked in a while."

"Today's my only day off," I say. "I need to catch up on my poli-sci project before we start tech tomorrow."

"That was some letter you sent Dad last summer."

"He showed it to you?"

"Yes."

"It was between me and him. It had nothing to do with you."

"He would like to come and see your show next weekend. What do you think?"

"Do *you* want me to say yes?" I ask.

"No, son, I drove all this way hoping you'd say no."

"I'm trying to figure this out, Mom. I've put a lot into this show. I don't want to spend the whole performance thinking about him."

"He's still your father," she says.

I think about the dream I recently had about him. I think about him taking me to rehearsals for *Carmen* at the Music Hall. I know that, despite his failure as a provider and his betrayal of my mother, any time I asked him to take me to an audition or rehearsal or play, he said, "Get in the car."

"Fine, he can come," I say. "Now, can I finish your French fries?"

The whole family comes up on Friday night. Aunt Amy makes me a wool herringbone scarf as a gift. My cousin Jack, a junior in high school, brings his girlfriend. And Mom comes with Aaron and Dad.

After the show, Dad says, "Son, I had no idea you were going to do a show about me and my buddies."

"Crazy, right?" I say.

"It made me feel like I was right back with Bruce and Stuey, riding up and down Woodward Avenue. You're amazing, son."

"Thanks," I say.

Grease is a lovefest between the performers and the audience. We sell out all three performances. After the final performance on Saturday night, Andrew and I host a party at our apartment. It's the best party I've ever attended. Everyone brings food, beer, and wine for this celebration. As I'm standing in the kitchen with the producers, one of them asks, "So how did you know how to do this?"

"What do you mean?" I ask back.

"How did you make this?"

"It's what I've been doing my whole life," I answer.

Chapter Sixteen

PEOPLE EXPRESS: ONE-WAY TICKET TO NYC!

A S THE LAST SEMESTER of senior year begins, I feel pride at what I've accomplished and fear of what the future will hold. While I know I'm graduating on May 3, I have no idea what will happen on May 4. Where will I live? What work will I do? How will I keep doing shows without the opportunities that a college presents? What are Andrew and I going to do when I graduate, and he has another year left?

On a Monday in January, Andrew comes home for dinner with big news. The musical theatre department is doing a new musical based on the movie *It's a Wonderful Life.* The book and lyrics are by Sheldon Harnick and the music is by Joe Raposo. I'm amazed that Sheldon Harnick, the famous Broadway lyricist of *Fiddler on the Roof,* is doing his new musical at U of M. Joe Raposo is the *Sesame Street* composer who wrote the theme song and "It's Not Easy Bein' Green" for Kermit the Frog. Andrew auditions for the musical and is cast as George Bailey, the lead.

I am proud of him, but I'm also jealous that he will be working with one of the greatest lyricists on Broadway. I try and think of a way to participate in this production and realize that if musical theater history is going to be made in Ann Arbor, then somebody needs to report it. I decide I'll write a series of articles on the making of this new musical. If I can get Sheldon Harnick to do an interview, it will be a journalistic coup. I call director Brent Wagner and pitch him the idea. He loves it. I make an appointment to meet with the arts editor of the *Ann Arbor News*. I show up at the newsroom and explain my idea. He offers to publish one article every Sunday. I'll write five Sunday arts stories in a row. The payment is thirty-five dollars per story.

I love the in-person interviews. I love coming up with the lede for each story and creating a narrative that can be tied together by quotes. I sit with all the creatives and attend a few rehearsals to observe them in action. Watching Andrew and his leading lady, Beth Spencer, rehearse is illuminating; Andrew's emotional immediacy is as potent onstage as it is in life.

Sheldon Harnick agrees to an interview, and we sit down in the theater office one afternoon. Harnick looks just as he did in old photos from the original production of *Fiddler*. He even seems to be wearing the same horn-rimmed glasses. I'm equally excited and nervous. The interview starts off a little dry because he's businesslike and reserved, which is not what I expected from the lyricist of warm, affectionate shows like *She Loves Me* and *Fiddler*.

We talk about the genesis of *A Wonderful Life*, how much he's enjoyed working with Joe Raposo, and the legal problems he encountered over attaining the production rights, which meant he could do a college production but not yet Broadway. He also explains he was attracted to the source material because he is intrigued by the do-gooder who's afraid he has thrown his life away by taking care of everyone but himself.

My mission is to uncover two things, both of which are touchy subjects: Why did he break up with Jerry Bock and why has he only written one Broadway show in the last sixteen years? And, consequently, what does a wealthy writer, who doesn't have to work, do every day?

I summon my courage and ask, "Why did you and Jerry Bock, one of the greatest partnerships in Broadway history, stop working together after *The Rothschilds*?"

I perceive that he hates answering this question. "Well, first of all, thank you for that compliment."

"I mean it."

"Jerry didn't want to do it anymore. I think he lost the drive."

"That must have been very disappointing for you."

"There was no animosity. We never fought."

"You weren't angry?"

"We had fifteen great years together. He was done. I wasn't." In fact, Harnick found other projects. He wrote a show called *Rex* with Richard Rodgers, a musical about King Henry VIII, that flopped. He wrote the book, music, and lyrics to another musical called *Dragons*, which was never professionally produced, and started doing translations, most recently for *The Merry Widow*.

Harnick doesn't express joy. Maybe he doesn't like doing interviews. Maybe he doesn't like student reporters. He doesn't look at me when he talks. He stares at a specific point in space over my head. It's almost as if he's reading his answers off a monitor I cannot see.

"Can you talk me through a day in the life of a lyricist?" I ask.

"Well, I try to write every morning. At least a couple hours. I might start with an image—like, for example, ice cream if I'm working on *She Loves Me*, or a piece of dialogue. And then I start building out from there."

"How long do you spend writing every day? Is it a nine-to-five job?"

"If I can sustain four hours, I've had a good day."

"And then what's the rest of the day like?"

"There are phone calls to make, lunch with my wife, Margie."

"What else?"

"Well, you'd be surprised how much work it is to keep up an apartment in New York City."

"What do you mean?" I am clueless. He can't mean that he cleans his own apartment.

"Well, you know, dealing with all the service people. You're always waiting for a plumber or electrician to show up. You'd be surprised how many things can go wrong in a New York apartment."

I walk out pleased. I've just had a professional conversation with a legend. I have touched a bit of Broadway. Though he wasn't as personable as I'd hoped, I am rewarded by his time and stories. I laugh with

Andrew that night that being a rich Broadway lyricist means waiting all afternoon for the plumber.

Over the past few months, though, our relationship has been challenged by numerous rifts. I want to act like we're married—safe and secure—while Andrew just wants a boyfriend. He doesn't have the heart to tell me it's not working for him, so we fight over what to eat for dinner instead. It doesn't help that he is consumed by the show. His role is an enormous responsibility, so he rehearses nonstop and sleeps for nine hours every night to rest his voice. We spend little time together. We rarely have sex. I feel alone.

Andrew is triumphant in *A Wonderful Life*. It's the best production to have ever played in Ann Arbor. While I'm proud of my stories for the *Ann Arbor News*, I feel like an outsider in this moment while Andrew is at the center of our little universe. When the show concludes, he is offered a summer stock gig at the Kenley Players in Ohio and a casting internship on Broadway. He is excited about what comes next for him professionally. And he wants to be free.

"I want to be alone," he says. "But I also know I'll be lonely if we break up."

"You're a selfish person," I say.

"And you won't let me have any friends," he retorts. "You're angry if I do anything without you."

"I thought we were a couple. I thought we were going to be together forever."

"You thought that, not me. I don't want to be married anymore, Jeffrey, I'm too young. That doesn't mean I don't love you. I just need my life to be about me."

"Big surprise," I reply.

"When you said you wanted to be with me forever, I didn't know what you were talking about. I was in the moment. I don't even know what forever means."

He goes to his parents' house for a few days. We make up.

As I finish my last classes of college, I feel like crying. What's my next step? College has been productive, but I have no mentor, no one to give me direction.

Graduation is on Saturday, May 3. My aunt Amy hosts a small party to celebrate. Andrew and his parents join, and they take a photo with my parents and me. Neither set of parents knows that we are a couple. After two years, I have never said the words *I am gay*. I've rationalized that I fell in love with a person who happened to be a man. My early fantasies of sex with women have allowed me to nurture the fiction that I'm bisexual. I know it's untrue and that I need to accept who I am. But my priority is to get a job; the first payment on my student loans is November 1 and I'm already nervous about it.

On the Monday following Saturday graduation, I make a plan. I will use my articles from the *Ann Arbor News* to get interviews at public relations agencies in New York. I go to the business school library and find a catalogue that lists all the public relations agencies in the country and identify the ones that might be interested in my skills. I write a cover letter that I tailor to each agency and attach three articles. Then I track every letter and start follow-up calls a week later.

The process is draining. I leave messages that are never returned. I am rejected by most. Some people compliment my writing and tell me they have no jobs to offer. One agency tells me my writing isn't strong enough. After one month, I've sent out sixty letters. By the first of June I've lined up a handful of interviews in New York. I will fly out on June 16 and stay at our roommate Nancy's mother's apartment in Sheepshead Bay until the nineteenth.

Every interview is instructive. I meet a woman named Pam at her apartment-slash-office on West Fifty-seventh Street. She works out of her living room and will need a second person if she gets a couple new accounts in the next few weeks. She talks fast and loud and seems fun. I meet an older man, wearing a three-piece suit, at a corporate agency on Madison Avenue, who is pure business. This one isn't for me. I go to another big agency that has more flair. The conference room has plush plum-colored walls and soft gray chairs around a black marble conference table. I'm interviewed by a handsome blond guy who is more interesting than the clients he represents.

My last interview is at a two-room office on West Forty-fourth Street between Fifth and Sixth Avenue. It's a firm run by two men, Alan Hale and Al Husted. Alan represents a performing arts festival called Pepsico Summerfare at SUNY Purchase. Peter Sellars will direct *Cosi fan tutte* in a diner, Eliot Feld will bring his ballet company, and a famous Romanian director will stage *A Midsummer Night's Dream*. Al talks about his years as Johnny Carson's press agent. They have one employee, a tall dark-haired man who sits in front of a computer in the outer office. His name is Daryl, and he has a deep, soothing voice. He's friendly. I like him.

With enough money to see one show while I'm in town, I line up at the TKTS booth and buy half-price tickets for Nancy and me to see Bernadette Peters in *Song and Dance*, Andrew Lloyd Webber's new musical. Bernadette beams when she makes her first entrance. She is pure love. She's playing a character who has just arrived in New York City proclaiming it's "the one place on earth I want to be."

When I get home to Ann Arbor, Alan Hale calls.

"Hello. We really enjoyed meeting you. Do you think you'd like to come here and work with us?"

"It's the one place on earth I want to be," I say.

"You're going to do just great," he says. "I think we'll be able to do a salary of 14,500 dollars plus health insurance."

This will be the first time I have health insurance since graduating high school. "I accept." We agree that I will start in July.

I make plans to move to New York right after July 4. I'll live with Nancy and her mom for the first few days until I find a place. She tells me to buy a copy of the *Village Voice* and scour the classified ads to find an apartment share to rent. She says I'll like Park Slope in Brooklyn. I go to the bookstore and buy the latest copy. The cover has a huge headline, "Scenes from an AIDS Ward." Gulp. I'm excited about going to New York, but I'm petrified of AIDS. I comfort myself with the knowledge that Andrew is the only person I have sex with.

Andrew goes to New York for two months to intern at a casting office. Our schedules prevent us from seeing each other for a couple of weeks, and I miss him. We have problems, and I don't know how we will resolve them, but that's for another time.

The night before my departure, I'm at home with Mom and Dad. Only two years after their divorce, Dad has moved back in with Mom. I think they're foolish but suppose it's better than being alone. At the dining table that has hosted countless talks, arguments, and fights, I take a deep breath.

"There's something I need to talk to you about before I go," I say. "This is really hard. There's no easy way to say it."

"That's OK," says Mom.

"What I want to tell you, is that, is that, Andrew and I are not just friends." I stop there.

"What do you mean?" she asks.

"We're . . . together. We're a couple. And we've been together since the beginning of junior year."

Mom looks at me with love, pain, and a little bit of relief. "I love you, son."

"I'm happy to hear you say that."

"I'm your mother. We always know. But I'm worried. I just don't want to see anything bad happen to you."

"Don't worry. We're in a monogamous relationship."

"You never know," she says. She knows what she's talking about.

Dad still hasn't weighed in. He doesn't look angry or disappointed. He looks fine. And then he speaks. "Well, as far as I'm concerned, it's no different than being a righty or a lefty."

I've never thought of this comparison. It's smart. Dad can be a perceptive and compassionate observer of human behavior.

"I'll only say one other thing," he adds. "After everything I've done in my life, I'd never be in a position to judge you, son. I love everything you do."

Graduated college. Check.

Found a job in show business with health insurance. Check.

Came out to my parents. Check.

Now it's time for New York.

JULY 5, 1986. I pack my suitcase. Dad's ready to drive me to the airport. I kiss Aaron and Mom goodbye.

"I'm ready," I say.

"Get in the car," he says.

On a quiet Sunday morning at the Detroit Metro Airport, he walks me to the gate. We stand near a window, watching another plane pull away from the jet bridge to begin its journey. We're both tentative, not knowing what to say. The gate agent makes the first boarding announcement. Dad speaks up.

"I know I'm a fuck-up, son. I know I've failed. And I don't know why I was lucky enough to get you. God knows, I didn't deserve it. But I want you to know, son, I love you and I'll never stop loving you."

"Mom told me once that it was your idea to adopt me. So I guess I wouldn't be here without you."

"Adopting you may be the only good thing I've ever done."

"I love you, Dad." Despite everything, it's true.

I sit by the window on People Express Airlines. As the plane takes off, I think about leaving Cardboard Village. How many times did I climb the tree in my backyard and look out over the crummy houses toward the gleaming sky and imagine flying away, over the clouds, to a better place? Now, I'm flying to New York City. One way.

An hour later, I look out my window and see the Brooklyn Bridge and the World Trade Center. It gleams in the hazy, hot sun. As we approach LaGuardia Airport, I see the Empire State Building, the Chrysler Building, and the Citicorp building that has only three legs.

A little girl is sitting next to me. She sees me looking out the window.

"Do you live there?" she asks.

"Yes," I say. "Yes, I do."

ACT TWO

Chapter Seventeen

"THE ONE PLACE ON EARTH I WANT TO BE."

I T'S NINETY-FIVE DEGREES OUTSIDE. I stand on the elevated subway station in Sheepshead Bay, Brooklyn, subway map in one hand,
street map in the other. While sweat drips down my armpits, Matthew
Broderick smiles at me with a look that says, *I'm cooler than you!* He's
not wrong. Posters for *Ferris Bueller's Day Off* surround the platform.
When the D train arrives, I hop into the car and head toward Park Slope
to look for an apartment share. Demand for rooms is high. Supply is
low. I'm looking for a room that's no more than four hundred dollars per
month, which will equal one half of my monthly pay.

I meet a variety of young people sharing apartments in unrenovated
brownstones on quaint streets like Garfield Place. These interviews feel
like applying for a job, auditioning for a play, and going on a blind date
all at once. Refrigerator usage and bathroom products are popular top-
ics. I try to impress them with my knowledge of the qualitative differences between Comet, Soft Scrub, and Ajax.

I meet two guys, Stuart and Chris, on Prospect Place, just off Flat-
bush Avenue. Stuart has been in New York for a year. Since graduating
from Stanford, which he loves talking about, he has been working at
a local foundation. He explains how much more fun it is to give away
money than to raise it. A light-skinned Black guy, tall and thin, he's both

153

friendly and a little bit smug. Chris is an easygoing native New Yorker, a few years older, who works in the computer business. He speaks with a Brooklyn accent. Both guys are handsome. It's easy to perceive that both are gay, but they don't talk about it and neither do I. They invite me to move in for 380 dollars per month, which means I've just saved twenty bucks!

My room is a makeshift third bedroom, the small alcove off the living room that has two huge sliding wood doors. It's about five feet wide by ten feet long, which means it can house a futon love seat that unfolds into a bed, and a desk. A small coat closet holds my clothes. One tall window faces Prospect Place. It's always noisy from traffic and the window is always open because we don't have air-conditioning. A woman who lives across the street screams at her husband every night about how badly he treats her. "I ain't gonna let you kill me," she says over and over. From the sound of her rants, I fear more for his life than hers.

Every morning, I crowd onto the 2 or 3 train from Bergen Street to 42 Street. I carry the *New York Times*, which I learn to fold vertically and read standing up. All the cars are old, some covered in graffiti, some renovated and painted dark red. The stations are so hot I feel like I'm baking alive. The Times Square station is like Dante's Inferno if Dante's Inferno also smelled like piss.

Welcome to New York City, summer of '86.

The guys at Hale & Husted are polite and dull. They don't have enough work for four people. I spend many hours talking with Daryl, who sits next to me. He used to work in a Broadway press office, most recently on Bob Fosse's last musical, *Big Deal*, which flopped on Broadway. He worked for Bob Fosse! He explains to me the insular ways in which production, marketing, and press work on Broadway. It's like a private club that requires knowing someone inside to gain admission. I wonder how to join.

Andrew has temporarily moved into the palatial West Fifty-sixth Street apartment of Judy Dow (yes, that Dow), an Ann Arbor native who spends time in New York and loves to help out talented students. We use Friday nights to see the musicals from the last few years: *Big River* depicts Huck and Jim's journey up the Mississippi River with gorgeous perspective scenery. The river shimmers. The show does not. There are a couple of rousing country tunes but the musical lacks drive, rhythm, punch. The smash hit of 1984, *La Cage aux Folles*, is the first musical about a gay couple. Two years after opening, it feels quaint—set in a world where AIDS doesn't exist, but gay stereotypes abound. It's stale. I ask myself, *Can I do better?*

Daryl recommends a new British movie, *My Beautiful Laundrette*, about a different kind of gay couple. If *La Cage* is old-fashioned and clichéd, this film is contemporary and surprising. Watching two handsome young men make out on screen is intoxicating. A romance about us. One character, Johnny, played by a hot young actor named Daniel Day-Lewis, swigs champagne from the bottle and then dribbles it from his mouth into the mouth of his lover, which is the sexiest thing I've ever seen.

After the movie, Andrew and I stroll through the plaza at Lincoln Center, sit on the edge of the fountain made famous by Erica in *All My Children*, then stop at David's Cookies on Broadway and Seventieth Street. Chocolate chip cookies make me feel at home. Sitting and eating on the bench out front, I look up at the old, ornate apartment buildings surrounding this corner in the heart of the Upper West Side.

"Will we ever be able to live in a place like this?" I ask.

"You'll see," says Andrew. "Maybe we'll wind up living in the same building as Sheldon Harnick."

"Ha!" I reply. "Only if I can learn to be the live-in plumber," I say.

"Come on, let's get home." We walk to the 72 Street station.

In mid-August Andrew must return to Ann Arbor for senior year. The thought of being apart for a year is agonizing. I miss him before he has even left. Our relationship hasn't improved, but I'm hopeful for the future, for the day when Andrew and I are permanently living together in New York. I romanticize our time together and dismiss our minor fights that foretell a rocky future: getting lost in the Village—my mistake—and him screaming at me because I wouldn't ask anyone for directions; arguing over arugula versus romaine lettuce at the grocery store.

Our last morning together is not a fairy-tale farewell. I make breakfast and Andrew yells at me when I spill the Raisin Bran. On the train to the station, I fall asleep, which I always do when I want to escape a difficult situation. In the middle of grimy Penn Station, another inferno buried underneath Madison Square Garden, Andrew and I say goodbye. We shake hands because we are afraid to hug or kiss in public.

"I miss you already," says Andrew.

The tears build up behind my eyeballs. A few drops find their way out.

"Goodbye," I whimper.

"Goodbye," he says.

I turn around and quickly walk toward the Seventh Avenue exit. I don't look back. After a zombie-like day at a zombie-like office, I come home and cry.

Saturday afternoon is solo exploration time. I go to Washington Square Park, observing this homegrown village carnival. Amid the chess games, weed sales, and children running through the fountain is a fire-breathing comic who cleverly builds a huge audience—teasing his act with jokes and banter to solicit coins, dollars, and subway tokens all placed in his dilapidated top hat—before he performs his pièce de résistance, which is sizzling hot, hard to swallow, and dizzylingly fun. Finding an audience isn't easy and I admire how this street performer employs his showmanship to build a throng of folks who reward him with a respectable payday.

Many evening conversations ensue with my roommate, Stuart. When he's not cross-examining me about my needs and wants, he's making proclamations about life in New York.

"The only way to live in New York is to get out on the weekends."

"What?" I say.

"To your country house."

"What are you talking about?"

"You know, your second home. In the Hamptons, or Connecticut," he says.

"You don't have a country house," I say.

"I don't have a lot of things," he replies.

Stuart has no boyfriend and never dates. He retreats to his bedroom for days at a time. He finds Andrew and me to be over the top: We're loud while he's quiet; enthusiastic while he's dry; quick to fight and make up, while he retreats when he's unhappy. Every night after dinner, I work out at a local gym. A hot guy with brown curly hair, a small waist, and carved shoulders split by a navy-blue Duke tank top works out nearby. I'm afraid to say hello. One night, he asks me to spot him doing shoulder presses. As he raises the dumbbells over his head, his hard lats graze my hands, which makes me hard. We talk as we walk out together. His name is Mike and he's in finance. He's subtly flirty. Stupidly, I let him go his way without extending the conversation. Was he interested? Before bed, I fantasize about Mike, then open my booklet magazine, *FirstHand*. It's all words, which are more titillating to me than magazine photos of guys with big dicks and dead eyes. Reading stories about fucking, I'm curious about this act that I've shied away from out of fear of pain and disgust with shit. The idea that I could ever host a dick up my ass seems anatomically impossible.

The weeks without Andrew are lonely. Talking on the phone is both soothing and torture. When he cries and tells me how much he misses me, I cry too, but I'm also reassured that he misses me as much as I miss him. I count the days until I see him again.

Work improves a little. Alan Hale lands an account to promote the Procter & Gamble soap opera, *Another World*. The mission is to rev up interest and ratings for an old, sleepy soap. *Another World* creates a storyline in which a "real-life" jury will decide the fate of a character accused of murder. My job is to produce the jury selection event in a real courtroom and maximize press coverage of this stunt. It's the first time on the job that I have a purpose and it motivates me to find a better job closer to the business of Broadway. In the new year, I sit down with my office mate, Daryl, and beg him to help me find job opportunities on Broadway. He's happy to help.

I interview for entry-level jobs with a couple Broadway pros. The first is a Broadway press agent named Jeffrey Richards, whose cluttered office near Carnegie Hall is filled with newspapers, books, and *Playbill*s that go back to *South Pacific*. Though I know publicity isn't a long-term answer, I'll do anything to get out of my present job. Jeffrey is an eccentric man—short and skinny, with thinning stringy hair. He wears a crumpled gray suit. He looks like he could have been the press agent of the original *South Pacific*. He's a little bit nervous, a little bit shy, a little bit caustic. But he also knows everything about Broadway. I offer enthusiasm, passion for the theater, and a desire to be productive. He offers me a job on the spot: two hundred fifty bucks per week, paid in cash.

"Does this include health insurance?" I ask.

He pauses. His face reveals surprise, embarrassment, and annoyance.

"Um, no. There's no health insurance," he says.

"What if I get sick?" I ask.

"Um, it's just not what we do in this business."

It's 1987. The AIDS crisis gets worse every week.

"Do *you* have health insurance?" I ask.

He pauses again. "Well, um, yes." His tone implies, *Why are you asking such a stupid question?*

"So it's OK for you to have health insurance but not your employees?"

"My insurance is paid by the union."

"What does that have to do with it?" I say.

"Well, unfortunately, you're not in the union," he responds.

"I can't work without health insurance." I walk out.

I interview for a secretarial position with a touring producer named Zev Guber, who has an office in another fancy building on Fifty-seventh Street and Fifth Avenue. Zev looks like his name: His curly dark hair and round blue eyes, fancy slacks and alligator loafers contain a hotshot. He seems like the kind of guy who would throw Jeffrey Richards into the locker in middle school. He runs the Westbury Music Fair, a job he inherited from his father, the producer Lee Guber, who was once married to Barbara Walters. He's producing *A Funny Thing Happened on the Way to the Forum* with Mickey Rooney and plans to tour it. This sounds terrific. But his arrogance doesn't feel earned. He's spoiled. Nevertheless, I do my best to persuade him that I'll be an asset.

"I know this may sound, um, strange," he says, "but how do you think you'd react if I asked you to get me a cup of coffee? Because, I've always had women, and I wouldn't want to make you uncomfortable."

"If you're asking for coffee? I'm happy to get you a cup of coffee," I say. "But I don't shine shoes."

"There might be a couple other things."

"Like what?"

"Picking up stuff at the cleaners, you know, scheduling my manicures and massages."

How to respond? I settle for, "I see."

It doesn't matter. He wants a woman he can comfortably order around.

One day in late March, Daryl tells me the Broadway producers Barry and Fran Weissler have an opening. He hands me a number to call. I have been reading about the Weisslers since they won the Tony for *Othello* in 1982. They were frequent subjects of the *Detroit Free Press* entertainment columnist Shirley Eder. They produced a big revival of the musical *Zorba* starring Anthony Quinn that toured the country. I loved reading about their plans to make *Carrie* into a stage musical with a score by Dean Pitchford and Michael Gore, the guys who wrote the hit songs from the 1980 film *Fame*, which I watched incessantly in high school.

The Weisslers' office is in the Actors' Equity Building on the corner of Forty-sixth Street and Broadway. The dark green marble lobby smells like French fries. A McDonald's occupies the first two floors, sending the sticky grease vapors of its fries and burgers into the lobby and up into the building through its elevators. I enter an elevator and push the button for the twelfth floor. A bronze sign on a solid wood door says "Barry and Fran Weissler."

I walk into a small waiting area that is lined with theater posters: *My One and Only, Your Arms Too Short to Box with God, A Christmas Carol,* and their current big show, Joel Grey in *Cabaret.* Behind a desk is a wall-size poster of *Othello* starring Christopher Plummer and James Earl Jones. I'm standing in the heart of Broadway. The man sitting at the front desk is smoking.

"Hi, my name is Jeffrey Seller and I'm here to see Fran Weissler," I say.

"Have a seat," he says.

Adjacent to the desk, against the wall, are two theater seats. Many calls come in and the receptionist answers each with annoyance, as if the callers are interrupting him from his real duties. Walking down the long, narrow, white hallway in front of me is a woman with high heels and a tight green skirt who's carrying a folder. With her dark hair and clenched face, she looks deadly serious. She briskly turns the corner, then speeds down the next hallway as if running to save a patient in cardiac arrest. She doesn't look at me or at the receptionist.

The phones ring nonstop. The receptionist puts people on hold and then barks to the recipient that so-and-so is on line six. At one point, I hear him call out, "Fran, Ruth Mitchell on line two." Ruth is Hal Prince's longtime assistant director. I wait a few more minutes, taking in the action at this theater office that seems more like a hospital emergency room.

A young woman greets me and invites me back to see Mrs. Weissler. I follow her down the narrow hall toward the corner office where Fran Weissler sits behind a white Formica desk overlooking Times Square. There is a small love seat against the opposite wall, a wicker chair next to her desk, and a tall corn plant. On a narrow table behind her desk sits the Tony Award for *Othello* as well as small framed photographs, including one of her and Barry with Chris Plummer. Billboards of Times Square are just outside her window.

When I enter the office, her assistant introduces me, but Fran does not get up. A big swirling brown hairdo envelops her face, which is perfectly painted with makeup. She has a deep yet feminine voice. She wears a fancy silk shirt and jacket that I may have seen Joan Collins don in *Dynasty*. She reminds me of the puppet known as Madame, who was a regular fixture on TV in the 1980s. Madame was fabulous, feisty, and fancy, and so, I will learn, is Fran.

She asks me to sit down in the chair next to her desk. I try not to be distracted by the corn leaf hanging by my left eye. I am awed and nervous to be sitting next to a famous, Tony Award–winning Broadway producer.

She looks at my résumé, squinting and frowning.

"So tell me about yourself," she says.

I describe my experiences directing, producing, writing, and teaching. I explain that I've been doing publicity for the last nine months.

She's not impressed.

"Well, you know nothing about the theater, but it's not your fault, you're only twenty-two," she says.

"I still think I could be useful. I can write letters, produce events, I pay attention to everything that's happening on Broadway, and I can talk to anybody."

"That's what everybody says."

"Everybody's not me," I reply.

Change of subject.

"How are you with numbers?" she asks.

"Pretty good," I say.

"I mean real math?"

"I took statistics my last semester at Michigan," I say.

"That's a class," she says.

Tough customer.

"I can balance my checkbook," I say, half joking.

"That's not hard until you're rich," she replies.

There is no right answer. I keep trying. "I thought when you're rich your accountant does it for you."

"Has anyone ever told you you're too aggressive?" she asks.

"Probably."

"And, by the way, you're right about the accountant."

"Mrs. Weissler, I've been following you and Mr. Weissler since I was in high school. I used to read about your shows in Shirley Eder's columns in the *Detroit Free Press*."

"I love Shirley," says Fran. "She's very good to us."

"I'll never forget the speech you gave at the Tony Awards when you and Barry won for *Othello* my senior year. I admire everything you've done."

"Well, you're not ready to work for me or Barry, but maybe you can work in our booking office."

I don't know what a booking office is.

Fran picks up her phone. "Diane, bring Susan in here."

A skinny woman with an intense face outlined by dark red eyeliner enters and sits on the small sofa. "Fran, I love that jacket," she says upon arrival.

"Thank you, darling," Fran responds. "This is Susan Weaving. She's the president of our booking company. Susan, this is Jeff. Maybe he can help you."

Susan explains that her job is to book Barry and Fran's shows all over the country. She's sort of like a talent agent, except her client is the show, not the actor. She books shows into places like the Fisher Theatre in Detroit, where I saw my first Broadway musicals. She explains that every market does about five shows a year and they always book whatever just won Best Musical. But that leaves four open slots and they have about ten shows to choose from. The booker's job is to convince the local promoter to do their show instead of someone else's and then juggle the schedules of about fifty different cities, making sure the show can close in one city on Sunday night and open in the next city on Tuesday night.

"To do this job, you have to be an amazing seller," she says.

"That's my name," I reply.

"What?"

"Seller. That's my last name."

"Really? I didn't even look at your résumé. Maybe this is fate," she says.

I like her.

"When do I start?"

"You need to be prepared for long hours and nonstop pressure."

"I'll do anything for this job," I say.

"No one wants to be the booker. It's the hardest job in the business, no glory. But know what? Every day I look out that window and see the line at the TKTS booth. It reminds me why I do this."

Two weeks later Susan calls me and offers me a job as her assistant. The salary will be 18,500 dollars, plus insurance, which is four thousand more than I'm earning now. I'm thrilled.

I'm also elated that Andrew is graduating and preparing to move to New York. He visits for a weekend in late April. We find a beautiful, renovated apartment to rent in Park Slope. Many windows look out on Seventh Avenue. The exposed red brick in the living room is polished. The wood floors are brand new. We sign the lease for a thousand dollars per month.

We see Richard Kiley in a heartbreaking production of *All My Sons*. We are flooded by the gentle affection that envelops the family in the beginning of the play and the tragedy that befalls them at the end. In the opening scene, when the father asks his son why he reads book reviews, he answers, "I like to keep abreast of my ignorance." We repeat that line many times after, along with "they were all my sons." I'm shattered by the dichotomy of a father who can be so caring and loving and yet so unethical, so immoral, so criminal.

I'm also unsettled by Andrew's behavior over the busy weekend. He seems tentative and less loquacious than usual. He leaves on Sunday night for his graduation and instead of feeling excited for our future together, I feel insecure. I call him Monday night and he acts like a different person; the man who never stops talking has little to say.

"What's wrong, Andrew? I can tell something's wrong."

"Nothing."

"Bullshit, you're never like this. What's going on?"

"You don't want to know."

"Of course I want to know."

"I had sex with another guy. His name is Tyler and he's a freshman."

I freeze. Hold my breath.

"I'm sorry, Jeffrey," he says.

"Me too." I can't tell if I'm more angry or hurt.

"I never wanted to be in a relationship. I just went along with it. And it felt good. But I never got to date, to slut around. And you know what? It was exciting."

That we've just broken up only registers when I put down the phone. My stomach is in so many knots I can barely eat. After waiting eight months, counting down the days, hours, and minutes, he's thrown me and our relationship away. I'm in agony. I cry every night. I call the landlord and cancel the lease on the new apartment.

One night, Stuart comes home with a video of a movie called *Parting Glances*. The movie begins with the camera following a hunky guy in his twenties running through Riverside Park. He's wearing a red Adidas tank top. He looks like Superman. It's a beautiful but slightly dingy park, with limestone monuments and stone pathways. He comes upon a cute guy who's sitting on a stone seat reading a book. The runner snatches his book and darts away; the cute guy chases after him. It's fun and flirtatious. They run up and down stone staircases, through meadows and pathways. It's a romantic jaunt. They cross Riverside Drive and enter a prewar apartment, where they drop their clothes, make out, and wind up in the shower together.

I'm transfixed by their connection and turned on by their sexiness. I want to have sex with either of them or, better yet, both. Their names are Robert and Michael, and we learn that Robert is soon to move to Africa to work for two years. Though their bond is strong, Michael is still emotionally connected to his former lover, who is homebound with AIDS, and goes to his apartment every day to care for him. Robert wonders where Michael's heart lies, and whether they should stay together during this long absence.

Is it possible to be jealous of movie characters? I love this couple horsing around in beautiful Riverside Park. I fantasize that someday I might live there with a boyfriend as handsome and sensitive as Robert. But I'm also frightened by the presence of AIDS, which lurks behind every corner.

When the movie is over, Stuart says, "What did you think?"

"I want Robert to be my new boyfriend."

"Tell me about it!"

"Was this movie supposed to make me feel better or worse?"

"You know, you need to be done with this Andrew obsession. You're too dependent on him. You just spent eight months waiting for him and look what he did to you. You're too young to get married."

"I thought we'd be together forever. I guess that was stupid."

"He was your first boyfriend. Move on."

I try to "move on" by running in Prospect Park. Each night I run farther and farther to release my loneliness.

But I have a great new job to start, and that gives me something to look forward to.

Chapter Eighteen

FRAN AND BARRY AND SUSAN

EARLY MAY. My first day on the job. When I arrive at Times Square, I hustle to the Actors' Equity Building with excitement.

After a short welcome and tour of the office, Susan sits me down at my cubbyhole that has a desk, a file cabinet, and an IBM Selectric typewriter. She barks orders nonstop. She's booking a tour of *South Pacific* starring Robert Goulet. It starts at West Point in late August and then plays one-week engagements all over the country. There's also a short tour going out in June of *My One and Only* starring Tommy Tune and Stephanie Zimbalist.

She gives me two tasks: 1) Type the contracts for all the *South Pacific* engagements on triplicate forms; and 2) Collect the daily sales for both shows, which are called "wraps." I distribute the wraps to Barry and Fran, and all the other partners via a new machine called a fax. I'm amazed by this magical new device that sends documents over phone lines to other devices in other places.

The Weisslers are "executive producing" *South Pacific*, which means they are overseeing it. Built to tour with no plans for Broadway, it's financed by another company, Pace Theatrical Group, which also presents Broadway subscription series in fifteen cities across America such as Tempe, Arizona; Houston, Texas; and Cincinnati, Ohio.

FRAN AND BARRY AND SUSAN

Robert Goulet doing any show sounds cheesy to me, like summer stock. Who wants to see this washed-up star in this old musical? Compared to shows like *A Chorus Line*, *Evita*, or *Dreamgirls*, it feels antiquated. I soon discover that many people want to see this star in this musical.

I ask myself, *What's happened to Broadway?* Turns out, few new musicals is what's happened. AIDS has cut short the lives of many promising creators and the rising cost of new shows has made raising money more difficult. Many Broadway theaters are empty: the Hellinger, the Minskoff, the Martin Beck, the Gershwin, the Nederlander. All the playhouses east of Seventh Avenue are also empty. The last two Tony winners of Best Musical, *The Mystery of Edwin Drood* and *Big River*, were humdrum. Neither were long-running hits. Neither had long tours. Few of the other shows produced between 1984 and 1986 were successful enough to tour.

Broadway isn't generating enough new musicals to fill five subscription slots every year. Though *Cats* is the biggest hit in the history of Broadway, it can't sustain the whole business. Consequently, the Weisslers and Pace are mounting revivals of shows that can tour the country without playing Broadway. Thus, Anthony Quinn in *Zorba* or Robert Goulet in *South Pacific*. *Les Misérables* has just triumphantly opened on Broadway, but it will take a year to plan a tour and get it on the road.

Our office is filling the gap. And it's hopping. Barry and Fran are producing a revival of *Cabaret* starring Joel Grey that Hal Prince is directing. It's on a pre-Broadway tour, currently playing in Philadelphia, and will open on Broadway in October.

Barry looks and acts like he is in a Shakespeare tragedy. A rugged complexion, black hair combed straight back, receding only above his temples, and a close-cropped black beard make him look like a viable Macbeth. Over a fit, short frame, he wears a navy blue suit, white shirt, and tie. A handsome man, his mission is to produce hits that make money and win Tony Awards; he works 24/7 in pursuit. He relies heavily on Fran—his Lady Macbeth—for support.

Susan is hyper—always on the phone, always spinning, her left leg wrapped around her right leg like a pretzel. All day, she shouts out tasks for me to complete. Holding her hand over the phone, she whispers and grunts instructions while smiling and listening to the person on the other end. She instructs me to start negotiating a contract but doesn't explain how to do it.

"The guarantee is 180,000 dollars plus 10 percent with a 60/40 split," she says. "Get their local expenses low low low."

"What's a guarantee?" I ask.

"I don't have time. Ask Bob. And don't forget to call everyone for their deposits. Miles is hounding me. It's 50K per city."

"I'm sorry, what does 'K' mean?"

"Thousand. Fifty thousand," she replies, exasperated. "Oh, and start with Frank Pierson in St. Louis. Miles doesn't trust him and wants his deposits immediately."

Miles Wilkin, the president of Pace Theatrical Group, has two jobs. First, he oversees his fifteen subscription markets throughout the country. Second, he is the lead producer of the *South Pacific* tour and makes all the business decisions. A producer and a presenter, he's one of the most powerful men in the business. From the way Susan talks, he sounds scary. Frank Pierson is the Broadway presenter (promoter is the old-fashioned word) in St. Louis and Columbus who has booked *South Pacific* for both markets.

Bob is Susan's other agent. He's a tiny, shy guy, around thirty years old, who works like a mouse in an office in the back of the suite. His energy is the opposite of Susan's. He is gentle. His primary job is to book one-nighters of *David Copperfield* and *The Flying Karamazov Brothers*, a new vaudeville show of comic jugglers. I ask him the meaning of these words and figures Susan just threw at me.

"Here's how it works," says Bob. "We're bringing the entire show— you know, the actors, the sets, the costumes, the lights. For all that, the local promoter pays us 180,000 dollars, plus 10 percent of the entire weekly gross, which is for royalties—the payments we make to the authors, director, and designers."

"That's coming out of the box office?" I ask.

"Right. But they have to pay us no matter what. That's why it's called a guarantee."

"Got it. What's the 60/40 split?"

"After paying us the guarantee and royalty, the presenter gets to be reimbursed for his local costs."

"What are those?"

"Stagehands, musicians, rent, advertising, all that stuff. If there's any money left over, then we split it. The producer gets 60 percent and the presenter gets 40 percent. That's the profit."

My head is spinning. I need to write these equations down on paper to understand how they work. Before I can do anything, Susan yells, "Call Frank!"

I dial the promoter Frank Pierson in St. Louis. He picks up the phone with a calm and genial demeanor. I explain that the producers would like him to please send his deposits for St. Louis and Columbus of fifty thousand dollars each.

"Is everyone making a deposit?" he asks.

"I believe so," I say, though, I'm not sure.

"Well, at least I deserve a contract first," he says.

"Of course, I'm getting that out tonight."

"Alright, send me the contract and I'll see what I can do."

We hang up. Next, I am on the phone with the presenter in Cleveland, a man with a fun name, Sam L'Hommedieu. When I ask him for his local expenses, he says 150,000 dollars and I say, "OK," and type that into the contract. Then I give Susan the contract to review.

She reads and then screams. "You gave Sam L'Hommedieu $150K for local expenses? Are you out of your mind?"

"I'm sorry," I say.

"The maximum is $135K," she says.

"You never told me," I reply.

"Miles will kill me," she says. "Call him back."

"Call Miles?" I ask.

"No, Sam. Are you listening to me?"

"OK."

"Right now," she barks.

I get up to call Sam.

"Did you talk to Frank Pierson?" Susan asks.

"Yes, we just talked."

"When is he sending the deposits?"

"He said he'd work on it," I reply.

"That's not an answer. You've gotta give him a date and get him to commit. Call him back."

Sweat drips down my armpits. Every other call I make seems to be to fix the call that preceded it.

I stay late and, with Bob's help, finish the contracts for Frank Pierson. We FedEx them so that Frank will receive them the next day. Getting on the subway after eight p.m., I'm tired but invigorated. I'm working in the business of Broadway.

I give Frank Pierson one day to the review the contracts, and then place a call to make sure he's sending the deposits. The receptionist takes a message. He doesn't return my call for several days and Susan keeps hounding me to follow up.

Finally, Frank's secretary answers my call but she's tearful and hesitant to talk.

"I'm sorry, is something wrong?" I ask.

She tells me that Frank died, and this is her last day. There is no money for the deposits or the shows. She hasn't been paid in three weeks. Apparently, he squandered the subscription monies and had no way to pay for the shows. He committed suicide.

I'm stunned. When I talked to him, he did not seem like a guy about to kill himself. Or a guy who would steal money from subscribers. This is a tough business. I walk down the hall afraid to tell Susan. She's going to flip out that there are two open weeks in the tour.

"Susan, I have something to tell you," I explain from her doorway.

"Did you talk to Frank?"

At that moment, Barry barrels down the hall, almost knocking me over. The individual offices are small and close together, and a conversation in one office is a conversation in all of them.

"Fran, get off the phone, this is an emergency!" he shouts.

Fran doesn't answer right away.

"I said get off the phone," he yells. "It's about Joel."

"What happened?" Susan says to me.

"He killed himself," I say.

"Oh my God, Joel killed himself?" says Fran.

"Joel killed himself?" blurts Alecia, the general manager.

"What are you talking about?" says Barry. "He lost his voice; he didn't kill himself."

"Well who died?" says Fran.

"I'm sorry," I say. "I was just telling Susan that Frank Pierson committed suicide."

"The promoter?" says Barry. "I don't care, my star is sick and I'm about to lose a fortune."

"Barry, Johnnie Planco on line two," announces the sour, smoking receptionist over the office intercom. Planco is Joel Grey's agent.

"Tell him I'll call him right back," barks Barry. "They want to know what we're going to do."

If Barry's focus is Joel, Susan's focus is Frank. She reacts to this news as if it's my fault. "This is a disaster," she says to me. "This will kill the whole tour."

"What's wrong with his voice?" Fran asks Barry.

"I don't know. He's sick. He's got some sort of infection."

"What are we going to do?" Fran continues.

"What are you going to do?" Susan yells at me.

"He says he can't do the show," says Barry.

"We can't put the understudy on," says Alecia. "The whole audience will ask for refunds."

"Alecia, how much money do we lose if Joel misses three performances?" asks Barry.

"We'll refund, like, I don't know, half the house. We'll lose a hundred thousand dollars."

"This is a disaster," says Barry.

It's a double disaster day.

"Why don't you get the understudy to lip sync for him offstage?" says Fran.

"Get Johnnie Planco back on the phone," yells Barry.

"Go to Miles's office and let him know about Frank," says Susan. "I need to find someone to take those dates."

I walk across the street trying not to shake. An assistant escorts me to a big corner office with floor-to-ceiling windows overlooking the Hudson River. Behind a perfectly clean desk sits Miles. He is a big guy, tall and wide. He is the opposite of Barry and Fran. They ooze theatricality and fabulosity. He's a little bit glum. People fear him. He doesn't say much and it's clear that, for him, theater is just a job. He's famous for the motto "Seeing the show only clouds your vision." When I explain that Frank committed suicide, it doesn't register. That the tour just lost two weeks registers.

"Tell Susan that she better rebook those dates. There's no fucking way I'm paying for two layoffs. I'll take it out of her commission."

A layoff, I learn, is when there is an open week in the tour with nowhere to go. What are you supposed to do with five trucks of scenery and costumes, plus a company of fifty people if you layoff? You send them home and pay them anyway. It's a fortune. The booker's job is to ensure there are no layoffs. I return to the office and report back to Susan, feeling like a birdie in a badminton game.

In the end, Joel's understudy performs his vocals with a mic offstage. Barry and Fran don't lose their "shirts" in Philly. And Miles and Pace Theatrical Group take over the subscription series in St. Louis and Columbus, which means the dates are filled.

SIX MONTHS AFTER TAKING THE JOB, Susan hands me the *South Pacific* tour and says it's my responsibility. She is laser focused on sales, box office, and profits. Every booking earns her a commission. The booking fee is 4,500 dollars per week. That feels like a lot of money, but the booker is the seller who makes the tour possible. My value to her is equal to how many bookings I obtain and how much commission I earn.

After one year, I know every major touring house in the country and can recite its capacity by heart. I can also remember what every show grosses in every city. This math is more interesting to me than the algebra classes I barely passed in high school. I'm excited to be in the middle of everything and learn about this side of show business. One day I even randomly come upon a letter from Hal Prince to Barry and Fran. He writes: "Only Ruthie is authorized to give notes. If you want to give notes, then you can take my name off the show, and I'll never return. Otherwise, let Ruthie do her job." I can't believe that I'm reading a letter from Hal Prince.

Chapter Nineteen

OUR FIRST NEW MUSICAL

A NDREW AND I FAIL at breaking up. A month after his arrival in New York City, during which he starts work as an elementary school music teacher, we get back together. Why? Because we're both afraid to be alone. Because we still like having sex, and we're both afraid of AIDS. Because we still share a passion for doing musicals together.

Working at the Weissler office is like getting a PhD in Broadway producing. But I need to make my own shows. I get a job directing *The Fantasticks* at a church group in Sheepshead Bay. I recruit Andrew to be the music director, and an actress who was in my acting class at Michigan to play the Girl. She is an exotic, emotionally powerful stage creature. With her long, flowing, and disarrayed black hair and wide-set brown eyes, she seems as if she might break into a thousand pieces at any moment, which is exciting. We rehearse and perform in a social hall that hasn't been painted, swept, or mopped in years.

I finish work by six p.m. so that I can run out the door, blow through cold, snowy Times Square, and get on the D train to the bottom of Brooklyn. Susan frowns when I leave at six p.m. Any departure before seven p.m. shows a lack of commitment. She resents my other theatrical pursuits but doesn't argue with my output. I eat my dinner, which I pack with my lunch in the morning, on the train, which is like my second home.

At the end of the run, one of Andrew's fellow teachers recommends we interview to direct the community theater at his temple, Rodeph

174

Sholom, one of the biggest reform synagogues in New York. Andrew and I show up at the imposing limestone building on West Eighty-third Street on a frigid night in late February. The tall, heavy wooden front doors remind me of the first time I walked into Temple Israel in Detroit when I was auditioning for the Purim play in fourth grade. Both have large lobbies with green marble floors. Both feel like the entrance to Oz.

In the temple study, furnished with plush couches and mahogany bookshelves filled with Judaica, we are introduced to a committee of board members. Though we've never met these folks before, we know this crowd. They're like our aunts and uncles and family friends. We are hired on the spot to direct *Annie Get Your Gun*, which the committee imagines will be a star vehicle for their favorite temple diva, Tennie Leonard. Yes, her name is Tennie.

The only problem is that they don't have the rights to *Annie Get Your Gun*, which is controlled by Rodgers and Hammerstein, who were the original producers. My booking responsibilities on *South Pacific* include regular talks with their head of licensing, Tom Briggs, so I give him a call.

"Jeffrey, no one's getting the rights to *Annie Get Your Gun* in New York," says Tom. "Irving Berlin's daughters are holding out for a revival on Broadway."

Plan B. "Why don't we take inspiration from your Jule Styne show at Michigan?" I say to Andrew. "We'll do a Frank Loesser concert."

"I love Frank Loesser," says Andrew.

Andrew and I dig up every Frank Loesser song we can find, including many for which he wrote lyrics to melodies by composers like Hoagy Carmichael and Johnny Mercer. The mission is to create a dramatic purpose for the songs that were not in his Broadway musicals—like "On a Slow Boat to China" and "Baby, It's Cold Outside."

To create a proper opening, we use the song "I Hear Music," which Loesser wrote with Burton Lane. We dramatize Frank's childhood in New York City, and then present vignettes of World War II, for which Loesser composed rousing tunes for the military, and poignant love songs about soldiers separated from their wives, like "Spring Will Be a Little Late This Year."

The second act comprises medleys from his shows. Tennie Leonard, a delightful, well-dressed, dramatic yenta of forty-five, sings "Adelaide's Lament." Jack Lichtenstein, an older member, provides the most touching moment in the show when he sings to his actual daughter "More I Cannot Wish You." Sweet Bob Levine, an "old-world" gay who has a "schmatte business" in the garment district, dons his snazziest vest, striped pants, and big round glasses and sings Hans Christian Andersen with a gaggle of temple kids who play the Little Ducklings. That he is embraced by this temple makes me love the place even more. Doing the show here feels like being with family.

Fran and Barry start work on a stage production of the movie musical *Hans Christian Andersen* to be directed and choreographed by Tommy Tune, who wants to stage the show on ice to depict "Wonderful Copenhagen," and feature the British Olympic skater John Curry as Hans. Tommy recruits his pal Maury Yeston, who helped save *Grand Hotel*, to write a new book, which is strange because Yeston is a composer, not a playwright. The original movie only had a handful of songs, and Tommy needs to find a half dozen more. I loan Fran all my Frank Loesser research, plus the cassettes of all the Frank Loesser songs that weren't in his big shows. Tommy loves them.

After Maury writes a draft of the book, I ask Fran's assistant if I can read it. The exposition is flaccid, there is no major dramatic question, and the show feels purposeless. It's inert. I write a three-page memo to Fran. She thanks me for my notes with a sly look on her face that implies, *you've got a lot of nerve.* Susan becomes infuriated with me.

"Who do you think you are, giving notes to Fran Weissler, not to mention Maury Yeston and Tommy Tune?"

"I gave them all my research. Tommy used my cassettes. I thought they might be open to my ideas," I say.

"Sell it, don't smell it," she says.

"What?"

"You're a booker. You're not the producer or the director or the dramaturg, whatever the fuck that is. Your job is to sell the show, don't tell them what's wrong with it."

She's right. I'm in the wrong place. But I don't yet know how to become the producer, the director, or the dramaturg.

Fran rescues me when she tells Susan, "It's OK, darling, he was right. The book is no good."

After sputtering on the project for a year, the Weisslers drop it. *Hans Christian Andersen* is a hard movie to adapt. Maybe they just needed fabulous Bob Levine of Rodeph Sholom, I think to myself.

Andrew joins the BMI Musical Theatre Workshop, which is chaired by none other than Maury Yeston. He teams up with a lyricist named Tommy Greenwald who has written a very funny musical about politics. Their task at the end of the first year is to write a ten-minute musical. I recommend to Andrew that they musicalize one of the vignettes from *Shtetl Tales*, a play for kids adapted from five different Yiddish folk tales by authors like Y. L. Peretz and Sholom Aleichem. The Ann Arbor–based playwright Rachel Urist hired me to direct a local production while I was a senior at Michigan. For Andrew and Tommy, I recommend the story of Sarah, a beautiful, snooty teenage girl whom three boys fight to win over. It's a sweet story of adolescent infatuation and love. Andrew and Tom write an adorable little musical. When I see it on presentation day, I recommend they expand the idea and make the whole play into a musical. Tommy and Andrew like the idea. I call Rachel and she's thrilled to adapt her play. I'll produce and direct. Rodeph Sholom agrees to present it in their auditorium and contribute ten thousand dollars toward the cost.

We're all excited about this new production—we're making our first new musical—and the timing feels prescient because Broadway is struggling. For the 1989 Tony Awards, there are only three shows nominated for Best Musical: a revue from Paris called *Black and Blue*, which isn't a musical; *Jerome Robbins' Broadway*, which is an anthology of old musicals; and *Starmites*, a flop, already closed, that featured a singing lizard. There are no nominees for Best Score or Best Book. It feels as if musical theater is dying.

Rachel, Andrew, and Tom dig in. The boys figure out where music will heighten the scenes. Their songs bring bounce and fun. The music adds an aural consistency to the whole show, and Tommy's lyrics add gentle, sweet wit. As summer progresses, Andrew also starts orchestrating the show. One Saturday in August, we sit on a blanket in the gay section of Jones Beach. I read and he writes orchestra parts while two hot guys play paddleball in front of us.

"You know what this is?" he asks.

"What?"

"Everything we love," he says. "Gays and musicals."

We laugh.

We decide we need to rename the show. We don't want to use Yiddish. The stories are unified by time and place but not storyline or theme. One of our tales, "The Wise Men of Chelm," satirizes the question "Which is heavier, a pound of bricks or a pound of feathers?" so we call the show *A Pound of Feathers*. I find an illustrator to make the poster.

We have auditions and recruit a team of young, passionate, and committed performers. Being director and producer at the same time as being a booker for a boss who screams at me all day is more pressure than I've ever handled. I don't hire a choreographer because the show doesn't have any "dances," and it turns out to be a big mistake. The songs have rhythm and need more movement, more gesture than I can provide. I enjoy masterminding the shape and tone of the evening but staging a musical without a choreographer becomes difficult. I can't physicalize the songs in a rewarding way. I feel as if I'm letting down Andrew and Tom. Everyone starts giving advice. I lose my confidence. We create a sweet show, but I take no pleasure in the process.

The audiences are small. The reactions are soft. Fran Weissler is kind enough to attend. I study her every movement during the performance to glean her reaction. On the way out, she smiles and says, "It was charming, darling, your team is so talented."

Her words are supportive, but I'm crestfallen. I stupidly dreamed she would immediately offer to move the show. Instead, she says, "charming," which feels like faint praise. To me, charming means it's not funny enough, or it's not deep enough, or it's not dazzling enough. It means it's not good enough.

Though I've just directed and produced my first new musical, I'm deflated on closing night. I feel like a failure because the show isn't a triumph that will move to an off-Broadway theater. But Andrew and Tommy come away with a handful of terrific songs and their partnership thrives.

With a little distance, I'm able to see it as a learning experience. I encouraged Andrew to start composing. I brought Rachel together with Andrew and Tom, commissioned them to write a new musical, and guided them through the writing process. I persuaded the temple to give us space and money. I cast the show, hired an artist to design a set, and found a carpenter to build it. But most important, I made something exist that didn't previously exist. I realize that my work as producer is essential and undeniable. I also realize that my work as director is not essential. I can find others to do it as well or better. I conclude that I will focus on producing.

In the new year, Andrew and I are unraveling. We've both just turned twenty-five—we went to see *The War of the Roses* on his twenty-fifth birthday, not a good omen—and we're both disappointed and dissatisfied. As winter progresses, Andrew becomes distant. I suspect he's angry at me because the show didn't go anywhere. We fight over the cooking time of rice. We talk less, stop laughing together, stop having sex. Being with him becomes lonelier than being alone. I start sleeping in the second bedroom. We break up again, and this time it sticks.

One Saturday morning in May, Andrew and a friend pull up in front of our building in a rented U-Haul. It's moving out day. He takes his stereo and piano. He leaves me the dining table. Our "War of the Roses" is over a couch we bought at Macy's. I agree to pay him for half the value.

As he packs, I go to work out at the gym—the only means of releasing my hurt. He's ready to leave by the time I return.

We look at each other. Neither of us knows what to say. I feel like crying. I miss him already.

"Goodbye," I say.

"That's it?" he says.

"What am I supposed to say?"

"I don't know, maybe good luck? Maybe, you will always care about me?"

"That's the problem with you, Andrew. You don't want to suffer any consequences for your actions."

"OK, forget I said anything."

"Here's what I'll say: I love you. I have always loved you and I will always love you."

"I've got to go," he says. "Or I'll never go."

"Goodbye, Andrew."

I fall on the bed crying, which is the only way to relieve the pressure I feel inside my chest. Crying unclogs my fear. Fear that I'm nothing without Andrew, fear that no one else will want me, fear that I'll always wind up alone, that the isolation I felt as a child is the home I will always come back to.

That night, I go to Private Eyes, the gay dance club in Chelsea. With walls and support columns clad in opaque white glossy squares that light up in different colors, it's snazzier than other clubs. It reminds me of Tommy Tune's set from *Nine*. Scared of initiating a conversation, I wander, hoping someone will notice me. How many times can I circle the dance floor? How many Perriers can I order from the intimidating bartenders whose expressions imply, *Hey loser, why aren't you ordering something more expensive?* How many times can I go to the bathroom just to pass the time? This exercise compounds my sadness. I give up and head for the exit when a tall guy leaning against a white column smiles at me.

He's the most handsome guy I've ever seen. His big green eyes, strong eyebrows, perfectly straight nose, and combed brown hair are anchored by a Clark Kent jaw. I walk over and say hello. His name is Bruce.

"That's my middle name," I say.

"That's really, um, you know, random," he says.

"Someone once told me Bruce is a gay name. Maybe that answers it."

"For both of us," he says.

"So, um, who you here with?" I ask.

"No one."

"Me too, or I guess I should say me neither," I say.

"So I guess now I'm here with you," he says.

"Lucky me."

We talk for a little while and then he asks me if I would like to go home with him.

Um, yes.

We walk to West Thirteenth Street just off Fifth Avenue. Nervous, I ask a lot of questions. He went to Harvard and then joined his dad's Wall Street banking firm. He hated it and now works at an ad agency as a junior copywriter. He explains that he lives with his boyfriend, who is out of town, and that they have an open relationship. My gain.

After the elevator ride to the sixth floor, we enter the high-ceilinged apartment and land in the bedroom, where he kisses me gently. Our tongues find each other slowly. His lips are soft, neither thick nor thin. I like the way they touch my lips. After our clothes come off, he straddles me. I'm rapt by his lean, softly outlined abs, and soft, sparse golden brown chest hair.

"Do you want to fuck me?" he asks.

"Um, ah, yes, I'd love to fuck you," I say. I'm nervous and excited. I've never had sex with anyone but Andrew. What about AIDS?

He leans over to his nightstand to get a condom and lube and puts it on me. Penetrating this handsome man releases me from the despair of Andrew's exit. The sensation of putting my cock in a warm, enveloping space that is both strong and soft is tingling and powerful; it sends tingles all the way from my fingers to my toes. It's the best feeling ever. We exchange phone numbers and agree to get together soon. When I call him a few days later, I'm greeted on the phone by his lover, Tom, who is warm and friendly. Their relationship confuses me.

We go out for dinner every month or so and always have sex at my place after. I like kissing Bruce. I like fucking Bruce. He makes me feel desirable. But it's hard to talk with Bruce. I can't figure out if he's shy, boring, or just "shut down." I wonder what other people talk about on dates. How do two people share stories, feelings, and opinions? Andrew never ran out of things to talk about. Bruce, a Harvard graduate, seems unable to initiate a conversation. Sitting at a two-top table at the Cottage Inn, I eat General Tso's Chicken quickly so that I can receive my reward—the pleasure of looking at his beautiful face as I touch his beautiful body. One night, he calls me on the phone, and after some uncomfortable small talk, lets me know that his boyfriend recently tested positive for HIV. He assures me that he tested negative. We've always played it safe, but I'm a little rattled. I decide that our unique relationship has reached its end.

I've been in New York the equivalent of one college cycle. I still count my life in four-year increments. Have I accomplished as much as I did in college?

After three years, Susan and I are like a warring couple. We fight over ten-dollar charges on my expense report. I write a scathing, sarcastic memo demanding a raise because, in my estimation, my earnings are not proportional to the revenue I generate. In her exasperated reply, she recommends I start looking for a "more corporate job." In a staff sales meeting, I openly question the reliability of a progress report she wants to send to a producer. Fran saves me from her attempts to fire me. I've come to hate my job, but I can't figure out how to make the leap to producing. How would I raise money? How would I earn money?

I'm lonely without Andrew. I miss talking with him every day, eating meals together, going to the movies, snuggling on Sunday mornings.

I feel lost.

I need to pause and think. I remember hearing people at Camp Tamarack talk about Outward Bound, a camp that is like a survival course, which pushes you further than you think you can go.

I ask Susan for a three-week vacation. In my three years at this office, no one has taken more than a week off. She miraculously agrees. She's as sick of me as I am of her. I write a check for 1,800 dollars to participate in the Outward Bound program in Maine. That's more than half my savings.

On a sailboat called a "pulling boat" that's thirty feet long and seven feet wide at the center, I join twelve other students and two leaders and paddle out into a cold, foggy sea. We learn to sail in the waters of Penobscot Bay. When there is no wind, and there are many days in which there is no wind, we row.

Our obstacles are many. We spend one night with no tents on a small island, left by our leaders to fend for ourselves. Most nights, we sleep on the boat at sea by spreading the eight oars over the deck of the boat, then covering the surface with rubber mats. We sling a tattered tarp over our heads. Fourteen strangers, lying head to foot like sardines, in a damp tent, in damp sleeping bags, in damp clothes, on a damp, chilly night.

One late afternoon, we dock in the cove of an island for a respite on land. I hike alone, away from the group, deep into an evergreen forest. In front of me is a beautiful resting area. Soft green moss that feels like shaggy carpet forms multiple mounds on the ground. Threadlike pine needles surround the green medallions of moss. Boulders, frosted in lichen, create a rolling effect in a forest that feels painted, like a backdrop from *The Wizard of Oz*. Lush spruce trees emanate the sweet smell of cotton candy.

I lie down under the trees and gaze through the canopy, charting pictures of leaves, branches, and sky. I inhale the mist of the forest and doze off.

When I wake up, I get up and walk in the direction I came from. I climb over fallen tree trunks and boulders, challenging myself to see how far I can traverse without touching the ground. I imagine the ground is a lake filled with crocodiles. I imagine Adventureland.

What starts as a pleasurable hike becomes an anxious trek to find my way back.

Nothing looks familiar. I change directions. I pick up the pace.

I'm running through the trees. Short of breath. Beads of sweat soak through my clothes. I run toward a small opening and hit a barrier of barbed bushes. The open floor of the forest has given way to prickly bushes and thorny plants that scratch, scrape, and cut. I change directions again. The sound of the ocean roars in front of me. I head toward it. The sound jumps. Now it's coming from behind. Next, it emanates from the side. Each time I change directions, I become a little bit more confused. It's getting darker and I'm in a maze of trees, bushes, and rocks.

I shout "Hello!" as loud as I can in all directions. No one answers. The sound of the ocean drowns me out. The area is too big for anyone to find me, and I have no idea in which direction to walk. Being alone in a place where no one can hear, see, or find me is scary. *Maybe this is death*, I think to myself. The absence of everyone.

My heightened anxiety forces bad decisions: I switch directions so many times that I have no idea where to turn. I finally conclude that I must choose a direction and then keep walking forward until I reach the ocean. I climb over, under, and through scrub, scratching my face along the way. I bound over tree trunks and large granite rocks. I don't stop. I don't look back.

I come to a swampy area with reeds six feet high and sink a little bit deeper into the mud and water with every step. When I reach the other side, the thick underbrush gives way to tall trees and open ground. I see an opening in the forest wall, beyond which is the ocean. The sea crashes against the uneven pink granite that separates the forest from the water. My heart slows down. I will circumnavigate the island back to the cove. One more decision: Clockwise or counterclockwise? I have no idea how big the island is or where the cove is in relation to where I am. I make a guess and go clockwise.

Heavy fog rolls in. Every step into the white mist sends a burning sensation to my sore toes. Up and down the slippery rocks, I fall on my behind. Each curve brings hope that just around this corner will lie the cove and boat. It's not around the first curve. Or the second one. Or the sixth. I feel like I'm in the movie *Planet of the Apes* where the sole remaining human rides his horse by the desolate shore.

The sound of the crashing sea begins to ebb. Terrain shifts. I have reached the opposite shore. I'm on a small cliff, about twenty-five feet above a quiet coast. I stay on the edge of the cliff, stick to the perimeter, and hold on to the trees so as not to fall over the edge.

Turning one more corner, I hear the blaring sound of a boat horn. Just around the bend is the cove and our team leader, Pokey, blowing it. I plop down onto the ground for a minute, relaxing with the knowledge that I've made it.

"I'm over here," I shout. "I'm OK."

When I get back to the boat, Pokey asks, "What did you do, circumnavigate the island?"

"Yep," I say.

He laughs. "Are you alright?"

"I'm a sweaty pig and my feet are fucking burning. But, yeah, I'm OK." I strip off my layers of clothes and raingear and jump into the cold water to purge my body and rejuvenate my spirit.

"That was a smart thing to do," Pokey remarks as I dry off.

"I figured it was the only way to find my way."

"I was a little worried about you because I know you haven't spent much time in the woods, but I knew you could take care of yourself."

"Thanks," I respond.

"I'm glad you got lost," he says.

Chapter Twenty

THREE MEETINGS THAT CHANGE MY LIFE

H OME FROM OUTWARD BOUND and reinvigorated, it's time to get
busy. Three meetings in the fall of 1990 are about to change my life.

MEETING #1

SITTING AT MY DESK on a Monday afternoon in September, I receive
a cold call from a man named Paul Blake, a name that sounds like a
character from the 1950s musical *Bells Are Ringing*. He is the producer
of the St. Louis Muny, the largest outdoor amphitheater in the country,
where every summer he mounts gigantic productions of classic musicals to a nightly audience of eleven thousand people. He also produces
other shows during the off-season that he wants to tour. He is engaging
and charming on the phone.

"Now darling, I've called around, done my homework, and I've heard
you're the best in the business."

"That's very kind of you," I respond.

He explains his goals. Though he spends the summers in St. Louis,
he directs and produces the rest of the year out of his home in Beverly
Hills. He has shows but no bookings. Midway through the call, it be-

comes clear there's another person on the line. Paul introduces him: "This is my can-do assistant, Kev."

"Executive producer," responds Kevin.

"Whatever," says Paul.

"Great to meet you," Kevin says in the self-assured voice of a talk show host. "I'm sure there's a lot we can do together."

"Now darling, we're coming to New York next week and we'd love to take you to dinner."

"There's no place I'd rather be," I reply.

I meet Paul and Kevin at the Broadway Grill. Paul is tiny. With his full beard and glasses, plaid sports jacket, and oxford shirt, he looks like an English professor but talks like an old-world theater queen. Old musicals are his specialty. Kevin, a handsome guy a little bit older than me, towers over Paul with his wavy brown hair and blue eyes. He is straight, but he exudes a love of theater that feels gayish.

"Darling, what I realized this summer is that I need a booking agent."

"Because it's all about distribution," adds Kevin.

"This *Bye Bye Birdie* production was mine," says Paul.

They are on a roll; I try to keep up.

"They totally screwed us," says Kevin.

"Kevin, let me tell the story."

"Well, tell it then."

"You see, I came up with this fabulous idea to get Tommy Tune to star in *Bye Bye Birdie* at the Muny. I call him up, and say, 'Tommy: Albert in *Bye Bye Birdie*. You were born to play this part. He says, 'Paul, you're such a gentleman, but I'm exhausted from *Grand Hotel* and I'm about to start this new show about Will Rogers. I need a break.' So I say, 'Exactly. This is going to be the best vacation you could imagine.' 'What do you mean?' he says. 'This'll be only a few weeks. Like a Mickey and Judy show.' Well, guess what? Tommy said yes. And then, to make it even better, I persuaded Ann Reinking to play Rose."

"That was my idea," says Kevin.

"The show was fabulous; it broke the box office record. Perfect for touring. Then Gary McAvay—"the biggest booking agent in the business"—flew out to see it and the next thing I know, he's booking a national tour that Pace Theatrical Group is producing. And I'm out."

"They stole it from us," says Kevin.

"They stole it from me," says Paul.

"I warned you to lock up the rights," says Kevin.

"Now he tells me." Paul rolls his eyes.

"I told you over and over."

"If charming young Jeffrey Seller were my booker, we wouldn't have lost that show."

"If we had proper distribution we wouldn't have lost that show," repeats Kevin.

"What do you mean?" I ask.

"Theater is just like the movie business. The studios make all their money in distribution fees. I just graduated from the Stark program at USC."

"So why aren't you doing movies?" I ask.

"I'm all about gathering. And, in the film business, they're all about money and power."

"Kevin, you talk in bumper stickers," says Paul. His gibes don't pierce Kevin, who doesn't even notice.

"No one cares about making anything good in Hollywood. I worked at Disney for over a year. I read the script to *Pretty Woman*, it was called *3000*, and I thought it would be a good musical. I told them they should be doing musicals. And they said, 'Kevin, it's never going to happen. If you want to make musicals, you should probably go somewhere else.'"

"Their loss, my gain," interjects Paul, who seems to love Kevin and be annoyed by him at the same time.

"We should start our own agency," says Kevin. He may not like Hollywood big shots, but he sure acts like one. Sometimes it seems as if Paul is working for Kevin.

"That's what we wanted to talk to you about," says Paul. "You could join us and book our shows."

"Kevin, what about you?" I ask. "What's a straight Irishman like you doing in the theater?"

"I'm Jewish!" he proclaims. "Didn't you know that McCollum is a Jewish name? It's in the prayer book. Baruch atah adonai, eloheinu mela-chollum!"

"Nice," I say, smiling.

"My mother was Susan Goldberg. My father was Thomas McCollum, but they divorced when I was a baby. We lived in Hawaii, and he left. My mother died when I was fourteen."

"I'm sorry," I say.

"My mother worked at CBS, so I got to meet the stars that came through to promote their shows. Mom was good friends with Jim Nabors and she played Phyllis in *Follies*. I ran the spotlight, so I learned to love Sondheim when I was ten."

"Where did you go when your mom died?"

"I went to live with my aunt and uncle in Chicago. I had never seen snow. But I basically raised myself."

"That's a lot," I say. Kevin talks about sad stuff without a whiff of sadness.

"Now, darling, we're here to talk about you. Where did you come from?" asks Paul. I tell my story, which he absorbs like an eager theatergoer. "Darling, what I see is that you're a big thinker. You're looking at the whole forest, not the individual trees. You're a producer."

I appreciate the way Paul sees me. He makes me feel wanted. Kevin is a lot. He fills every open space with words. He says stuff that makes no sense. And yet. He's insightful about the booking business. And he's fun.

The three of us part ways, each tasked to think this opportunity over.

Three weeks later, Paul calls and tells me he has an investor to pay for this endeavor. He sends me to his Wall Street friend who might be interested. His name is Allan Gordon. I call him to set up an appointment. He's curt and gruff.

I show up at his office on Lexington Avenue and Forty-third Street. A receptionist leads me into a conference room with high-backed leather chairs situated around a table cluttered with papers and folders. Allan is giving instructions to his secretary. Something to do with the New York Stock Exchange.

"Take a seat," he says. "So what's the deal with you and Paul?"

I explain that my role would be to "sell," or book, Paul's shows on the road.

"And you know who to call to sell this shit?" he asks.

"I've been doing it for three years."

"Did you see that show *Phantom*?"

"Of course I saw *Phantom*."

"The most boring piece of shit I've ever seen. Intermission came and I told the people we were with I was going out to have a cigarette. Never came back. I dragged my wife out with me."

I listen to him and smile.

"I mean," he continues, "it's all about getting laid, right?"

"What?" I ask.

"I mean, unless you're getting a blow job all day long, it isn't worth it, right?"

I try to explain why I love theater and the business, which has nothing to do with blow jobs.

He responds, "You can't make any money doing this shit, can you?"

"You know what they say, 'You can't make a living, but you can make a killing.'"

"It's all shit," he says. "Why does anybody do this? It's gotta be because they're getting a piece of ass."

I disagree in a friendly way. The conversation lands on *Cats*, because in 1990 every conversation about theater lands on *Cats*.

"I hated that piece of shit too," he says.

"For what it's worth, it's the most profitable show of all time."

"I don't understand how anyone makes money in this business."

"How do you know Paul?" I ask.

"I was his landlord when he lived in New York. I own a lot of real estate."

"So you and Paul became friends?"

"I liked him. He was, you know, different."

It's hard to imagine that this vulgar, gruff money guy appreciated Paul Blake. This seems as likely as Sylvester befriending Tweety.

"So, you think you want to get involved with show business?" I ask.

"Lemme tell you something, if the company works, you're going to leave. Why would you stay? You don't own it. So it'll never work."

Allan is entertaining. He doesn't invest in the agency, but he'll return to our lives soon. His statements about the agency and me turn out prophetic.

MEETING #2

LATER IN SEPTEMBER, Beth Emelson, Barry's assistant, comes into my office with a flier that says "BOHO DAYS, a rock monologue by Jonathan Larson." She says she met him at Naked Angels, a theater group downtown, and asks if I want to go with her. I'm intrigued by the idea of a rock monologue, so I agree to go.

That night, we climb two flights of stairs to the ninety-nine seat Second Stage Theatre on Broadway and Seventy-fifth Street. We sit on the right side of the small auditorium. On the stage is a piano, along with a band setup for drums, guitar, and bass. The back wall of the theater is brick. There are no wings.

A tall, lanky guy named Jonathan enters from stage right. He has curly brown hair that rises over his head like the branches of a tree. His ears are big. He wears black jeans, dirty canvas sneakers, and a loose shirt. He sits down at the piano, pauses, and then launches his story through a cycle of songs.

It's his thirtieth birthday and he feels like a failure, as if he's missed the deadline to be successful. Inside his head he keeps hearing, *tick, tick, boom!* He writes rock musicals that no one wants to produce. He has an agent who doesn't return his phone calls. He's broke. He has a girlfriend whom he isn't in love with, but he'd be lonely without her. His best friend is a successful executive at an ad agency and offers him the chance to be a copywriter. It's a real job with a real salary. He wouldn't have to live in a fourth-floor walk-up with a bathtub in the kitchen. He doesn't know what to do.

Jonathan exudes passion and vibrancy. He's especially full of life when he's enraged by it. He hates how "the theater" treats him, as if "the theater" is a person, but he refuses to give up on it. He hates his job waiting tables at the Moondance Diner. To show the absurdity of hipsters who wait on long lines to eat eggs and French toast at Sunday brunch, he writes new lyrics to Sondheim's "Sunday" satirizing New York culture. It's hilarious.

"Green Green Dress" expresses his obsession with a sexy woman whose tight bodice hugger he wants to "unwrap." Its vamp evokes the theme song from the TV show *Batman*; the snappy melody embeds itself in my brain. He and his girlfriend sing through a "Therapy" session—"I'm OK if you're OK"—that is both witty and true. Struggling with a copywriting job offer, he sings "Johnny Can't Decide." It feels like he's singing directly to me: *Jeffrey can't decide.* Jon is driven, industrious, and self-absorbed, which is pointed out by his best friend, who reveals in a gut-wrenching moment that he's HIV positive.

By the time he gets to the line "what a way to spend a day," in a song recounting his love of doing theater as a boy, the dam behind my eyes breaks open. I cry because I don't like my job, but I don't know how to move on to the next one. I cry over my breakup with Andrew. I, too, am frustrated by "the theater" but I don't want to stop making it. I've never met this man and yet his musical feels like my life. How did he know my story? His songs make the hair on my arms stand up, make me laugh and cry, fill me with awe and hope. The entire show is like my own cathartic therapy session.

After the show, Beth takes me to the opening night party at a bar downtown. When Jonathan arrives, he is surrounded by friends. I'm too shy to meet him and I'm not sure how to express the profundity of this evening. I go home without talking to him, but the next day I write a letter:

Dear Jonathan,

I saw your play, Boho Days, *and was bowled over. Your work— music, lyrics, and spoken word—has an emotional power and resonance that I rarely experience in the theatre. You're also insightful, perceptive, and very funny.*

I'm writing because, like you, I also want to do great things in the theatre, but from the producing and directing side. And, in thinking about Boho Days, *and your predilection toward rock musicals, I hit upon an idea I want to share with you.*

I've always wanted to develop a musical, or you might say, chamber opera, about an American family in crisis (I realize Bernstein did something of the sort with Trouble in Tahiti*): a domestic drama that touches on the dissolution of the American dream that's all sung—where the events and emotions are so fierce that music provides the only viable channel for communication. Let's say the parents are in their late forties or early fifties and grew up in the early years of rock 'n roll (Buddy Holly, Elvis, etc. . . .), the children are in their teens or early twenties, growing up on contemporary rock 'n roll and all of them sing in the genre that's in their blood. Thus their generation gap, their communication barriers, and everything else that separates them is reflected not only in their words but also in their music. And when they collide in duets and trios and quartets so do these musical genres.*

The point here is to motivate the use of rock music. Use it to tell story, convey its themes, and flesh out its characters. Rock is

inextricably linked to the American dream; it's one of its byprod-
ucts. And it's the perfect medium for a musical about a group
of people who all grew up on it, albeit at different periods in its
evolution.

Food for thought.

From the looks of your impressive résumé, I figure you
probably don't need to get involved with low men on the totem
pole like me. You are obviously well connected in the New York
theatre community. However, getting a show up is damn near
impossible no matter what the connection.

So I figure it's worth a try.

A little about me:

I'm a theatrical booking agent for producers Barry and Fran
Weissler. That means I sell weeklong engagements of their shows
(Gypsy, Cabaret, Fiddler) to road promoters when they go out
on tour. I've also produced and/or directed several off-off Broadway shows in my spare time. Last year, I produced and directed
a new musical called A Pound of Feathers that was written by
two BMI students, Andrew Lippa and Tom Greenwald. I worked
with Tom and Andrew throughout the development process,
raised the money for the production, and basically put the whole
package together. It was an enormously challenging and satisfying process that I look forward to tackling again.

My bread-and-butter job has served as a valuable training
ground for my aspirations as a producer. I know I have a knack
for producing shows and I think I've got some valuable artistic
ideas as well.

I'd love to get together and talk. I've got about a thousand
ideas to share, and I'm sure you do too. Here's my card—I hope
you'll give me a call when you have a spare moment.

Best regards,
Jeffrey Seller

MEETING #3

TWO WEEKS LATER I'M sitting in the conference room eating my lunch—a salami sandwich, sliced carrots, and an apple. I'm reading an article on the front page of the *Times* about the obscenity trial of 2 Live Crew for their rap lyrics when Susan comes into the conference room and closes the door.

I look up and say hello, but I see she's looking at me like she's caught me stealing, as if reading the *New York Times* while eating my lunch is a crime.

"We need to talk," she says. There's an envelope in her right hand. She sits down kitty-corner to me, at the head of the table.

"What's up?" I ask.

"It's clear to me that you don't want to be a booking agent. Your heart lies somewhere else. You don't want to do this. We both know you want to be a producer. And I think it's time for you to just go and do what you want to do."

She's right, I think to myself. But that doesn't stop my internal panic. My heart plunges from my chest to my toes. Blood drains from my head. I'm shocked. I'm scared. I can't even form words to respond.

The office intercom buzzes, and the receptionist calls out, "Jeffrey, Jonathan Larson on line three."

I spring from my seat, hurrying to the phone and my future. "Tell him I'll call back," I say to the receptionist. "Please take a number." Jonathan Larson is calling me while I'm being fired—this is the definition of irony.

Susan puts the envelope in front of me, tells me that it holds two weeks' severance pay but that I should get my things together and leave immediately. My body feels like it's either so numb I can't walk, or so shaken I can't sit down. I grab a friend in the office and go to the closest bar, McHale's, and order a glass of Scotch, something I've never done before. I down it. The drink steadies me enough to return to the office, get my few belongings, and exit. I feel humiliated, but also relieved. Susan just did what I didn't have the courage to do myself.

When I get home, I call Jonathan.

"Hello?" he says.

"Hello Jonathan, this is Jeffrey Seller."

"How are you?"

"That's an interesting question. I was just fired."

"Wow. Is that a good thing or a bad thing?"

"If I believe anything you wrote in your play, it's a good thing."

"So now you'll have time to produce my play," he says.

I laugh. "You said it. Do you want to get together and talk?"

We make a date to get together a week later at a pub on Bleecker Street near Broadway.

The much-awaited day arrives and Jonathan and I sit opposite each other at a banquette as I tell him again how much his show meant to me. How deeply it moved me. How much I loved his songs. How hard it made me cry.

"I like your idea for a musical," he says. "But first I want to get *Boho Days* on. So, do you want to produce it?"

"I wonder whether it'd be able to find a wide enough audience. It's so theater-centric."

"It's not about theater," he responds, "it's about staying true to yourself. Pursuing your dreams and not giving up and selling out."

"I know, but . . ."

Jonathan's passion is irresistible. By the end of our meeting, I tell him that I will think about producing *Boho Days*. I offer him one piece of advice.

"It shouldn't be called *Boho Days*. Your character keeps repeating 'tick, tick, boom' the whole show. That's your title."

"You think about producing it and I'll think about changing the title," he says.

A month later I visit Jonathan at his fourth-floor walk-up on Greenwich Street. There's a tiny kitchen table against the wall right next to the front door and the bathtub is under the window. The paint is peeling off the walls. We sit at the table, drink tea.

"I work at the Moondance Friday through Sunday, which gives me four full days to write," he says. "I can't wait until I can finally dump that waiter job to just be an artist."

"And I'm a fired booker who wants to be a producer."

"You're gonna be my producer."

"Just like Cameron and Andrew," I say.

"I love *Jesus Christ Superstar* but I can't stand Andrew Lloyd Webber."

"I memorized every word to *Evita* in high school," I say. Have you seen *Phantom*?"

"Hell no. Who could afford it? Those aren't our stories, those aren't our characters, that's not our music. I'm making musicals for our generation."

I'm thrilled by his enthusiasm for the form.

We talk about other shows. I recently saw the Mozart opera *Don Giovanni* directed by Peter Sellars. He placed the story on the streets of present-day Harlem. I wonder if it would be fun to make a contemporary Don Juan musical using the sounds of present-day Harlem.

"I think that sounds like a good idea for someone like Madonna," Jonathan says. "She could play Don Juan."

He tells me of another project he is contemplating—a modern-day *La Bohème* that takes place in the East Village. Mimi has AIDS instead of tuberculosis.

"I love that idea," I tell him.

"I want to do a show about people living with AIDS and not dying from AIDS," he says. "So, when are you seeing Flora about *Tick, Tick . . . Boom*?"

"As soon as I can get your fancy agent on the phone," I say.

"Tell me about it."

Stephen Sondheim's longtime agent, Flora Roberts, is legendary and reputed to be tough. After half a dozen tries, she takes my call and invites me to her office to talk. It's in a small building on West Fifty-seventh Street. I walk into a dark, tiny room with papers and books everywhere. The room is illuminated by one lamp. A short, plump woman with gray hair piled on top of her head and round black-framed glasses sits in a swivel chair in the center of a half round table that curves around her. She looks like a hard-boiled egg sitting in its special cup.

I sit down and she immediately starts talking in her raspy voice. No small talk.

"So, do you think anyone will come see it?" she asks.

"When I went to see it, I had never heard of Jonathan Larson, but he was telling my story. I think he's telling everyone's story, at least everyone trying to make it in New York."

"What do I know? I'm an old lady."

"I'm honored to be sitting here with you," I say.

She doesn't respond to compliments. "OK, get out your pencil. Here's the deal: He gets 2 percent for music, 2 percent for lyrics, and 2 percent for the book. That's 6 percent of the gross, but I'm going to let you use a pool as long as you pay him a weekly minimum of twelve hundred bucks. He needs an advance of 2,500 dollars, immediately, which will at least help him pay the rent in that godforsaken apartment of his. It doesn't even have a buzzer, you know."

My head is spinning. I need to figure out what a "royalty pool" means. I write it all down and then haggle a little, after which we come to an agreement: She lowers the advance by one thousand bucks. We shake hands and I leave trying to figure out where I'm going to get fifteen hundred dollars.

In my next meeting with Jonathan, I summon the courage to make another big suggestion.

"I think you need a new opening number," I tell him. "'Boho Days' is your weakest number. It's too repetitive, all the energy is downward. It's not melodic enough."

A month later, he gives me a cassette of a new song called "30/90." It's a lively pop-rock song about turning thirty years old in 1990. I love it. I tell him it sounds like a Billy Joel song.

"I'll take that as a compliment," he says.

Jonathan invites me to his Peasant Feast, a dinner he hosts for his friends every year around Thanksgiving. His bohemian apartment is packed with people, the plates are in every shape and size, and there is mixed silverware from every corner of the city. I'm an outsider, but his friends are loud, celebratory, and full of life.

I sit next to Jonathan's best friend, Matthew O'Grady, who is the real-life best friend depicted in *Tick, Tick . . . Boom*. Matt is a handsome guy—blond hair, blue eyes, strapping. But *Tick, Tick . . . Boom* reveals his HIV status in one of the show's most tragic moments, and all I see when I look at him is "HIV+." And that scares me. He tells me stories of going to high school with Jon (which is what he calls him) and getting high together. On my other side is Janet, Jonathan's former girlfriend, who tells me about her modern dance company. I feel like I'm in a scene from *Tick, Tick . . . Boom*. I'm struck by the way Jonathan uses his own life experiences—his friends and family—as narrative material for his art. He's doing something no other musical writer is presently doing: He's musicalizing what it's like to be alive in 1991. His characters are real people who happen to be singing their feelings—their hopes and fears, their joys and frustrations, their victories and defeats.

Now I just have to figure out a way to produce *Tick, Tick . . . Boom*. But before I can do that, I need to get a job so I can pay the rent.

Chapter Twenty-One

THE BOOKING OFFICE

I CALL PAUL AND KEVIN to tell them that I have no job and I'm available for anything.

Paul is too scared to put up eighty thousand dollars to start an agency so Kevin says he will put up half for 50 percent ownership. Paul agrees on one condition: Kevin must contribute his share first. Paul will contribute his share when it's needed. Kevin, a twenty-eight-year-old assistant, one year out of graduate film school, uses forty thousand dollars from his savings to start a booking agency in New York—a city in which he has never lived or worked—because he's convinced, "It's all about distribution." I ask him why he's doing this.

"Because we're going to be a big success. We're going to do great things together."

"Where did you get forty thousand dollars?"

"I bought stock in Disney when I was in college. I knew Eisner would turn that company around. The brand was too powerful to fail."

"Where did you get the money to buy stock?"

"It was my insurance money from my mother's death."

Kevin likes making bets. He and Paul offer me six hundred dollars a week, which is less than I was earning from the Weisslers, but it's better than unemployment so I accept.

We start our agency in January of 1991. We decide to call it The Booking Office, a nod to the olden days when bookers worked out of old-fashioned offices behind wood-framed doors with opaque windows and transoms. Miles Wilkin and Pace Theatrical Group rent us one room that was vacated by a subtenant. On my first day at the office, I put together two oak dining tables to use as desks even though I'm the only one in the office. A leftover burgundy couch sits against the wall. I buy four chairs from Conran's.

A couple of weeks later, I fly to Los Angeles, which feels backward because I'm flying away from the center of the theater business to work with my colleagues. The plan is to spend a week working in person with Paul and Kevin. They use a long, low-ceilinged room on the second floor of Paul's home on Coldwater Canyon in Beverly Hills. It has two dormer windows bringing in light from outside. Paul works at the far end and Kevin works at an adjacent desk. It reminds me of the house Natalie Wood covets in *Miracle on 34th Street*. I sleep in a large guest room on the first floor off the living room. I love Paul's home. I love eating breakfast in the kitchen every morning. I love reading in his cozy study, with walls lined with green wallpaper.

Paul and Kevin love to brainstorm. Kevin spends much of the day spouting ideas and telling Paul what he should be doing next.

"Darling," Paul says to Kevin, "if you know everything there is to know, then why are you sitting in that chair and I'm sitting in this chair?" Through their bickering, they sound like kids dreaming up ways to put on shows in their backyard.

The next day, Paul receives a call from his friend Hugh Martin, the composer and lyricist of *Meet Me in St. Louis*, who famously wrote "The Trolley Song" and "Have Yourself a Merry Little Christmas" for Judy Garland. Hugh is upset because his Broadway musical was to launch a first-class national tour this coming summer, but the producer just informed him that it's too expensive and they are going to reduce it to a non-Equity bus and truck, which means using non-union actors, which means lower salaries and inferior talent. With Hugh's encouragement, Paul concocts a strategy to take over *Meet Me in St. Louis* as an Equity tour. He talks to agents and music directors and set designers. Kevin spurs him on. I explain from my experience at the Weisslers that this won't be easy. The show was a flop on Broadway, and the road presenters don't think it will sell that many tickets. But they still need it to fill out their subscriptions after another crummy season on Broadway. They want a less expensive production on which they won't lose money. But Paul is an optimist.

"Darling, nobody wants a cheap production of *Meet Me in St. Louis* with amateur actors. I should know. I'm the David Merrick of St. Louis!"

"I love your chutzpah, Paul," I say.

"Do you know what I do?" says Paul. "I wake up, have my hot water and lemon, and then go up to my office. I can't just sit here and wait for the phone to ring because it won't until I get things started. No one's calling to offer me the next big show. I have to do it myself."

"We do it together," says Kevin, who seems to enjoy poking at Paul.

"The phone starts ringing after I start calling people and putting things together."

"I get that," I say.

"I invent myself every day," he says.

We brainstorm ways of making a tour of Rodgers and Hammerstein's *Cinderella on Ice* starring Randy Gardner and Tai Babilonia, America's favorite ice-skating couple, who were world champions in the late '70s. Paul's idea is to cast Phyllis Diller as the Evil Stepmother, Georgia Engel as the Fairy Godmother, and two more older stars to play the King and Queen. I'm game to give it a shot.

"Darling, I did a small tour of *She Loves Me* a year ago. And in ten weeks I made half a million dollars. Imagine what we can make if we do a forty-week tour?"

"Two million dollars," says Kevin.

"Thank you, Kev," says Paul, rolling his eyes, "my human calculator."

Kevin invites me on Sunday to his house in Van Nuys, which he says is "Sherman Oaks adjacent," where I meet his wife, Michele, his black lab named Cole, and a group of his friends. Kevin seems to exaggerate everything—his job title, his zip code, his job at Disney. He shows me his garage, which he and a friend made into a production office to work on new shows. We talk and eat lunch. I like Michele, an actress with whom Kevin studied at the Cincinnati Conservatory of Music. She is not like Kevin. She's of the earth and modest. Michele and Kevin are a testament to the cliché that opposites attract.

Kevin suggests we go to a nearby racetrack. I've never been to a racetrack. Like a big macher, he places bets on numerous horses. I have no idea how any of this works, and Kevin loves explaining how to bet on the horses and how the odds work. It's his way of taking charge. I can barely follow but am happy to be in a group.

I get back to New York feeling embraced by my new employers, but also scared. The tiny business of Broadway is built on friendships, alliances, and favors. At twenty-six years old, I'm still treated like a nobody. I'm only as good as the shows I'm selling. No one is going to buy a show to do me a favor.

Paul's mission, "I invent myself every day," rings in my head. I pick up the phone and start calling people. They listen to my pitch with interest.

"That sounds interesting," says one.

"Not a bad idea," another responds.

The presenters are warm and supportive—at least they take my calls—but not one of them says, "I want this show next season." I try not to get discouraged.

I need the same courage that brought me from the temple Purim play to Stagecrafters to Michigan Opera Theatre and New York.

Paul calls for updates.

"How's it going, dear boy?"

"There's a lot of interest, but no commitments yet. Everyone's focused on *Grand Hotel* and *City of Angels*."

"Don't worry. You know how to talk to people, you know how to listen," says Paul. "You don't hit them over the head with it."

I strike a five-week booking in Fort Lauderdale and Palm Beach for *Sammy Cahn in Person*, another Paul Blake production, and he is delighted. I'm less successful with Rodgers and Hammerstein's *Cinderella* but it doesn't matter because Paul pulls off the impossible: He clinches a deal to produce a twenty-week tour of *Meet Me in St. Louis* starring Debby Boone. We are off and running.

Then a seismic shift happens that alters the state of the business. With no advance notice, Susan Weaving quits Barry and Fran's booking agency claiming a contract dispute. She takes steps to start her own agency. Barry obtains a court injunction to stop her until they reach a settlement. She won't be able to work for a year.

With no one to lead Barry and Fran's booking agency, two of their shows come my way: *A Chorus Line*, which is in its final tour post Broadway, and *Love Letters* starring Stefanie Powers and Robert Wagner. Another producer hires me to book *The Odd Couple* starring Tim Conway (the popular costar of *The Carol Burnett Show*) and Tom Poston (a costar of *Newhart*), and a new tour of Hal Prince's production of *Evita*. Six months after opening the doors and we are the second-biggest agency in New York. Paul never puts up a penny.

Progress at work eases the loneliness I feel at home. I miss having a partner and playmate. I don't have a group, a posse to go to the beach with, to go dancing with. I spend many nights alone at home. On a Sunday in May, I'm on the phone with my mom when I blurt out that I've never felt like I could express my true feelings and that I've felt lonely my whole life. I tell her I wonder if it's because I was adopted. She wonders if it's because I'm gay. This exchange about my feelings becomes an argument over whether she's to blame for my unhappiness.

"Do you think I was a complete flop in raising you?" says Mom.

"For Christ sakes, mother, I don't think you were a flop."

"You sure act like it."

"Why is this always about you?" I ask.

"Don't turn this around."

"You can't see me separate from you. I say I feel like I was 'thrown away' at the start of my life, and you take it personally. You think it's a reflection of you. Can't you just separate us for a second and just support me as me?"

"Maybe you should be thankful for what you had," she says. "It could have been a whole lot worse."

I ask her why they chose to adopt a child.

"We didn't want an only child."

"So it had nothing to do with me." I know this isn't a fair reply, but I feel the need to strike at her.

"That's not what I'm saying," she says.

"Well, then what are you saying?"

"Did you ever think of finding your biological female to find out if there's any homosexuality in her family?"

"My what?" I ask.

"Your biological female."

"What the fuck is that?" I ask, fury building.

"You know what I'm talking about," she replies.

"It's my biological mother, Mom."

"The woman who had you is not your mother."

"The only thing more offensive than your question about homosexuality—it's as if you're trying to make sure you're not to blame for it—is you denying the word *mother* to describe the woman who happened to conceive me, carry me, and give birth to me."

"I am your mother!" she shouts.

"I guess you really can't acknowledge that I came from another woman."

"Son, I can't take any more burdens."

It's true. She has had too many burdens. So many burdens, in fact, that I think she never actually saw me growing up. She always says, "You practically raised yourself."

OCTOBER 16. MY TWENTY-SEVENTH BIRTHDAY. Mom calls to wish me a happy birthday, as if the previous conversation never happened. But today I wonder about my birth mother. Did she think about me today? Did she remember that she gave birth to me twenty-seven years ago today? I long for her today, perhaps for the first time. Being innately connected to someone I don't even know makes me feel lost. It makes me wonder if everyone feels as alone as me. Are these feelings caused by my adoption or my upbringing? I've ignored this my whole life. Maybe this is why I've always felt a little bit sad on my birthdays.

The Booking Office continues to grow. My job expands when I start not just booking shows but suggesting to my producer clients shows and stars that I think could successfully tour. We pursue Marie Osmond to star in a tour of *The Sound of Music* and she says yes. I also meet the Broadway legend Manny Azenberg, who produced every Neil Simon play since the early '70s. He hires us to book *Lost in Yonkers*, which just won the Tony Award for Best Play and the Pulitzer Prize for Drama. Over the coming years he will become advisor, mentor, and friend.

In November, there's a conference of the Broadway League in Newport, Rhode Island. A couple hundred industry bigwigs get together every other year to talk about issues facing the industry. The theater owners, producers, and road presenters all attend. Paul and I drive together. This dapper short gay man seems like a fish out of water at the McDonald's on I-95. He complains about Kevin the whole way. Upon arrival in Newport, Paul and Kevin get on the phone. They are arguing and I can't tell if Kevin is quitting or Paul is firing him as his executive producer. Paul has run out of patience for Kevin's compulsion to tell him what to do every minute of the day. Kevin has run out of patience for Paul's idiosyncratic way of producing and making decisions.

"I felt like I was working for him," says Paul. "He forgot that I own the company, and he works for me."

"Well, Paul, maybe he found it too confusing to be your employee in the producing company and your partner in the booking company," I say.

"You're right. He's not confused anymore," says Paul.

Most of the conference panels and meetings are self-congratulatory, which is incongruous with the state of Broadway. Few new musicals are being produced each season and there are barely any new plays. There's only one new musical this fall, *Nick & Nora*, and word of mouth is terrible despite its legendary creative team: composer Charles Strouse, lyricist Richard Maltby Jr., author and director Arthur Laurents. The word on the street is that it's bland and boring, which I soon learn is true. Broadway is stale.

ON THE LAST DAY of the conference, there's a speech by playwright Terrence McNally called "Where Are the Producers?" followed by a "Town Hall" session where anyone can get up and say what's on their mind. During his keynote, McNally beseeches the industry to develop and produce new plays, take more risks, and stop relying on revivals.

"The new American play is an endangered species," he says. "Five new plays opened on Broadway last year. Five. Forty years ago, thirty new plays opened. Sixty years ago, over sixty new plays opened. We are losing Broadway as a home for plays. And without new American plays, there is no American theater. We need you to take the lead. Please. Produce them. Book them in your theaters. Present them in your roadhouses. Our art form depends on it. We can't rely on helicopters and chandeliers."

Following McNally's speech, industry leaders take seats on the dais: Barry Weissler, my former employer; Rocco Landesman, the producer of *Angels in America* and the president of the third-largest theater chain; Tom and Jack Viertel, brothers who are producer and dramaturg, respectively; and finally Gerald Schoenfeld, the stentorian chairman of the Shubert Organization, who acts like he's the mayor of Broadway. There's a lot of talk about load-ins, labor costs, the high cost of producing new musicals, and the difficulty of finding directors to mount large musicals with huge pieces of moving scenery. To me it all feels beside the point.

From the back of the room, I raise my hand.

"Comment in the back," says Rocco Landesman.

"I'm looking around at this room and hearing talk about the state of the industry and the sad truth is that only one new musical is opening this fall. And I think that what's not being talked about is where our new musicals are going to come from. It's not about a director moving big scenery around. It's about finding the next generation of writers who are going to create the musicals that keep our business going. We barely have enough musicals to fill out the Tony categories every year. And it's because no one here is doing anything to develop young talent. What does it cost to bring three writers together to work on a new musical? As Mr. McNally says, we just need the producers."

My speech is passionate, a little angry. Rocco looks at me like, *Who the fuck are you?* Gerald Schoenfeld, the chairman of the Shubert Organization, looks like he has no idea what I'm talking about. What I glean from the panel is, *Sit down, kid. Stay in your place.* I feel humiliated. Exiting the ballroom at the end of the session, I see Terrence McNally in the lobby and introduce myself.

"Mr. McNally, hello, I heard your speech, and I couldn't agree with you more. My name is Jeffrey Seller. I want to produce musicals."

"And I agreed with everything *you* said, Jeffrey. That took a lot of guts. Forget about those guys on the panel. Do it yourself."

I try.

The goal is to produce *Tick, Tick . . . Boom* at the Actors' Playhouse on Seventh Avenue. It has about two hundred seats, which will be ideal for a one-man show. I would need to raise about 350,000 dollars. Jonathan and I review all the possibilities at our next meeting.

"You mentioned that you sent the cassettes to Sondheim," I say. "What did he think?"

"He said it's a rant about my disappointment over *Superbia.*" *Superbia* was Jonathan's last musical that he was convinced would take him all the way to Broadway. Playwrights Horizons did a one-week reading, after which many folks, Sondheim included, affirmed that he was "talented," but then nothing happened.

"What do you think?"

"He's missing the point," he says, "It's about being an artist and staying true to your dreams, not selling out."

"I never even saw *Superbia*, but your show was also my story."

"Exactly."

I plan a reading at a rehearsal studio on West Fifty-fourth Street and get about thirty people to attend. This time, there's no stage, no band, and no lights. Just Jonathan at his piano.

The new opening number is terrific, but as he begins telling the story, it feels smaller than I remember, more solipsistic. Playing himself plus all the other characters, from his girlfriend to his best friend to his agent, Jonathan's presence becomes overwhelming. The baldness of this reading exposes his earthbound voice. He sings well for a composer, but as the sole performer in a sung-through show, his singing doesn't have enough color or beauty. How can anyone be Pete Townshend and Roger Daltrey at the same time?

The invited guests are supportive, but the enthusiasm I witnessed at Second Stage has evaporated. Now, they pose a lot of questions: "Who really cares about someone whining because he's turning thirty? Woe is me."

"He's a great songwriter. Tell him to find a story."

"It feels a little inside baseball."

"There might be a way to do this, but you need to get a real actor to play the part."

I'm unsure of whether it's worth bringing this criticism to Jonathan, and I make the mistake of broaching the topic of the role. Jonathan is adamant.

"But Jonathan, if this is a musical, then shouldn't the role be able to be played by anyone?" I ask.

"No. It has to be played by me; it's a one-man show about me."

"I thought you said this is a real musical, not a one-man show," I say.

"It's a musical, but I have to do the first production because it's my life."

"You know that some of the people whose lives were portrayed in *A Chorus Line* weren't even in it?"

In the end our disagreement doesn't matter because I can't raise a penny.

Jonathan settles for some gigs of the show at downtown bars. His best friend, Victoria Leacock, promotes the hell out of it. The next time I see it, the spark is missing. I think it's because Jonathan has moved on. Maybe Sondheim was right. The good news is that he's working on his new version of *La Bohème*.

Chapter Twenty-Two

BOOKING WARS

A YEAR AFTER I AM FIRED, Barry Weissler calls and asks me to come back and take over his booking agency. The call feels great. But talk about selling out? I politely decline.

Then Miles Wilkin asks if I'll stop by his office to talk about something. I enter his vast corner office that looks out over the Hudson River. He shuts the door.

"You know I don't do small talk. I'll just cut to the chase. Do you think you'd be interested in heading up a new booking agency that would be owned by Pace and International Creative Management? ICM will package the shows, you'll book them, and we'll produce and promote them in our markets."

Wow. I'm impressed by the breadth of this idea.

"If so, I'll set you up with Sam Cohn to talk about it."

"I'm definitely interested," I say. "But I have a contract at my current job, and a bunch of good clients."

Miles doesn't care about any of these things. "This is not about your company. It's about you." I'm flattered. He continues, "They need someone who knows the road and can train their concert agents at booking legit."

"How do we proceed?" I ask.

"Call Sam Cohn's office and make an appointment. They're expecting your call."

To say that Sam Cohn is the most powerful agent alive is to underrate his pivotal role in show business. He represents actors Meryl Streep, Sigourney Weaver, Robin Williams, and Macaulay Culkin. He represents directors Mike Nichols, Woody Allen, Tommy Tune, and Robert Benton. He was Bob Fosse's agent and friend. He represents playwrights and screenwriters Peter Stone and Nora Ephron. His ability to make Broadway shows happen is as powerful as his ability to make big Hollywood movies happen. He's respected, admired, loathed, and feared.

I walk to the offices of ICM on West Fifty-seventh Street and am escorted to Sam's suite. I am nervous. Two assistants sit at desks outside his office. One places calls while the other takes messages, even though Mr. Cohn is infamous for never returning them. I listen to the action for about ten minutes and then one of the guys says, "He's ready for you."

I open the door and walk in.

A short man with gray wispy hair barely covering his crown sits in a leather chair with a chrome frame behind a black marble desk. He has wire-rimmed glasses and a scrunched, wrinkled face speckled with brown spots. He wears a tattered, navy blue wool sweater with a white collared shirt underneath, gray slacks, and fancy black loafers with no socks. He looks like a crotchety math professor. His feet are on the marble table along with a pack of Parliament cigarettes.

"Take a seat," he says.

I sit across from him while looking at the pictures on the wall behind me. There's a Hirschfeld drawing of him as Little Orphan Annie, with a cigarette in his hand and ashes falling to the ground. Sandy the dog sits next to him.

"I understand you're an excellent agent," he says.

"Thank you."

"Tell me about yourself."

He puts a cigarette in his mouth and then looks all over his table for a lighter. He finds a pack of matches, lights up, and takes a long drag while he listens to me. He smokes with his right hand and crumples little pieces of paper into balls with his left hand and then pops them into his mouth, chewing in between inhales of the cigarette.

I tell him about the University of Michigan and my work history.

"The Weisslers, huh? That must have been its own drama," he says.

"I guess you could say I had a front row seat," I reply.

"What do you want out of this?" he asks.

I explain that I love putting teams together; that I want to be a producer.

"You can produce right here. It's what I do every day. You'll be my partner."

I look at him in amazement.

"You get good ideas, and we'll put it all together. I have the directors, the writers. And our talent side will bring the stars."

I'm trying not to fall out of my chair. I'm trying to think of something smart to say.

"That Hirschfeld is amazing," I say.

"It was a gift from Mike Nichols."

"Really?"

"I got Mike to produce *Annie*. The producers didn't know what they were doing. I told Mike to see it at Goodspeed. I pulled together the financing and he revamped the show. He made more money from *Annie* than any movie he'd ever directed."

"Mr. Cohn, I have one hesitation, and I don't want it to be a deal-killer, but I also need you to know I don't want to be a booker for the rest of my life."

"That's what I'm telling you. You can produce anything you want."

One of the most powerful men in show business is taking me under his wing. He is affirming what I always thought about myself. I'm not crazy. I'm not deluded. He is offering to be the kind of mentor I never had in high school or college. The meeting ends with smiles and a handshake, and I walk out of the contemporary, chic ICM headquarters pretty sure I could own the whole thing someday. I walk back to my office elated about what's to come and concerned about the messy process of getting there.

I need to talk to Paul and Kevin. I signed a letter of agreement when I took the job, even though the salary was only six hundred dollars per week. I feel a little bit guilty and a little bit scared. Paul gave me a job after I was fired. His tour of *Meet Me in St. Louis* gave the agency its first stream of income. But it's also true that I did 100 percent of the work and was responsible for signing up all the other shows. I was the motor of an agency that I didn't own. Paul and Kevin, who haven't spoken to each other since the firing, get on a call. I explain that I've been offered this new opportunity.

"See, I knew this was going to happen," says Paul. "Allan Gordon was right."

"Allan is a Wall Street rich guy who owns a lot of parking garages and gets a kick out of trashing theater people," I say. "He's not a serious person."

"You know why he wouldn't invest in this company? Because he said you'd leave," says Paul.

"I'll get them to buy you out," I explain. "You'll make a nice profit, and I'll get on with my life."

"What if I don't want to be bought out?" says Kevin.

"I hope you can think about this from my perspective," I say.

"Darling, Sam Cohn is an awful man," says Paul. "He's just saying these things to get you."

"You mean like you got me?" I ask. "What's so wrong with that?"

Kevin is more pragmatic. He doesn't get angry. He talks about all the reasons why I should stay and how much more successful we will be if we stay together.

"Stay together? You two don't even speak to each other," I say.

"That has nothing to do with this," says Paul.

"You are going to be so much more successful than anything Miles Wilkin and Sam Cohn can offer," says Kevin. "They're just going to pigeonhole you."

I listen and try to be patient.

"If we stay together, we can do anything. We'll own this entire business," says Kevin.

Kevin has just moved to New York with his wife, who is starting rehearsal for a new Broadway musical called *Crazy for You*. He has no New York experience and doesn't know any of the players on Broadway. But he owns half of a booking agency, or more precisely, half of me. He likes what he's got. And he's not going to let it go easily.

Over the next week, I try to make clear to Paul and Kevin that I want out. I call Sam and Miles and suggest they buy the entire company from Paul and Kevin thus freeing me from my commitment and inheriting all the commissions that will come over the next year and a half.

Paul wants the buyout.

Kevin wants me to stay.

Miles wants to get rid of those "losers" and start this new venture.

Sam Cohn wants the boost that youth and new business enterprises will bring to his agency, which is losing ground to Mike Ovitz and the Creative Artists Agency. It's been poaching Sam's clients from every direction. It's a lot of wants. I'm the middleman in a multi-pronged negotiation between egomaniacal men who only want to win. I work to please all of them while also getting what I want: a high-paying leadership role at one the world's most powerful agencies, where I'll be sitting in an office next door to its iconic leader.

What complicates this negotiation is that Kevin knows that Barry and Fran blocked Susan Weaving from working for a full year after she walked out on them. Kevin uses this as leverage and ICM won't proceed without a full release.

I meet with Paul's lawyer, Loren Plotkin.

"This whole negotiation makes me want to throw up," I say. "It's all about buying and selling me. The company has no value without me. If they won't sell it, I'll walk even it means doing something else. They'll have nothing."

Loren understands every side of this equation and proposes a reasonable compromise: ICM and Pace pay Kevin and Paul a buyout of 200,000 dollars for which they receive my services and the contracts to all the shows I'm presently booking. I try to sell it to both sides. Sam is agreeable; Pace doesn't want to pay that much; Paul is happy to take it; Kevin is basically immovable. He thinks the agency is being undervalued. I'm not sure there is any number he will accept. The negotiation drags on past the holidays and deep into February.

No one will budge and I need a break.

It's Saturday night. No plans. I put on a pair of Levi's and a T-shirt and take a taxi to the Roxy on West Eighteenth Street. It's the biggest dance club in New York, occupying a former roller rink. Saturday night is gay night. Shirtless muscle guys dance on bar counters. A DJ named Frankie Knuckles spins the throbbing music. The place is filled with young men of every stripe—muscle studs, pretty boys, goth and grunge types, and guys like me who don't feel at home in any of these groups. I wander the club. I order a Coke. I stand on the side of the cavernous room, holding the rail that separates the dance floor from the sitting areas, watching men dance. Out of my left eye I see a cute younger guy who looks like Jason Priestley from *Beverly Hills, 90210*. He's tall and broad, loose and relaxed. He's pretty and masculine. He looks at me and smiles with the brown eyes of a puppy. I smile back. Then he confidently walks over and asks me to dance.

He takes my hand and leads me to the floor, and we dance to a remix of "If I Could Turn Back Time." He's a sexy mover, easy and fluid. He smiles when he dances. He exudes fun. He takes charge of me on the dance floor, and I like it.

"What's your name?" I ask.

"Jesse, what's yours?"

"Jeffrey."

"I can't stop looking at your beautiful eyes," he says.

"That's very sweet of you," I reply.

We get a drink.

"So what's your story?" I ask.

"Just hanging out with some friends. Can I kiss you? I really want to kiss you."

"Yes, please."

He bends down a little because he's taller, which makes me swoon. His lips are pink, soft, and curvy. He touches my lips with the perfect balance of plushness and pressure. I invite him to come home with me. We make out in the cab. When we get to my apartment, we slowly take off our clothes.

"Can we just camp out?" Jesse says as we're hugging and touching each other on my futon. He doesn't want to have full-on sex. His question is endearing and makes me like him even more.

"I'm just happy to be lying here with you."

We keep making out and eventually fall asleep.

The next morning, I wake up and run out to buy some bagels and orange juice at the corner store while he sleeps. When I return, he's awake.

"I was worried you left, which would have been weird because this is your apartment," he says.

"I got us some breakfast," I say.

"I like you," he says.

"I like you too," I reply.

"And can I tell you something else?"

"Sure," I reply.

"You're even hotter with your clothes off."

I've wished someone would say that to me since I was sixteen years old.

Jesse is a new kind of gay guy. He's comfortable expressing the masculine energy of a strong, tall man and the campy fun of effeminate gays. What I glean is that younger gay guys are less compartmentalized by homophobia and self-loathing.

Over the next six months we become boyfriends. Our relationship is built on physical attraction and play—throwing the Frisbee in Central

Park, running, playing board games. Jesse is easy to be with and snuggly to sleep with. On Saturday mornings, he eats Cheerios with lots of sugar on top, and watches cartoons. I read the *New York Times* and obsess about closing the ICM deal.

Jesse is twenty-one years old and acts like a kid. I'm twenty-eight years old and seesaw between kid and middle-aged man. Jesse served in the army for a couple of years, didn't go to college, and arrived in New York City where he got a job assisting a production manager at a men's clothing company. He works hard and is achieving success.

Our sex makes me euphoric. I love his body. I love his mouth, which has a small vertical scar that crosses his upper lip. It makes his beautiful face a tiny bit rugged. Jesse craves being penetrated, and our intercourse makes me feel more whole, more alive. But Jesse is needy, which starts to repel me. He wants me to call him constantly. He wants my undivided attention and I'm unable to oblige. I'm distracted because I'm focused on developing a new working relationship with Sam Cohn.

March is occupied by countless meetings and phone calls. Each step forward is muddied by new hurdles. Everyone is frustrated and fed up. It becomes clear that this whole negotiation is about Kevin and me. I invite him to talk one night at my apartment.

"I figured we're never going to get this done until you and I talk," I say. "This whole thing is really about my desire to leave and your desire for me to stay."

"It's about what's best for both of us," he says.

"Kevin, I need to say something."

"Of course."

"You don't own me," I say.

"I never said that," he replies.

"Then stop trying to force me to stay."

"I'm not trying to force you. I'm trying to make you understand how much I value you."

"Kevin, you're a nice guy. I like you, I really do. I enjoy your company. But you're not in charge of me."

"It's because I like you and respect you so much that I don't want to lose you," he says.

"This is my life we're talking about," I say.

"And mine."

"Kevin, you can't force me to be your dutiful booker. You can't force me to show up and sit at a desk and pick up the phone every day and call Judy Lisi and use my talent to get her to book your show."

"I know that."

"You're treating my talent like some sort of commodity," I say.

"It's because I understand exactly how talented you are that I'm trying to make you happy," he replies.

"Quit saying that. If you want to make me happy, then let me go."

"I've already said I'll sell them the company for $300K."

"That's fucking crazy."

"I'm asking you to remember that you made an agreement and you're the one trying to break it. I'm just trying to do what's best."

"For you, not me," I say.

"But it has been good for you. You called and said you needed a job. I took the risk. I put up the capital. And without that, we wouldn't be sitting here having this conversation."

"That's a stretch."

"You're not showing any respect for capital," he says.

"That sounds like one of your bumper stickers."

"Companies don't happen without someone taking a risk. Shows don't happen without someone taking the risk. Did Paul take the risk? No. I took the risk. You know that."

"Stop lecturing me," I say.

"I made it possible for you to go to the office to start booking. I paid for your desk, for your chair, and for the phone you talk on. Sam Cohn didn't do that."

"Kevin, you were Paul's assistant."

"I was his executive producer."

"A title you gave yourself," I say.

"Not true."

"I'm glad they taught you all about film distribution at USC. Maybe your instinct about booking was smart, but you're not a producer. You're an assistant who was recently fired."

"Not true."

"And you might own half a booking agency, but you don't know anything about booking. And I'm supposed to stay here with you instead of going to ICM, working in the office next to Sam Cohn at triple the salary?"

"It's not about the money, it's about the future."

"Kevin, you have your relationship to money, I have mine, and if you think I'm going to walk away from $120K a year, you're out of your mind."

No progress. I'm not sure if I want to kill him or commend him for his tenacity. He manages to get in my head, though, and I wonder whether I am selling out. Is this my *Tick, Tick . . . Boom* moment? Maybe I should just focus on being successful with Kevin.

After he leaves, the phone rings.

"Hey, cute man," says Jesse. We haven't talked in a while.

"Hey, handsome. How are you?" I ask.

"Can we go to dinner? I thought maybe we could go to Elephant and Castle tomorrow night."

"Your favorite."

"Unless you're too busy having dinner with Sam Cohn."

"Ha, ha."

"So is that a yes?" he asks.

"You bet. I'll meet you after work," I say. He doesn't sound like himself.

In the narrow back room of the cozy restaurant in the West Village, we sit at a two-top against a wall in the back.

Jesse looks at me with his puppy dog expression, which makes me melt a little.

"I miss seeing you more often," he says.

"I still want to hang out," I respond.

"Hang out? That's all this has been to you?"

"Sorry, bad choice of words. I was just using your word. It's what you said the night we met."

"I thought I meant more than that," he says.

"I just don't want to disappoint you, Jesse. I can't be with you in the way you want."

Silence. Jesse looks at me like he's going to cry. He pauses.

"I need to tell you something," he says.

A blast of heat shoots up my back. "Please," I say.

"I don't even know if I can say it."

"You know you can tell me anything."

"I went to my doctor a couple weeks ago, and, well, I got tested for HIV."

"I see." I'm about to explode.

"I got the results yesterday and, um, I guess I'll just say it. I'm positive."

Shaking in my chair, I feel like I'm having a heart attack. I'm going to die of AIDS. Struggling to form words of sympathy as I crumble under my own fear, I blurt, "I'm really, really sorry, Jesse. I don't know what to say."

"I needed to tell you."

"Do you know where you got it?" I ask.

"I don't know, doesn't matter. Maybe from you."

He's not wrong. The last time I tested was more than a year ago.

"Oh God, I'm so sorry you're going through this," I say.

"I'm sorry we're both going through this."

"I'll go see my doctor immediately." My mouth is dry. My stomach is clenched. Eating is impossible.

The rest of the dinner is a blur. The relationship was already winding down. This will end it. The shadow of AIDS will make having sex with Jesse impossible.

I sweat through three T-shirts that night. I see my doctor the next day, who asks me a bunch of questions about exposure. When I explain in detail what we've done, he says, "I doubt you have HIV. But we need to make sure." After taking my blood, he tells me to call him in a week.

It's the "making sure" part that devours me. "Doubt" leaves a hole for being positive. I think back to every time we had sex. We were safe and used condoms, but how do you have sex without exchanging at least some body fluids?

My body is in turmoil. I make extra trips to the laundromat to wash cold sweat–soaked T-shirts. I run longer and farther. I focus on work intermittently. I can't even masturbate. The thought of my semen carrying HIV is petrifying. I try to imagine life with HIV. I think about everyone I've ever known who has died. I think about hospital rooms, funeral homes, and coffins, which scare the hell out of me. I don't share my anxiety with anyone. I want to talk to Andrew, but I don't want to bother him or scare him. I avoid talking to my mother or father. Though I count down the days, I dread calling the doctor on the appointed day. How do I pick up the phone and ask the doctor if I'm going to die? Being put on hold by the receptionist is agony. What am I supposed to do if he says positive? Are there false positives? After I'm on hold for a few seconds, he jumps on.

"Your HIV test was negative."

Like a dam bursting, my body releases and I start crying.

"But you need to come back. Your cholesterol is a little high. I want to check that."

"Thank you, Doctor, I think I'm going to go throw up now."

"You're OK. Just keep doing what you're doing."

I go downstairs to the deli and treat myself to a Häagen-Dazs ice cream bar. And then I sign up with a friend for a weekend seminar at the Gay Community Center called "Making Safe Sex Fun!" More like "exhausting," I think. It's difficult to talk about boundaries with men I'm having sex with. I'm hesitant to say I'm not comfortable taking their dick in my mouth. Jerking off with hot guys in the steam room of the gym seems easiest. Bottom line, the connection between sex and death doesn't go away.

IN LATE APRIL, I've finally aligned all the parties and we have a tentative deal. Sam calls to congratulate me. Then Kevin walks into the office and drops a bomb that explodes the whole thing.

Over the last four months, Kevin has become friends with the producer of *Crazy for You*, Roger Horchow, who is new to Broadway. He's slightly famous as the purveyor of the beloved Horchow Home Collection, which he recently sold to Neiman Marcus for 125 million dollars, and he's now enjoying life as a producer. No one on Broadway had high hopes for another musical of repurposed Gershwin tunes, but when it arrived on Broadway, Frank Rich declared that *Crazy for You* reclaimed "the effervescent confidence of the great American musical and ended the era of the British blockbuster." It became an instant hit and a shoo-in for Best Musical.

Kevin says, "Roger Horchow is loaning me the money to buy Paul out. And he's granting me the booking rights for *Crazy for You*."

Nothing comes out of my mouth.

"This is just the beginning of what we can do if we stay together."

"Kevin, you're either the smartest person I've ever met, or the stupidest," I say.

"We'll see," he says.

Kevin is now the sole owner of The Booking Office, which now has the booking rights to the hottest show on Broadway. He has no intention of selling it to Sam Cohn, ICM, Pace, or anybody else. The deal is off.

I'm exhausted. And impressed. I don't implode. I don't scream or shout or cry. Instead, I get busy working on *Crazy for You*.

In the weeks and months after, I come to some conclusions. I have always assumed that I can bend the world to my will if I try hard enough. I've also assumed that failure would result in catastrophe. This negotiation made me realize that I can't always change people's minds, and not making a deal doesn't mean the world is coming to an end.

Kevin and I start a genuine collaboration, and the agency grows. I still like Kevin. I enjoy his company; I enjoy his ambition and enthusiasm. He appreciates my knowledge, insights, and realistic assessment of the business. He also agrees to sell me half the company, which is essential to my self-esteem and our partnership. Because I have no cash, he lets me pay him out of my share of the profits for the next two years.

"We can do anything together," Kevin states.

I'm starting to agree.

Chapter Twenty-Three

THE REAL LIVE BRADY BUNCH

I GO TO A NEW off-Broadway show called *The Real Live Brady Bunch* at the Village Gate in the fall of 1991. It's a silly, satirical trip back to one of my greatest childhood comforts—the Bradys, where the parents are perfect, the kids are good-looking, and the house is beautiful. *The Brady Bunch* was my favorite TV show for the same reason it was a favorite of so many kids born in the '60s: We all wanted to be a Brady.

The brainchild of sisters Faith and Jill (now Joey) Soloway, the stage show uses comic actors in their twenties to reenact, word for word, episodes of the TV show. The ingenious Soloway Sisters created it in a tiny theater in Chicago and had audiences lined up around the block. They had full houses, but they didn't have the rights. In short order, the original creator of *The Brady Bunch*, Sherwood Schwartz, flew out to see it. He liked it so much that Paramount, the owner, granted them a license. Then, legendary NYC rock promoter Ron Delsener brought them to the Village Gate off-Broadway.

I'm jealous that I didn't think of it myself. But I get an idea. I'm sure the show could sell tickets all over America. It's a magnet for press. Many of the journalists now writing about entertainment grew up watching *The Brady Bunch*. It would also be inexpensive to tour.

I cold-call Delsener and ask for a meeting. He tells me to show up the next day at his office, which is in a handsome brownstone in the East Seventies off Madison Avenue. He works in the high-ceilinged, stately living room with a large oil painting of himself behind his desk. It makes him look like a rock star. Ron is in his fifties, a small, wiry guy with wispy, long white hair. It's curious that many of the big machers I've encountered—Barry, Sam, Ron—are all small. Ron has a nervous twitch and blinks a lot. He talks in incomplete sentences. He's profane.

I propose he license the show to Kevin and me, then we book and produce a national tour.

"Why do you want to do this?" he says. "They're a couple of bitches, you know."

"Who?" I ask.

"The Soloways."

"I like bitches," I say.

"I'm just kidding," he says. "I love 'em. Faith's nice, but that Jill, she's tough. Watch out for her."

"I think I'll be OK," I say.

"What do I get out of this deal?"

I explain that he'll get 10 percent of the gross and do none of the work. Our company will produce, manage, and book the show. It's our chance to emulate Barry and Fran's business model—doing everything in-house.

"Go do it," says Ron. "Just don't forget to send me my checks. And good luck with that Jill Soloway. I'm telling ya, she's a fuckin' ballbuster."

"It's my specialty," I say.

I bring the deal to Kevin, who loves it. We plan a tour that will launch in Boston and then travel to San Francisco, Washington, and Chicago before doing one-nighters at colleges.

We need to raise $300,000. We team up with some friends who run Theatre by the Sea, a summer stock theatre in Kingston, Rhode Island. They're tired of doing shows like *The Music Man* and want to branch out to younger shows. They agree to put up the capital and build the show in their scene shop.

The Charles Playhouse in Boston is five hundred seats and has had many long-running off-Broadway hits, most recently *Nunsense*. I call the owner, a Broadway producer named Michael Frazier, who is delighted to book us in February. We agree to the rental terms, and then sign up a local press agent and advertising agency. We'll go on sale in January.

Jill and Faith cast the show with some of their veterans and a bunch of new actors. We'll rehearse at Theatre by the Sea. We need a place close to Boston to tech the show and warm up with a few public performances. There's a grungy former porn house in Providence called the Columbus. *California Pizza Girls* was its most recent engagement. It's cheap and available.

"You're putting the Bradys in a porn house?" says Jill.

"It's a theater that used to be a porn house," I say.

"Now we know why we picked you," says Faith.

"It'll help sell tickets," I say.

A week before we start rehearsals Michael Frazier calls and says we can't come to his theater.

"What are you talking about? We're going on sale next week," I say.

"Sorry, he says, "I booked this Patsy Cline show for the holidays. I thought it would play four or five weeks. But who knew? It's a hit, I'm extending it indefinitely."

"We have a contract," I say.

"I haven't signed it yet."

"But we're capitalized, we're cast, I already reserved an ad in the *Globe*."

"Sorry." Click.

CHALLENGE #1: FIND A NEW THEATER

WE SEARCH FOR ALTERNATIVES in Boston. Nothing works.

I turn my sights to San Francisco. The Marines' Memorial, which does off-Broadway shows, is booked. An old Masonic Temple called the Alcazar has recently been renovated. It sits on a derelict section of Geary Street where drug dealers, prostitutes, and homeless folks populate the front sidewalk. This may be too much irony. I call the owner, who tells me it's available for eight weeks. We take the deal.

I hire a local ad agency and publicist named Carla Befera, who specializes in shows like *Beach Blanket Babylon*, which has been running since the '70s. She assures me that the timing for *The Real Live Brady Bunch* is perfect. February is great in San Francisco and there are not many shows opening.

Now we must truck the lights, sound, costumes, and scenery across the country, and provide housing for the company in an expensive town. This raises our costs.

Carla pitches news articles. There are many newspapers in the Bay Area, and my hunch proves correct: They all agree to big features profiling the show. They all use graphics of the original show logo. The *San Francisco Chronicle* devotes its entire Weekend cover to the Brady Bunch grid, using photos of our cast.

The first performance is a sold-out sensation. When Marcia is hit by the football and cries, "Oh my nose," the audience whoops and hollers. Standing in the back of the house and watching the audience go wild is thrilling. That my favorite TV show from childhood provides my first opportunity to produce feels surreal and right.

The show sells out for four weeks. The young audiences who cheer for the show's silly shenanigans are like helium keeping a balloon aloft. But the helium runs out. Sales decline every week thereafter. When eight weeks are up, we haven't paid back any of our capitalization, so our partners quit. They agree to forfeit their entire investment and we agree to indemnify them against any future losses. They have no more financial risk, and we don't have to pay back the money they already invested. We're back at zero: No money, and no theater.

CHALLENGE #2: FIND A NEW CITY AND NEW CAPITAL

WE PIVOT TO WASHINGTON, DC, which is a strong theater town. The Kennedy Center has a five-hundred-seat venue that's empty. In all my years as a booker, they've never been interested in my shows. Revivals of *South Pacific* with Robert Goulet and the fourth national tour of *Evita* were too down-market for them. That they might be interested in *The Real Live Brady Bunch* seems foolhardy. I call Max Woodward, their longtime programming director, who is more partial to Richard Rodgers than Sherwood Schwartz.

"Max, you're not going to believe why I'm calling."

"I have no interest in *The Odd Couple* or the thirteenth national tour of *A Chorus Line*."

"What do you have against *A Chorus Line*?"

"It robbed *Chicago* of the Tony in 1976. An unforgivable crime," he says.

"Max, what would you say if I told you I need a theater for *The Real Live Brady Bunch*?"

"*The Brady Bunch* at the Opera House? Barbara Bush would fly up from Houston and fire me herself."

"Not the Opera House, the five-hundred seater," I say.

"You mean the Terrace?"

"Yes, just for the summer. It'll get tons of young people into the building."

"That's not the worst idea I ever heard," he says.

"Does that mean maybe?"

"We'll talk about it."

We need 100,000 dollars to reopen the show. We call Paul Blake's friend Allan Gordon, the profane Wall Street guy I met two years ago who didn't invest in The Booking Office because he said I wouldn't stay. He invites us to his messy office where we show him a TV spot that Kevin's friend Karey, from USC film school, just cut. He made a parody of a traditional testimonial with terrific graphics and the Brady soundtrack. It's funny and entertaining—like the show.

"What's this?" asks Allan. "Looks fun."

"It's our new show, it's called *The Real Live Brady Bunch*, and we're doing it at the Kennedy Center this June."

"Like the TV show?"

"Exactly. It's actual episodes performed by really funny actors."

"That sounds so stupid it might work," he says.

Allan is not an aesthete or arts snob. He's looking for a good time.

"And the best news is that we only need a hundred grand to get the show going."

We explain the deal. And then we explain it again. Allan holds us hostage because he's bored with his life and enjoys being in the presence of Kevin and me. After exhaustive discussion, he agrees to put up the hundred thousand we need to open in DC.

The Washington newspaper features are as enthusiastic as they were in San Francisco. The review in the *Washington Post* declares the show "great fun." Ticket sales are decent. We take the big step of buying TV airtime for our spot. And luck be a lady, the TV spot moves the needle from decent to great. The show ends the five-week run with a small profit.

Progress.

The Charles Playhouse in Boston is free in the fall. We book eight weeks with landlord Michael Frazier, even though he weaseled out on the previous deal. Business is solid but Frazier stiffs us for twenty thousand dollars in box office receipts which basically means he steals our money. It's not enough to sue over, and he knows it.

"Once a philosopher, twice a shmuck," says Allan.

"What does that mean?" I ask.

"Think about it."

"I guess it means we're idiots for allowing him to screw us a second time."

"Precisely," he says.

On to the college one-nighter tour.

CHALLENGE #3: MAKE A DEAL WITH A HAS-BEEN POP STAR

THE COLLEGES WANT TO book the show, but they say they need someone to help sell it. A star. We recruit Davy Jones, lead singer of the Monkees, and famous Brady guest star. I'm suspicious when I learn that his agent lives in Kalamazoo, Michigan. She is also the president of his fan club. I'm not joking. We have a couple of friendly conversations. I make an offer. She asks for a little more, and we agree on the phone to split the difference. The next day she calls and says Davy needs more money. I remind her that we've verbally agreed to a deal. She denies she ever agreed. This silliness ensues for a week, after which I am fed up talking with a fan club president who is either a) stupid, b) a liar, c) the agent of a total asshole, or d) all the above.

"Please tell Mr. Jones that he can go fuck himself," I finally say.

She calls back and accepts my last offer.

We open in Springfield, Missouri, which may be the ugliest Springfield in America. There is no Main Street or any city center, only strip malls where the Olive Garden is the best restaurant to take the cast to dinner.

Davy Jones joins our caravan of actors on a sleeper bus that drives all night to get to the next stop the following day. The truth is that, at age forty-eight, he is still handsome and has a good voice. His rendition of "Daydream Believer" slays.

This classic bus and truck tour goes smoothly until Mr. Jones starts bedding several women in the cast, which I can't imagine could have been easy to do on a moving sleeper bus.

Still, our tour happily ends in Chicago, the city where the show began. Sherwood Schwartz joins us for the final performance and cast party. When all is over, we send Allan Gordon $10,000 in profit. It is good practice for what comes next.

Chapter Twenty-Four

RENT PART I: THE READING AND WORKSHOP

THE OFFICE IS BUSY. Kevin is raising money for a revival of *Damn Yankees*, which will get him producer billing on the poster and our agency the booking rights. This is a new development on Broadway. Because it's so hard to raise capital, producers are offering investors who put up large sums of money the title of "producer" even though they don't actually produce the show. I'm booking four shows at once.

The receptionist rings me. "Jonathan Larson on line one."

Jonathan keeps in touch regularly and I'm excited anytime he calls. Booking pays the bills while Jonathan promises the future.

"Hello friend," I say.

"Guess what? I'm finally doing a reading of *Rent*." Jonathan has transported Puccini's penniless bohemians from Paris in the 1800s to the East Village in the '90s where, of course, they can't pay the "Rent."

"Amazing."

"It's going to be at New York Theatre Workshop on June 10."

"I'm there."

"Just so you know, this is going to be the *Hair* of the '90s."

"From your mouth," I say.

This reading of *Rent* gives me something to look forward to. The timing is excellent. It's a pivotal moment in the theater industry. *Kiss of the*

233

Spider Woman just beat *Tommy* for Best Musical, and the two shows tied for best score at the Tony Awards. The business is seesawing between traditional music by guys like Kander and Ebb and contemporary music by guys like Pete Townshend. Jonathan wants to tip the balance.

The day before the reading, Kevin brings a young producer wannabe named Peter Holmes à Court to the office. They met standing in the teller line at Chemical Bank. He has a childlike face—small nose, small blue eyes—with soft, perfectly combed brown hair that sits atop his gangly six-foot-three body. Peter is from Western Australia and dresses in fancy clothes. His mother owns the largest theater chain in London. He's in New York to form a production company. I invite him to join me at the reading in the hopes that, if he likes it, we can get him to invest. Kevin has a meeting with the *Damn Yankees* producers and can't join, but another friend who is a director, Rod Kaats, tags along.

We take the subway from Times Square to Eighth Street and Broadway and walk to the Workshop. The auditorium has about 150 seats. The stage is big for off-Broadway. Music stands are set up in front of fifteen chairs and there's a band set up on the side. A group of actors take their seats.

They perform the opening number, "Rent." It slams like a jolt of energy. The action shifts to a group of homeless people near Tompkins Square singing about life in Santa Fe, followed by two lesbians in a full-out argument. As we move through the songs, the energy dwindles. I can't latch on to any characters. I can't find the plot. I am not experiencing the elation I felt the first time I watched *Boho Days*. This cycle of songs doesn't electrify. It numbs. It feels like we're lost in the East Village and can't find a way out. There's no air-conditioning, and the theatre gets hotter as the first act drones on, clocking in at over ninety minutes.

Peter stands up at the intermission and says, "I'm sorry, I didn't know it was this long, I have another appointment to attend." He's polite in a British way but his words belie his face, which signals loudly and clearly that he hates it and wants to get out of this hot theater as soon as possible.

The second act is no better. At the end of the show, my other guest, Rod, leans over and says, "Well this show can't be saved. I love Jonathan but he should just work on something else."

I'm deflated and a little bit embarrassed. Though there were good songs, they were untethered to any identifiable story. The cast never faltered, but their energy had no focus. I didn't walk away thinking about any of the characters. I had hoped *Rent* would be the answer—to musical theater, to my professional life. Instead, it felt like a mishmash.

When Jonathan calls me the next day, eager to hear my thoughts, I punt. We make a date to have dinner at Diane's on Columbus and Seventy-second Street, a small hole-in-the-wall where two people can have a burger, fries, and a Coke for ten bucks. It's the kind of burger joint where people carve their initials into the tables.

Jonathan and I are seated at a two-top near the front. There is space around us. I feel like we're all alone on a tiny island and that he's going to cast me off it if I express what's really on my mind. This is made worse by his needy eyes and floppy curly hair. His big ears stand up like a German shepherd's. "I'm all ears," he says.

No shit, I think to myself.

I'm scared. How do I be encouraging and still tell the truth? I'm afraid of hurting his feelings. I'm afraid that he'll reject me and not want to be my friend anymore.

"I love the songs," I say. "I love the location of the East Village. I love the grittiness of the opening number."

"That's good," he says. "What else?"

I buy some time while the waitress takes our order.

"But then I'm lost. It's a presentation of songs that don't seem to have anything to do with each other. No sooner do you establish the time and place with the opening song, before jumping to a song about homeless people and Santa Fe. I don't get it. None of the characters are coming through."

Jonathan blinks.

"I'm not sure what you're trying to do. Are you just trying to compose a collage of life in the East Village? Or are you trying to tell a story?"

Jonathan's ears turn red, his eyes turn down, his shoulders hunch. He's deflated. I've hit him. I've bruised him.

"I'm not writing a collage," he says.

"Then you need to tell the story of *La Bohème*. I need to understand the beginning, middle, and end. I need to be able to follow Roger and Mimi."

"I'm going to do this," he says. "You'll see."

"Good, because if you don't do this, I think I'm going to have to leave this business."

"You'll be taking me with you," he adds.

MY THIRTIETH BIRTHDAY—October 16, 1994—is not the subject of a rock monologue. I don't hear the tick tock of the clock; I don't feel my head about to explode. I'm just lonely. And down on musicals. And sick of booking.

The night before, some friends and I go to dinner at Trattoria Dell'Arte, the Italian restaurant near Carnegie Hall with the giant white plaster sculpture of a nose in the front window. The two guys with whom I've had the most intense relationships, Andrew and Kevin, both join. Over the past year, Kevin and I have become like brothers. When he and his wife broke up, he called me first. I told him to come over and sleep at my place. I made breakfast for the two of us every day. His vulnerability and bewilderment made him more lovable and me more sensitive to his feelings. Andrew and I have forged a close friendship in the years since our breakup. After a painful first year, in which I missed him so much I couldn't bear to talk to him on the phone, we have found a way to renew our bond and work together on new shows. This past year, I produced the first incarnation of his new musical, *John & Jen*.

At a long wooden table in the wine cellar, Kevin plays the macher and orders two bottles of red wine from a "sommelier." I don't know what that is.

"He's the wine expert. His job is to make sure we get the perfect bottle," says Kevin.

"That's a job?" I ask.

"He's really here to make sure we spend a lot of money," says David Stone, my friend from the Weissler office, who is also a fledgling producer. He rolls his eyes at Kevin's need to be a big shot.

When we came here for Andrew's twenty-fifth birthday five years earlier, we were splurging at a place we couldn't afford. Now Kevin orders bottles of cabernet brought by a "sommelier."

"Who went to the invited dress last night?" asks David.

"*Sunset Boulevard*?" someone asks.

"I've been waiting two years to see what all the fuss is about," says Richard, a friend who owns Theatre by the Sea in Rhode Island and shares the same birthday.

Andrew Lloyd Webber's new musical, *Sunset Boulevard*, is the most anticipated new musical of the season. It's also the only new musical of the season. A revue called *Smokey Joe's Café* is coming in, but it has no book and uses songs from the '50s and '60s.

"What does it say about this business when there's only one new musical and it's an American movie adapted by a British composer and playwright?" I ask.

"And they've already fired two leading ladies," says David.

Patti LuPone was signed to play the part on Broadway after originating the role of Norma Desmond in London. But the production got poor reviews. When Lloyd Webber subsequently opened it in Los Angeles with Glenn Close as Norma, Vincent Canby of the *New York Times* creamed all over her performance. Lloyd Webber promptly dumped Patti and signed Glenn for Broadway. Patti sued Lloyd Webber and received a million bucks. Separately, Lloyd Webber fired Faye Dunaway days before she was supposed to take over the role in Los Angeles.

"This shit's fucked up," says someone else.

"It's not that good," says David.

"The way they kept singing the words, 'Sunset Boulevard,' gave me a stomachache," says Beth, a friend from college.

" 'Boulevard' just doesn't sing," someone says.

"What it really is, is two good ballads surrounded by a lot of crap," says Richard.

"I heard Sondheim and Prince were once thinking about doing it with Angela Lansbury," says Andrew. "I wonder what that would have been like."

"What did you think of Glenn Close?" asks someone who wasn't at the dress rehearsal.

"She's riveting," I say. "But I'd still rather hear Patti sing those songs."

"I think Patti's gonna have the last laugh," says David. "She'll be the only person who makes money from this."

"Why does everyone spend so much time knocking the only new musical on Broadway?" asks Andrew.

"Because we care," I reply. "Because we want to do better."

We enjoy many bottles of Kevin's expensive wine. We eat lots of pasta, chicken, and steak. I blow out the candles on my carrot cake and, when all the couples have gone home, Kevin takes my friend Beth and me to another bar for more drinks. All three of us are single—Kevin and Beth each recently divorced—and none of us has anyone to go home to.

"So, what are you going to do in your thirtieth year?" asks Beth.

"I don't know. Maybe find a boyfriend?" I answer.

"That's easy," says Kevin.

"Do you know Bobby Lambert?" I say. "He played Tulsa in the Tyne Daly *Gypsy*. So fucking handsome. I saw him in the lobby of the Minskoff last night, didn't even know I exist."

"Make him know," says Kevin.

"Why would a Broadway actor want me?"

"Because you and I are going to own Broadway," says Kevin, who is always encouraging when I'm feeling pessimistic or down.

"You know, Kevin, there are barely any shows. And the few shows that make it are so bloated and expensive. How are we ever gonna raise five or ten million dollars?"

"It'll happen," he says.

"I don't think I'll ever be a producer. And I fucking hate booking. I hate working for producers who aren't as smart or talented as me."

"This is going to be the best decade of your life," says Kevin.

"Yeah, right." I say.

"And, by the way, it's midnight."

"Happy birthday, sweetie," says Beth.

The next morning, on a warm, blue sky day, I walk to the newsstand and tell myself that I'm on track. I tell myself to be happy and content. I plop down two dollars and fifty cents and pick up the Sunday *Times*. On the front page, below the fold, is a Hirschfeld drawing of Steven Spielberg, Jeffrey Katzenberg, and David Geffen. The front page! I read the story of their new movie studio and entertainment company, DreamWorks. I'm awed and jealous. I want to be them. At fifty-one years old, Geffen has started two huge record companies and produced *Dreamgirls* and *Cats*. This serves as another reminder that I have work to do.

Mom and Dad call as I eat Cracklin' Oat Bran. They sing "Happy Birthday" on the phone.

"How are you going to celebrate, son?" asks Dad.

"I went to dinner with friends last night," I say. "It was nice."

"You're the luckiest thing that's ever happened to your mother and I," he says.

"Thanks, Dad."

"I wish you a top-notch day," he says before hanging up the phone.

I read the paper; obsess about DreamWorks and my measly accomplishments; fritter away time, wondering why I'm alone on the day I turn thirty years old. With dinner approaching, and no plan beyond arugula and a half eaten can of tuna fish in the refrigerator, I go to the New York Sports Club on West Eightieth Street.

All trips to the gym start and end in the basement—the location of the men's locker room. It's long and narrow, lined with red lockers brightened by fluorescent white lights. At the midway point is the entrance to the wet area: Straight ahead are the sinks and mirrors; stalls and urinals to the right; showers, steam room, and sauna to the left. There are a couple of guys that are getting ready to go upstairs and start their workouts. Another guy is closing his locker to leave. The goal is to spot a hot guy who is also starting his workout and then hope our routines align well enough to finish and shower at the same time.

I warm up on the VersaClimber for twelve hard minutes, which makes my heart speed up and my wrists sweat, then I start a rotation of bench presses and dumbbells for chest and arms. I watch the clock and cruise the room, pushing hard for forty-five minutes. Seeing no prospects upstairs, I head down to the men's locker room in the basement.

As I approach my locker, a sweaty guy with smooth wet skin and a drenched towel around his waist emerges from the wet area. He's a little bit younger, probably in his mid-twenties. His brown hair is wet and wavy. He has a cherubic face—freckles; cute, small nose; juicy, curvy lips—sitting on top of a robust body. He's tall—at least six feet, with broad shoulders and muscular legs. He's not ripped, just perfectly proportioned. He swigs water from the fountain and clocks me approaching my locker. We make eye contact. He nods slightly, and heads back to the steam area.

I pull off my shoes and socks, then my shorts and shirt, and drop them under the wooden bench; grab a towel from the shelf. My heart starts accelerating—as if I'm back on the VersaClimber. I wrap the towel around my waist and shower quickly. Approaching the steam room is exciting because the opaque glass door hides what you'll find when you enter this milky-white space clad in ceramic tiles. I open the door to find the guy sitting on the top level to the right. His towel covers most of his crotch—there's a gap below where the two ends meet. I pull off my towel and place it on the adjacent bench and sit down. When I used to go to the steam bath with my father when I was little, none of the older Jewish men wore a towel. Why start now?

The guy glances at me, then looks at my package. I look back. We both sit for a minute. He spreads his legs a little so that his knee grazes mine, and his towel cracks open some more. I see his cock. It's proportional to the rest of his tall, broad body. The touch of his knee and the beauty of his cock make me hard. He gently strokes his cock. The door opens and another guy enters. We pause. The new guy is shorter than me, but thicker: muscular round pecs, defined lats and shoulders, narrow waist, dark hair. He sits to my right; spreading his legs forces his towel to open just a little. I play with my dick, and the first guy strokes his. The new guy watches. He unlatches the tuck in his towel, and it drops to his sides. The electricity emanating from these two guys makes my dick stand at attention. The first guy leans over and wraps his right hand around it. Then the other guy puts his left hand on my thigh. I take hold of both their dicks and start slowly pumping. I love the sensation of touching both their cocks at the same time, using the sweat we're all generating as lube. The first guy lowers his head and takes my dick into his mouth. I inhale with surprise. It feels like the first time I received a blow job. His lips, his tongue, his dripping saliva make my dick vibrate. I can feel the pulsing sensation all the way up my back to the base of my neck.

Two hot guys touching me at the same time is a revelation. Not one, but two guys want to touch me—my legs and my cock and my chest. I forget about everything else. Here, in the sexy, sweaty steam room, nothing else exists. I explode into the mouth of the first guy. He drips my cum onto his cock and strokes it. Soon, both guys explode as well.

Almost immediately, the miracle of escape evaporates. Now I'm just in a steam room on my birthday with two guys whose names I don't know. I put the towel around my waist and exit to the showers feeling a little bit ashamed.

Climbing to Eightieth Street, I smell the bagels baking at H&H, which is on the corner. I buy an onion bagel to eat on my way home. The nibbles of onions that cover the outside are crispy, its crust makes the perfect crunch between my teeth, and the warmth inside provides comfort to my insides. This bagel is my company, a birthday companion for this lonely thirty-year-old.

A YEAR AND A HALF LATER, in the fall of 1994, Jonathan wins an award from the Richard Rodgers Foundation to pay for another workshop at New York Theatre Workshop. James Nicola, the artistic director of NYTW, recruits rising director Michael Greif, whose career has taken off after directing an acclaimed production of *Machinal* at the Public Theater. Michael's raw, urban, industrial aesthetic, combined with searing honesty, is exactly what Jonathan wants for *Rent*.

My excitement leaps when Jonathan invites me. Despite my previous criticism, I am hopeful that he has cracked this musical in a way that will liberate him from his waiter gig at the Moondance Diner.

I tell Kevin and he's happy to join me. On a rainy Thursday night in November, we head back to the East Village and rush into a pizza place on Eighth Street to inhale a quick slice before walking to the Workshop. We take two seats in the first row. Kevin loves to sit in the front row. The house is about half full. Stephen Sondheim makes his way down the aisle and sits two rows behind us. I try not to gawk. He pulls out a newfangled device, the Apple Newton, on which to take notes. I'm impressed by his embrace of new technology. There's a band stage right and a couple of metal tables with metal folding chairs stage left. Right before it starts, I feel the need to manage Kevin's expectations, particularly after the reading with Peter Holmes à Court.

"Look, this is either going to be brilliant or a piece of shit," I say.

"It's going to be brilliant," he replies, "I can feel it."

"We'll see." My heart beats faster. That was what I thought the last time I saw this.

Two young guys take the stage. One is blond, hair almost white, wears wire glasses, and exudes the presence of a bohemian intellectual. The program says his name is Anthony Rapp. I remember him as one of the teens in *Six Degrees of Separation*. The other guy, with long brown hair and a deep voice, is thick, trapezoidal, but he's not flabby. They sing the opening song, "Rent," which is as dynamic as I remember it from eighteen months ago. Then a young Latina woman—small, sexy, with overflowing brown hair and a curvy catlike face—sings a rock song

242

called "Out Tonight." Her name is Daphne Rubin-Vega and her deep voice growls with gravel and gold. She's Mimi. She sings like a boxer in a ring using her voice to knock out her opponent.

A drag queen visits Mark and Roger's loft and sings another high-spirited, flashy number describing how he recently earned a bunch of money. Though the plot isn't yet discernible, these downtown bohemians express themselves in vivid, riveting ways. After the introduction of two lesbians, who sing another fun song, Roger has the space to himself where he tries to access his creativity, to summon inspiration, and start composing again through a song called "Right Brain." He has a dark, rumbling rock voice that shares one trait with Daphne—it's nothing like the sounds that emanate from the current Broadway voices. The story cracks open when Mimi knocks on the door and meets Roger. They court each other in the most ingenious rock duet I've ever heard, "Light My Candle." It's flirtatious, it's catchy, and it perfectly sets in motion the love story of this piece. The sound of this show pricks my ears in a whole new way—it's like nothing I've ever heard before. Kevin and I look at each other with the same expression: *Holy fuck.* Kevin whispers, "That's the best musical storytelling I've ever seen."

Inspiration and brilliance are on this stage. It is messy, but that's a problem for another day. With "Light My Candle," *Rent* is declaring itself.

The musical unfolds with power and ingenuity. The woman playing Maureen sings a performance piece in the style of Laurie Anderson while accompanying herself on the cello. At one point she picks the cello up and frames her head with it. It's zany and surprising.

Act One ends in the Life Café with a rousing number about Bohemia called "La Vie Bohème." After the blackout, Kevin turns to me. "Get out the checkbook," he says.

"Are you joking?"

"We have to do this show."

After the unfortunate first reading, I'm relieved. "Slow down, just let me introduce you."

We walk up the side aisle. I glance at Sondheim, who is scribbling notes on his Newton. Jonathan greets us, eager to hear our reaction.

"You've found the story," I say.

"Told ya."

"This is my partner Kevin I was telling you about."

"Hey, thanks for coming," says Jonathan.

"No, thank *you*," says Kevin. "This is, like, one of the best musicals I've ever seen."

Jonathan is like a puppy about to receive the best treat ever. "Really?"

"We have to do this with you. What do you need?" Kevin takes out his checkbook, which kind of embarrasses me, then continues, "What do you want? We just want to help you get this on."

"Don't you want to see the second act first?" asks Jonathan.

"I already know it's great. This show must be seen," says Kevin.

By the end of the show, after Mimi comes back to life, Kevin's mission becomes an obsession.

"Seriously, what do you want?" he asks Jonathan.

"Well, if you're offering, I need to make a recording of this workshop before everyone goes away."

"Done," says Kevin. "No problem."

He can't stop talking on the subway ride home. "This is going to be huge," he says.

If we want to produce this, we're going to need financing. Kevin calls our investor from *The Real Live Brady Bunch*, Allan Gordon, and invites him to join us at the final workshop performance on Sunday night. The house is packed, mostly with young people. Tony Kushner, the celebrated author of *Angels in America*, shows up. The electricity that accompanies crowds who have heard the show is great crackles in the air. Allan is fascinated by this scene, which has nothing to do with his life. Though he's exactly the kind of old rich guy Jonathan satirizes in the show, he likes being around this youthful vibe. I doubt he "gets" the show, but he seems to "get" the room. He absorbs the emotional temperature. And he declares after intermission that he wants to join us on this endeavor.

Jonathan introduces us to director Michael Greif. Clad in jeans, tennis shoes, and a baggy black sweater, he has a face that's defined by the kind of round glasses that Harry Potter, still in the imagination of J. K. Rowling, will popularize in another two years. Michael is intimidating and cool. He talks with a trace of sarcasm. When he says, "Nice to meet you," I'm not sure he means it. That he is the perfect director for this show is proven by this workshop.

The performance is triumphant. The audience is vocal, their cheers are hearty, and the smile on Jonathan's face is brighter than any I've ever seen. In a taxi on the way home, we offer Allan 40 percent of the profit in return for 50 percent of the capital. He barks the reasons this makes no sense, reminds us that we're worthless shmucks and that he went to Harvard, and I went to Michigan—a safety school—and then, accepts. We fail to consider that this deal will ultimately give Allan a bigger share than either of us individually.

The Sunday before Thanksgiving, Jonathan and the cast go into a recording studio and make a high-quality cassette of all the songs. At a cost of eight thousand dollars, it becomes the definitive record of this workshop and the soundtrack of our lives.

Kevin listens nonstop. I am enthusiastic but cautious. Jonathan keeps saying, "This is going to be the *Hair* of the '90s." I tell him not to say that out loud.

We schedule a meeting with Jim Nicola, the artistic director of New York Theatre Workshop. His cluttered office is in the dilapidated Candler Building on Forty-second Street, just east of the crumbling New Amsterdam Theatre. Jim is a large man with penetrating blue eyes who has his own methodical rhythm that contrasts with our fast, bubbling energy.

Jim listens to us passionately talk about *Rent* and thinks carefully before he speaks.

"I agree with you, Kevin, and I think it has a ways to go," says Jim.

"It's already better than anything running on Broadway," says Kevin.

"I had hoped we could just do it ourselves, but our board isn't willing to take the risk," he says. "This show is more than twice as big as anything we've ever done."

"I think we can create a nice partnership," I say. "Jonathan loves it here and wants more than anything to keep going."

"We'll pay for all the costs that are over and above what you can afford," says Kevin.

"That's a reasonable offer," says Jim. "I need to think carefully about what it means to work together."

"You'll be able to open it at your theater, and then we'll move it off-Broadway when it ends its initial run," I say.

We make two agreements: an option agreement with Jonathan for the commercial rights to *Rent*, which will cost two thousand dollars, and an enhancement agreement with New York Theatre Workshop in which we will give them one hundred thousand dollars to pay for half of the production downtown. We will own the sets, costumes, and props and have the exclusive right to move the show wherever we choose.

Our lawyer, Loren Plotkin, is scared for us. "No one has ever paid this much money to enhance a production in New York," he says. "They moved *Driving Miss Daisy* with no financial enhancement."

"There's no other way to get the show on," I say.

"And we got Allan Gordon to pay for half of it," says Kevin.

"I think you guys are crazy, but I'm not here to tell you how to run your business," he says.

We decide that we need a total of 125,000 dollars to pay for Jonathan's advance, the recording we just financed, and our legal and development fees. With Allan putting up half, we take our share—62,500 dollars—from our booking business.

Kevin and I discuss the show for hours and write three pages of critique—observations and questions about the characters, the plot, the songs, and the flow—that we send to Jim Nicola, who reviews them with Jonathan and Michael. We bring Jonathan to a performance of *La Bohème* at the Metropolitan Opera to help demonstrate the clarity and simplicity of the storytelling. At this point, Jonathan's adaptation of *La Bohème* is longer and more complicated than Puccini's opera. We clock how many minutes pass before Mimi enters the loft to meet Rodolfo

(Roger). In *La Bohème*, it's about fifteen minutes; in *Rent*, it's about thirty.

Kevin's motto, "This is going to be huge," becomes our standing joke. At a meeting at Loren's office to discuss the rights agreement, Loren makes a cover page that says, "*Rent* rights: This is going to be huge."

I fantasize about where we might do this show. I imagine an empty garage on Second Avenue where we can set up 350 chairs and play to a downtown crowd.

I hear about a building on East Fifth Street that's for sale. It's around the block from the Workshop. It used to be a sound studio. It's a huge open space—the size of a grade school gym—with arched wooden beams holding up a curved, concave ceiling. I bring Jonathan, who says it's exactly what he imagined: "And it'll sound amazing with these vaulted ceilings." I bring Kevin and Allan. My fantasy is that the three of us can buy it with Allan's money and house the show in our own off-Broadway theater.

The owner is happy to sell and doesn't have any other offers, but the price is prohibitive because there are also air rights, and it doesn't make sense to buy a theater before we know if the show is a success.

In the summer of 1995, Jonathan goes away to work with a dramaturg on the book, music, and lyrics. They return with a new draft. In October, we do a small reading of a revised script on the fourth floor of the new Workshop annex. The only attendees are the production team and a few staff members of the Workshop. Kevin is out of town that night. The story is now framed by Angel's funeral, with the narrative unfolding as a series of flashbacks seen through Mark's lens. The first half hour is so full of information about every character that it's impossible to latch on to the arc of the story. No one is in focus. Mimi seesaws between hopeless heroin addict and righteous truth-teller. As the sing-through proceeds, everyone in the room slowly sinks into their chairs. The show has gone backward.

There are a few winning new songs: "Happy New Year," which kick-starts Act Two, when the group breaks back into their building after Benny has locked them out; "Tango Maureen," a witty metaphor for Mark and Maureen's relationship written in a traditional musical theater style; and "What You Own," a rock duet for Mark and Roger, which is the "eleven o'clock" number. Great tune, great hook. I question whether the story can hold another political theme, "We are what we own," at this late stage of the evening, but recognize that the song provides an electric jolt that will help catapult us to the finale.

A couple new songs are not good: "Love of My Life," a duet for Maureen and Joanne that pays homage to Porter's "You're the Top" with lines like "You're the hepatitis in my clam," and "Your Eyes," the song Roger sings to dying Mimi. The lyrics are generic ("Your eyes, as we said our goodbyes . . . took me by surprise"), the melody flaccid. That it's the song Roger has been working on all year makes it lamer. It can't be the final number.

I compose a three-page letter to Jim detailing my concerns. I conclude with the following:

> Rent *is still in search of a skeleton that holds it together. There*
> *is still no central story. It's there and we all know it: It's Roger*
> *and Mimi. But it seems as if Jonathan, in the spirit of equal-*
> *ity and community, and in his desire to express many of his*
> *socio-political views, is giving equal time to everything. This new*
> *version of* La Bohème *is three times more complicated than the*
> *original and sometimes incoherent. It must be simplified. It must*
> *be clear. I'm not trying to sound dire, and I don't think there's*
> *a crisis here. I think the piece is begging for heavy editing, some*
> *thoughtful scene shuffling, and a couple new songs to replace*
> *"Love of My Life" and "Your Eyes." It demands dramatic disci-*
> *pline.*

Jim and Michael Greif talk. Jim seriously considers postponing the production. Michael, who recently became the artistic director of La Jolla Playhouse, can't change his schedule, which would mean postponing for a full year or getting a new director. Jonathan, who has already given notice at the Moondance Diner, is infuriated and scared. His chance to finally get a show on is about to slip away.

I call Manny Azenberg, the rabbi of Broadway, and ask for advice.

"Don't start unless you're sure the script is ready," he says. "You have no idea what you're going to discover when you put it in front of an audience, but if you're not absolutely certain it's in the best possible shape before you start, you'll never catch up."

"I think Jonathan will explode if we postpone for a year."

"It's better than a flop," he says. "Remember, if you have two or three weeks of previews, it's nothing. There's very little time to make changes when you're performing every night."

Manny's advice is tough to absorb. Postponing feels impossible and going ahead feels foolhardy.

Jim gives my notes to Jonathan. He calls and invites me to dinner. We meet at an Italian restaurant I love on Eighty-third and Broadway and eat fried calamari and pasta. I feel like every time I go to dinner with Jonathan I'm criticizing his work and making him feel bad.

"Your notes stung," says Jonathan. "They made me really defensive, like 'what the fuck do you know?' Then I called Sondheim, and he told me that if I want to work in this business, I have to collaborate. Or at least listen. So I read them again."

"You're right," I say. "None of us know what we're doing. We're all new at this."

"I'm going to get this right," he says.

"I believe you."

"I know it's too complicated," he says. "I'll make the beginning clearer. And I know what you're saying about Mimi."

"That's good," I say.

"But 'What You Own' is a fucking great song and I'm not cutting it."

"Fair," I respond.

"Let me drive you home," he says. He recently bought a beat-up old green station wagon. "This is Rusty," he says. "Three hundred bucks! I figure, if the show doesn't work out, I can get the fuck out of here and drive to Santa Fe."

"Touché!"

"Good rhyme," he says.

I go to sleep hopeful, once again, that this show might finally come together.

Chapter Twenty-Five

RENT PART II: REHEARSALS

ON A SUNDAY NIGHT in mid-December, a few days before rehearsal, Jonathan invites Kevin, members of the new cast, and me to his apartment for his annual Peasant Feast. Michael Greif is there, along with Daphne Rubin-Vega, who is comfortable in any situation.

"This show is going to be fucking hot," she says.

I meet a wiry, muscular guy with blond hair, blue eyes, very long eyelashes, and red lips. To quote Daphne, he's fucking hot. It's Adam Pascal, our new Roger. If this guy's voice is as good as his looks, we've found the perfect leading man.

"I'm a trainer on the Upper West Side," Adam tells me, "but I'm really a rock musician." He's affable, laughs a lot.

"How did you hear about the auditions?" I ask.

"Idina told me," he says. "Idina, come here." A sexy young woman with flowing brown hair and tight jeans encasing a valentine ass walks over. She's our Maureen.

"Hey," she says.

"We went to high school together," says Adam.

"Syosset," says Idina, exaggerating a Long Island accent.

"And you both wound up in this show?"

"This is the first play I've ever been in," he says.

Our win.

"Idina, what were you doing before you got this job?" I ask.

"I sing at bar mitzvahs," says Idina. "Only until I get my first recording contract."

Two kids from Long Island who wanted to be rockers are now the leads of an off-Broadway musical.

Anthony Rapp is there. He's a theater veteran, having already appeared in several plays on Broadway, and he reveals he's been working in a coffee shop lately. "This is the best show I've ever been part of. It's going to change everything."

Jonathan stands on a chair and makes a toast. "I do a Peasant Feast every December for my friends and this year I decided to do it for you. It feels like everybody broke up this year, and two close friends died of AIDS, and since I wrote this show about my friends, you know, my family, I thought I would do it for you. Because you're my family now."

We drink wine. We eat dinner.

"You need to know something," Tim Weil, the music director, says to Kevin and me. "No one fucking wanted to do this show except you. The only reason we're here is because of you guys."

A SNOWSTORM BLANKETS NEW YORK the day of the first rehearsal. It's mostly a day of orientation; everyone introduces themselves in a warm but tentative way. In the adjacent kitchen, I meet the set designer, a small, skinny man named Paul Clay, who is working the nerdy hipster vibe better than anyone I've ever met. Paul is a visual artist and sculptor who lives in the East Village. He's like a character in *Rent*. He shows us his drawing of the set, which is a big sculpture of junk held aloft by scaffolding. It feels less like a fleshed-out design and more like a few scribbles on the page, but this show is different.

The actors learn the score and Michael starts staging scenes and dances over the holidays. I return on January 2, 1996, for the first singthrough of the show.

Adam is wearing denim overalls—he looks more like Pippin than Kurt Cobain. When the sing-through of the first show in which he's ever acted begins, he never looks up from his music stand. But that doesn't even matter. His voice soars with a muscularity that's thrilling. When he lets it rip during his first song, "One Song Glory," a new lyric set to the tune of "Right Brain," I get goose bumps down my back.

At this straightforward sing-through, as each actor sings and reads from their scripts, the show makes sense for the first time. Every scene is like a building block placed intentionally over the one below it.

Act Two is even better. The first act, which dramatized Christmas Eve, leads to a second act that starts on New Year's Eve and then follows the next year through the seasons and holidays: Valentine's Day, spring, Halloween, and then a return to Christmas Eve one year later. I'm still not crazy about the last song, "Your Eyes," but I'll harp on that another day.

At the end of the show, I'm satisfied and relieved. Jonathan has solved the "math" of the plot—it all adds up—which makes the songs more rewarding and the characters more engaging. I realize I'm not viscerally moved at the end. After all this analysis, criticism, and change, I know the magic trick: I know how the magician cuts the woman in two.

"You did it," I tell Jonathan after the sing-through. "It works, it makes sense."

He smiles with pride. He knows it as well.

"I have one more song to write. It's for Maureen and Joanne in the second act."

"I can't wait," I say.

On this first workday of the year, I walk out into another snowstorm feeling optimistic.

As the show progresses, I touch base with Jonathan, who is pleased by the progress. He's written the new song for Maureen and Joanne that he looks forward to sharing. Michael and choreographer Marlies Yearby spend a day with the cast to talk through the fifty-plus "toasts" or references in "La Vie Bohème" and then stage it as if they're all at a party and everyone is doing their thing. Then, Michael and Marlies shape it into a dynamic climax to Act One.

During tech, Jonathan gets sick with a stomach bug and goes to Cabrini Medical Center. They examine him and determine that he had food poisoning. I touch base with Jim, who also tells me things are progressing well, except that Jonathan felt sick to his stomach again two days later and went to St. Vincent's Hospital, where they examined him and sent him home to rest.

"Why didn't he go to his doctor?" I ask.

"He doesn't have a doctor," says Jim.

"He doesn't have a fucking doctor?"

"He doesn't even have health insurance." This news stings, sending me back to college when I didn't have health insurance and constantly worried about getting sick.

The dress rehearsal is on January 24, a Wednesday. When I walk into the theater, it's already filled with 199 people and the air is thick with anticipation. I'm by myself because Kevin is away. The stage is organized clutter, like an abandoned lot in the East Village. There are two metal tables with red chairs arrayed around them, and a scaffold sculpture of East Village detritus is up left forming a Christmas tree. The brick back wall is painted blue. Most prominent is a thick yellow extension cord that runs from the center to off stage left. The band is under a platform stage right. Three standing mics on either side of the stage apron indicate that this will be a hybrid between a musical and a rock concert. The set is raw and beautiful at the same time. Its minimalism is jarring at first, and then its parts come into focus. With attention to texture and color for accent and buoyancy, Michael and his designer have created an evocative environment for this story to play out in.

The show is electric, the cast is on fire. Daphne and Adam are fierce. Wilson Jermaine Heredia, who plays Angel, is adorable and feisty, a strong young man and a sexy drag queen. The duet, "I'll Cover You," that he sings with Collins, the warm and buttery Jesse Martin, is glorious. "La Vie Bohème," the finale of Act One, is dinner party, dance, and rave, all in one. The Act Two opening, "Seasons of Love," is rapturous, and Jonathan's new song for Maureen and Joanne, "Take Me or Leave Me," stops the show. Michael's staging of "Contact," a song dramatizing the ups and downs of every couple having sex, which evolves into Angel's death, is riveting. Angel's funeral is sad, powerful, and earned. At the end of the run-through the audience whoops and hollers, clapping, whistling, and stomping their feet. Granted, these are friends and family—not a real audience—but it still feels good.

I approach Jonathan after the show and tell him how great the show is. He smiles a little, as if to say, *I told you so*, but also with some pain on his face. He's a bit distant.

"I've been kind of sick," he says. "I'm sure it's stress related."

"Are you going right home to sleep?"

"Right after my interview with the *Times*," he says. Our publicist persuaded the *New York Times* to do an article on the hundredth anniversary of *La Bohème* and its staying power as reflected by *Rent*.

"Feel good, my friend. It's going to be great."

I offer up some compliments to Michael after the performance, and he thanks me with his customary coolness.

"Wilson is spectacular as Angel," I say.

"Yeah. I was thinking about firing him."

"Not now, I hope," I say.

"He came a long way tonight," says Michael.

I'm pleased by his steady focus and the fantastic world of the play he has created.

Exiting the auditorium, I see Jonathan sitting behind the window of the box office talking to Anthony Tommasini, the chief music critic of the *Times*. I walk to Third Avenue and call Kevin, who's returning from a business trip, and report on the evening. He's thrilled.

"I'm glad you're back," I say.

"I have one more thing to tell you," he says.

"What?" I ask.

"This is going to be huge," he says.

This time I enjoy it and respond, "From your mouth."

I wake up on Thursday filled with anticipation for the first preview. I spend more time than usual picking out my outfit. I don't want to wear a jacket—too formal. I settle on a cashmere sweater and wool pants. I begin my trek to my therapist's office on Eighty-eighth and Madison. I walk through the Great Lawn, covered in snow, which is midway through a reconstruction project, big piles of dirt blanketed in white around the fields. Passing the Delacorte Theatre, I think about *Tick, Tick . . . Boom* and Jonathan's song, "Louder Than Words," which transpires on the ground I'm traversing. In my head I'm singing,

Cages or wings?
Which do you prefer?
Ask the birds
Fear or love, baby?
Don't say the answer
Actions speak louder than words.

Everything is coming together on this cold, sunny morning in January.

When I get to Dr. Fine's office, I take a seat and wait for her to emerge from her office to welcome me inside. I've been in therapy for three years, four times a week. Dr. Fine and I are in the slow process of decoding my childhood. I wonder if it will take eighteen years to process my first eighteen years.

"Tonight is the first preview," I begin. "I'm excited, I'm nervous, I have no idea what's about to happen. I just hope Jonathan isn't mad at me."

"What do you mean?"

"He wasn't his usual self last night," I say. "He was a little bit absent. I don't know, I feel, like, maybe he's still mad at me because of all my critical comments."

"Isn't that part of your job?"

"I know. I'm just, I don't know, scared, I guess. The crowd at the dress last night went crazy, but I know that doesn't mean anything."

I talk and talk and when forty-five minutes pass, she says, "We're done for today."

I get up, put on my coat, and walk to the subway stop at 86 Street. I get on a local that drops me off at 59 Street, where I switch for the R train to Times Square. I bound up the escalator in my office building, eager to start the workday. When I enter The Booking Office, the receptionist is looking down. Silence. I walk by two more employees, both looking away from me. As I pass the office of John, our contract manager, he stops me.

"Jeffrey, I have something to tell you," he says. He looks serious.

I stand in the doorway of his office, my coat still on.

"What's up?" I ask.

"I don't know how to say this."

"What?" I ask.

"Jonathan Larson died last night."

Blood drains from my head. I fall against the frame of the door.

"Jay Harris called this morning to let you know."

"What?" I feel like I'm falling backward.

"I'm so sorry to be the one to have to tell you this. He collapsed after he came home from dress rehearsal. His roommate found him on the kitchen floor."

I freeze, like when my father almost drowned in the Au Sable River. I want to blurt out the words "I can't believe it," but I do believe it. Jonathan has become a character in his play. He's now the narrative. I flash back to David Merrick announcing on opening night of *42nd Street* that Gower Champion has died. With that announcement *42nd Street* became a legend. Jonathan will become a legend. I sit down at my desk, still wearing my winter coat. I try to quiet my body, which won't stop shaking. I need to tell Beth Emelson, who is a friend of Jonathan and the person who introduced me to him when she brought me to *Boho Days*. I walk out the door and start walking to Lincoln Center Theatre, where Beth works. Walking helps me not shake as much.

I reach the office at Lincoln Center in what seems like minutes.

"Can you please let Beth Emelson know Jeffrey Seller is here?" I say to the receptionist.

"Hold on," he says. I hear him reach Beth. Almost instantly, she appears.

"What's up? What's going on?"

We walk to the back where her desk is right outside producer Bernie Gersten's office.

"What's wrong?" she says.

We go into Bernie's office.

"Jonathan died last night," I tell her.

"No!" she screams. She hugs me. We both drop onto Bernie's couch. I tell her the few facts I know. We hold each other. We shake and cry. Bernie enters. He was Joe Papp's deputy and partner for thirty years. He executive produced *A Chorus Line* and helped Michael Bennett get his show on. Then he watched dozens of young men, including Michael Bennett, die of AIDS.

"I'm sorry, kids."

"Jonathan was barely even sick. He had a stomach bug."

"Here's what you need to know," says Bernie. "Death doesn't give a fuck. Feel bad, grieve, and cry when you need to. But you have one job to do: get the show on."

I pick myself up from the couch and walk back to the office. Kevin arrives. We talk to Jim Nicola, who tells us that Jonathan's parents are flying to New York right now. Instead of doing a first preview, Jim wants to do a reading of the show for family and friends. He thinks it wouldn't be safe to do a full run-through under these circumstances. We agree.

Kevin and I go for a walk in Bryant Park.

"Know what's weird? We're here feeling like it's the end of the world, and everyone else is going about their day as if nothing happened. For them it's just a normal Thursday."

The theater is somber. No one talks in the lobby. It's hard to absorb that this is the same place in which Jonathan watched an audience go crazy for his show at dress rehearsal last night. Tonight it hosts his memorial service. We take seats in the second row. Another downtown producer, Anne Hamburger, sits next to me.

Jonathan's best friends, Jonathan Burkhart and Eddie Rosenstein, walk on stage. Their eyes are red.

Holding back tears, Eddie says, "This show was the most important thing in Jonathan's life."

"We're not supposed to be here right now, Jonathan is supposed to be here," says Jonathan Burkhart, rubbing his eyes and nose.

"The only way we could think of to honor Jonathan right now is to do the show. So the actors are going to sing it but not do the staging. They're also in shock and we don't want anyone to get hurt," says Eddie.

"Thanks for being here," says Jonathan Burkhart.

"This is for Jonathan," says Eddie.

The actors, led by Anthony Rapp, enter to a silent audience. They sit in the red folding chairs around the two metal tables with their street clothes and head mics. The show starts gently. When Adam starts singing, "One song, glory, one song before I go," we all start crying. It's as if Jonathan was writing his own life and death. With each song, the actors commit a little more fully to the moment. When we reach "La Vie Bohème" and Collins announces, "Mimi Marquez, clad only in bubble wrap," Daphne leaps out of her seat and jumps onto the table dancing. Then Wilson joins. Within seconds, the entire cast is doing the full choreography of "La Vie Bohème," and what started as a reading has blossomed into a full-out performance. The power of Jonathan's words and music take over the theater. The first act finishes with an ovation bigger than dress rehearsal.

A man I don't know approaches me. "Are you involved with this show?" he asks.

"Yes," I reply.

"I love these people. I just want to hang out with them."

I'm pleased that, even under these circumstances, he's connecting to the show.

Kevin and I get up to meet Jonathan's parents, Al and Nan. I'm frightened. I don't know what to say or how to encounter the pain they must be feeling.

We shake hands. We offer our condolences.

"He believed in you guys," says Al. "Talked about you all the time."

"Please. We just want you to do the show," says Nan.

"That's right," says Al. "You have to do the show."

"We won't let you down," says Kevin.

"We loved your son, and we love his show," I say.

The beauty and pain of "Seasons of Love" kicks off Act Two. The cast performs full-out. The "I'll Cover You" reprise, written as Angel's funeral, is about Jonathan tonight. For me, it will always be about Jonathan. When Adam and Anthony sing, "We're dying in America at the end of the millennium," the prescience is searing. If, indeed, we are what we own, then Jonathan is *Rent*.

At the end of the performance, there is extended applause and the cast exits. Silence. No one moves, no one says anything. The woman sitting next to me takes my hand. Anthony emerges from the door upstage center and sits down at the table. The other actors return and sit down. We are one community sharing grief. No one knows what to do next.

"Thank you, Jonathan Larson," I say out loud.

There is a long, powerful applause.

We file out of the theater quietly and go home with the hope that the show that starts previews tomorrow night will honor Jonathan's vision.

Chapter Twenty-Six

RENT PART III: PERFORMANCES

THE DAY OF THE FIRST PREVIEW, Kevin and I meet with Jim Nicola and Richard Kornberg, the publicist who arranged the *New York Times* interview. It's Friday and Jonathan died less than two days ago but it already feels like ages. We still don't know the exact cause of death, but we know it was a form of heart failure. We look over the ticket sales for the next three weeks; it's about half sold. The joy and anticipation of starting previews of our exciting new musical has given way to sadness and loss.

The *New York Times*, whose photographer Sara Krulwich took the last photograph of Jonathan just two hours before his death, is preparing an obituary, and Anthony Tommasini is writing his feature story as planned. We will perform two-and-a-half weeks of previews and open on February 13. The *New York Times* article is scheduled for Sunday, February 11.

Audience members are quiet as they take their seats for Friday night's first preview. Some are aware of what has transpired, many are not. This is the type of crowd that supports downtown theater but is also reserved. We must earn their favor. The seats are about two-thirds full. The performance lacks the exuberance and adrenaline of the dress rehearsal and the intensity of the memorial. It's a little messy. With an audience of newcomers, the plot is hard to follow. Roger's HIV status isn't clear. Mark's relationship to Maureen and Joanne is confusing. When Mark meets Joanne for the first time, the woman behind me whispers to her friend, "Why is he helping that girl set up speakers?" It's hard to locate where each scene takes place. At intermission, I hear someone say, "I feel lost in a maze."

Many songs receive no applause or tepid applause. I think it's because they don't have traditional endings or "buttons." They lack "punctuation" that allows the audience to exhale, applaud, and then move on to the next scene.

The actors express no joy in Act One. They are too beaten up. The previous night, when the cast sat together at the table and sang the show, the first act was warmer, clearer, and more connected by a strong community spirit. Tonight, the characters seem more distant.

The second act, which begins with a soaring "Seasons of Love," finds its rhythm. The story is easier to follow, and the characters come into focus.

At the end of the show, the audience offers applause that is better than polite, but less than enthusiastic. Kevin and I go to dinner with his girlfriend, Lynnette, and we discuss what we've just seen. The man who proclaimed that "This is going to be huge" is no longer optimistic.

"There's no joy, there's no pleasure," says Kevin. "This is a disaster."

"Kevin, it's not a disaster, it's a first preview."

"Adam never opened his eyes when he sang," Kevin says.

"Don't worry, he will," I reply.

"I know, I'm just, you know, sad, frustrated; I want this to be good."

We drink a couple glasses of wine. Kevin starts reading his program. We try to find something, anything, to laugh about.

"And who the heck is Pickle?" he says.

"What?" I reply.

"I'm looking at the staff page and it says, 'Props by Pickle.'"

"Well, who knew? Pickle is both a funny word and a propman."

We finally laugh and have some chocolate mud pie with vanilla ice cream.

I fax another round of notes to Jim on Sunday that urge Michael to clarify and focus—the audience can't track time and place; that urge Tim to musically punctuate the numbers—to ensure there are satisfying, clear endings that give the audience a chance to breathe, to clap. He meets in the morning with Michael, Tim Weil, and the dramaturg, Lynn Thomson, to decide what changes to make to Jonathan's words and music. The Larsons have given them permission to implement any changes they think will improve the show.

When I arrive on Tuesday night, I greet two women sitting behind me: Elizabeth Williams, the coproducer of *Crazy for You*, and her friend Liza Lerner, who is both a board member of New York Theatre Workshop and a daughter of Alan Jay Lerner, the creator of *My Fair Lady*. Sitting in front of me is Kevin's teacher, Worth Gardner, who famously ran the musical theatre program at the Cincinnati Conservatory of Music. He's over-pumped from weightlifting, he's over-tanned from sun machines, and he's known for hating anything he doesn't direct.

At the end of a jittery Tuesday performance, Elizabeth and Liza look at me with expressions of support and sympathy. Their words are generic, but their subtext is, *I'm sorry your friend died, and I'm sorry that his musical isn't very good*. I'm deflated. Then Worth grabs me.

"It's a fucking mess," he says. "Way too many problems to fix. The entire cast is horrible, and the worst one, that guy who plays Roger? He's actually the best, because at least he isn't even trying to act."

His criticism feels sadistic, a barrage of negativity that delights him as it destroys me.

I go home feeling terrible. The looks on the faces of Elizabeth, Liza, and Worth haunt me.

But as the week progresses, the show starts to find its rhythm and focus. Michael devises an ingenious way to help the audience know where each scene takes place without adding a word to Jonathan's text: He has Mark read the stage directions out loud. The cast gains confidence with each performance. Anthony is a sensitive storyteller who provides an excellent point of entry to this community. "Light My Candle" is a playful, sexy seduction that makes both Mimi and Roger irresistible. Tim gives the songs more conclusive endings, which lets the audience applaud.

We hold a memorial service for Jonathan at the Minetta Lane Theatre on Saturday, February 3, another cold, snowy day during a winter in which it seems to blizzard every week. Jonathan's friends speak, Marin Mazzie sings "Come to Your Senses" from *Superbia*, and Adam sings "One Song Glory," which is eerie—as if he's channeling the ghost of Jonathan. The least experienced member of the cast, Adam has grown physically and emotionally every night. Today, for the first time, he opens his eyes when he sings "One Song Glory," which is now a powerful, agonizing expression of Roger's yearning and fear. After the service, we return to the rehearsal studio at New York Theatre Workshop for a small reception. I stand in the kitchen with Jim, eating cupcakes and talking about the show.

"I still wish we could replace 'Your Eyes,'" I say. "It drives me crazy that, after all those great songs, we end on that one, which is supposed to be the song Roger's been writing all year."

"Well, maybe Roger wasn't that great a songwriter after all," says Jim.

I smile. I appreciate Jim's mild-mannered analysis. We both know that we can't change the song and that we will be OK. After the reception, I start walking uptown to process my grief. It's freezing and snowing outside but putting one foot in front of the other is soothing, simple. It releases sadness and nerves. I don't stop until I reach my apartment uptown.

On Sunday night, my good friend David Stone calls and says that Joe Mantello, the actor and director, saw the Sunday matinee and wants to call me. I'm thrilled because a) I've had a crush on Joe since seeing him in *Angels in America*, and b) he's a rising star director whose first Broadway effort, *Love! Valour! Compassion!*, just won the Tony Award for Best Play.

"Hello," I answer.

"It's Joe," he says.

"How are you?"

"I saw your show today."

"Thank you."

"It's the next *A Chorus Line*," he says.

"What?"

"There hasn't been a musical like this since *A Chorus Line*."

"Wow. You should see some of the dour faces I've seen after the show."

"Don't listen to a word they say," he says. "This is the best musical in twenty years."

This one conversation improves my entire outlook. At least for a bit. My mood goes up and down with every person who tells me what they think:

"I haven't heard a score like this since I don't know when."

"I don't know who I'm supposed to be rooting for."

"This is like the opposite of a Broadway musical. And I mean that in a good way."

"I'm lost. I can't tell what's going on."

I'M EXCITED. THEN I'M SCARED. I think it's brilliant, then I think it's a piece of shit. I'm afraid the critics won't appreciate the organized messiness of the staging.

Michael and Tim carve the show like sculptors. It grows a little bit every night. It becomes more electric, more dynamic, more emotionally satisfying. The whole is becoming larger than the sum of the parts. Standing in the back of the theater, the wide stage exploding with music and energy and youth, Kevin and I realize that what we're witnessing is a Broadway musical, not some off-Broadway show. Its story, its themes, its sound are big. For the first time, we imagine a different path, one we had never even discussed with Jonathan—going to Broadway.

Six days before the opening, on a Wednesday, I receive an advance copy of the Arts & Leisure section of the *New York Times*. On page five, there's a huge photo of Jonathan and Michael sitting on the metal table on the stage. Jonathan's smile shows the confidence of someone who is finally touching his dream. This set is his home. He's happy to be a man of the theater, no longer a waiter at the Moondance Diner serving Sunday brunch. It's a powerful feature with several quotes from Stephen Sondheim. While the writer is careful not to offer any opinions about the piece, its very existence, size, and placement make the reader feel as if the show has a future. At the end of the piece, Tommassini writes, "On the last night of his life, Mr. Larson talked of something he had learned from a friend with AIDS: 'It's not how many years you live, but how you fulfill the time you spend here. That's sort of the point of the show.'"

The critics from numerous newspapers come to see the show over the last weekend of previews. I stay away.

By Monday morning, the day before the opening, my stomach is twisted. I'm too anxious to eat. Manny Azenberg calls to check in.

"How are you feeling?" he asks.

"I can't even eat my breakfast."

"Welcome to the theater," he says.

The publicist Richard Kornberg calls me with updates every morning around ten a.m.

"Are you ready for this?"

"What?"

"It's good news and bad news," he says.

"I always want the good news first."

"The *New Yorker* just published John Lahr's article."

"And?"

"It's part feature on Jonathan, part review of the show, and it's all terrific."

"What's the bad news?"

"They broke the embargo against publishing until the day after opening. I'm afraid the *Times* is going to be pissed."

"OK, so I'll enjoy the good news and you make sure the bad news doesn't happen."

"You got it," says Kornberg, who is endlessly enthusiastic.

I pick up the *New Yorker* on the newsstand. Jumping off the page is a color illustration of Jonathan: His curly dark hair is a tree holding the many characters and symbols of life in the East Village. It's a beautiful metaphor for the many stories that rose from his head. Lahr loves the show. This feels like a good omen. I'm able to eat my lunch.

Monday night, our final preview, I sit on the steps in the auditorium of New York Theatre Workshop and watch the show with Jonathan's big sister, Julie, who is gracious, courageous, and visibly pained by her brother's death. Sitting knee to knee, I can feel her body vibrate with exhilaration at her brother's achievement and pain at his absence. We hold hands during Angel's funeral when Collins sings the "I'll Cover You" reprise. For Julie, this is Jonathan's memorial service.

On opening night, Kevin and I show up early and greet our guests. My plan is to watch the opening number from the back of the house and then go across the street with Kornberg to have a glass of red wine to calm my nerves. I can't sit still.

At a small, inexpensive Italian restaurant, I'm sitting at a table with Al and Nanette Larson and Kornberg. We eat and drink to pass the time until we can get in a taxi and go down to the headquarters of the *New York Times* to buy a copy of the early edition that comes out around 10:15 p.m.

Richard tells me that Peter Marks wants to talk to us later tonight. Peter is the *New York Times* theater beat reporter who writes a column called "On Stage and Off" every Friday. Peter has already seen the show and is an enthusiastic supporter. This can't be bad, I figure. Peter has undoubtedly read the review and wouldn't be setting up a call if it was negative.

I eat rigatoni and broccoli and drink red wine until my blood is warm and my heart is calm. I check my watch every ten minutes. The show comes down around 10:45 p.m. At 9:50 p.m., Kornberg and I walk to the Bowery and hail a cab.

We head up Third Avenue, turn left on Forty-second Street, then another right on Sixth Avenue and another left on Forty-third Street. My heart races faster with every left turn. It feels too much, too big, too momentous. When the taxi pulls up in front of the building, I jump out of the right side and walk to the kiosk and insert four quarters into the slot. I pull out one paper.

"Get two!" shouts Richard from the window.

I do the whole thing again. I return to the cab.

Hands shaking, heart pounding, I find the Arts Page, buried in section C. Turning to page eleven, my eyes scan the first paragraph. I see two words: "Exhilarating" and "landmark." I scream with relief and happiness. "Electric current of emotion" is the next phrase I take in. The fear that was vibrating through my body is replaced by joy.

"He did it," I exclaim. "He got his review in the *New York Times*." Critic Ben Brantley ravishes the cast and score with praise. He calls the choreography witty. His euphoric review ends with the following two sentences:

"People who complain about the demise of the American musical theatre have simply been looking in the wrong places. Well done, Mr. Larson."

We hug, we cry, and we head back to the Italian restaurant, while the second act is still transpiring across the street.

"It's a rave, Al. Your son got a rave from the *Times*."

Al and Nan beam with pride. We hand them a paper and Al savors every word. Peter Marks calls us via Richard's cell phone. He's looking for any news he can get about a transfer.

He talks to Nan first.

"Jonathan should have been here," she says. "He would have loved every minute of it."

When I get on the phone, Peter jumps right in.

"So, Mr. Producer," he says, "what happens next?"

That he's calling me "Mr. Producer" is a dream come true.

"Let's enjoy tonight," I say. "Tomorrow, we get to work."

We walk across the street and stand in the back during the rapturous applause and cheering. There's a celebratory party upstairs. Grief is suspended for a moment of celebration. We all imagine what might come next.

Chapter Twenty-Seven

RENT PART IV:
BROADWAY

THE NEXT MORNING, Kevin and I return to the theater to talk with Jim Nicola, his staff, Kornberg, and his associate Don Summa. We sit on the tattered couches and mismatched dining chairs in the room that has housed readings, sing-throughs, rehearsals, memorial receptions, and the opening night party. Our job is to decide what happens next.

"Broadway, we must go to Broadway!" I shout.

"I think you're absolutely right," says Jim, a cautious man. His fervor surprises.

"If this show can't work on Broadway, then I'm going to have to pack it up and go home," I say. After all, the reviews are spectacular. "The first original breakthrough rock musical since *Hair*," says Linda Winer in *Newsday*. "If I owned an available Broadway theater, I'd just 'Rent' it," says Clive Barnes in the *New York Post*.

Today is February 14. To qualify for this year's Tony Awards we must move the show to Broadway and open before the cutoff date, May 2. We need to find the right theater, negotiate the rent (no pun intended), and then move the entire production uptown. Simultaneously, we must create a marketing campaign and start selling tickets. All in less than four months.

Before making a final decision, we bring this conversation to our more experienced colleagues.

"Do you think you'll be able to fill all those seats?" someone asks.

"You always said this was going to go off-Broadway," says another.

"It will run forever off-Broadway," says our lawyer, Loren Plotkin.

"Are you sure the Broadway crowd wants to see a show about AIDS, heroin addicts, and homeless people?" says ad guru Nancy Coyne, who coined the tagline "Now and forever" for *Cats*.

"Is the audience for *Rent* going to come to Broadway?"

"I don't get it because I'm old, but this is your golden opportunity," says Manny Azenberg. "Of course you should go to Broadway."

I ask myself, *What if we move the show to Broadway and it runs as long as* Tommy, *the last rock musical? Tommy* got great reviews but ran less than two years. It recouped but did not become a huge hit. Will we be satisfied if that's the trajectory of *Rent*? Would that be better than going off-Broadway and running for five years? Our answer is yes. This show needs to be on Broadway. This show needs to change what we think is possible on Broadway. If the downside is a small success that only runs for a year or two, it will have been worth it.

In the Friday *New York Times* "On Stage and Off" column, Marks quotes me: "This is not about Broadway or Off-Broadway, it's about finding the right house." My quote is bullshit. I'm creating suspense around our plans to move the show. The truth is that we don't yet have the answers.

But Kevin and I are fueled by the zeal of two men on a mission to prove that a show about downtown bohemians can play uptown, which currently offers British mega-musicals and a stage version of the movie *Victor/Victoria* that is an unfortunate imitation, albeit with Julie Andrews, of the inspired original movie.

In one week, Kevin and I have gone from being two hardworking bookers to being the producers of the hottest new show in town. It feels amazing. But not just amazing. It feels right. It feels like my outside is finally matching my inside.

BOOKING A THEATER

THERE ARE THREE LANDLORDS on Broadway, and they all want the show. Kevin and I ask Manny Azenberg to join us as an informal advisor—our rabbi. We visit the Shuberts at their mahogany wood-paneled offices on the top floor of the Shubert Theatre. We enter the inner sanctum of the largest and oldest theater chain via a tiny elevator still operated by an attendant. After a slow ride up to the fifth floor scrunched into a tiny cab, the attendant pulls the metal door to the right, and we open another door into a reception room that looks like an old-fashioned library with a cherrywood desk, where a female receptionist sits in a conservative skirt and blouse.

She announces our presence, and we are asked to sit down. Going to the Shuberts is like going to see the Wizard. The fancy, dark office was designed to project wealth and power. It reminds producers who is really in charge of this business. That tiny elevator doesn't just take us to the fifth floor of an old theater, it takes us back to 1947.

Bernie Jacobs and Gerry Schoenfeld, the president and chairman, look like they've been here since 1947. They took over in the early '70s after the last Shubert heir, drunken Lawrence Shubert Lawrence Jr., ran the business into the ground. They remind me of the *Muppet Show* hecklers, Statler and Waldorf, except they are not even a little bit funny.

"As you know, Mr. Seller, *Big* is getting ready to open downstairs at the Shubert," says Gerry, a short, rotund man about seventy years old with white stubble on his pate. "And the only theaters that are available are the Lyceum and Belasco."

"What about the Broadhurst?" says Manny to Bernie, the dour president with a permanent scowl, known for forging close relationships with Michael Bennett and Bob Fosse.

Bernie and Manny practically growl at each other. They are holding back years of partnership, friendship, discord, and animosity. They used to be close. Manny married his wife, Lani, in Bernie's living room. But they haven't spoken in several years. Manny detests Gerry Schoenfeld, whom he calls "a poser," and with whom he almost got into a fistfight a few years back.

"The Broadhurst has a booking," says Gerry in a pretentious voice that echoes the voice of God in *The Ten Commandments*. Manny looks at him incredulously. The booking about which he's talking is a murder mystery by George Furth and Stephen Sondheim that recently opened to negative reviews and no sales.

"You can have the Belasco for fifteen thousand per week flat, plus expenses," says Bernie.

This is a good offer, but the theater doesn't have enough seats for this musical. Manny has explained to us that two-balcony houses are terrible for long-running musicals. No one wants to buy tickets in the second balcony and there aren't enough good seats in the orchestra.

"There's something else you should consider," says Gerry. "*Big* is getting ready to open in late April, so you might want to think about opening after the Tony deadline so that you qualify for next year's awards."

"Why would we want to do that?" says Kevin.

"Well, you might recall that *Chess* came in the same season as *Phantom*."

"What does that mean?" I ask.

"I just think that *Chess* would have had a better chance had it not been up against *The Phantom of the Opera*."

"With all due respect, Mr. Schoenfeld, *Rent* is no *Chess* and *Big* is no *Phantom of the Opera*," I say.

"Just some wisdom gained from many years of experience," says Gerry.

"Save it for the next guys," says Manny. "We're out of here."

Manny is furious. In the tiny elevator, he starts shouting: "You have the biggest hit in years, and they offer you the fucking Belasco?"

"He was trying to persuade us to not open until after the Tony cutoff," I say.

"When he said, 'the Broadhurst has a booking,' I wanted to punch his teeth in," says Manny.

We won't be working with the Shuberts.

Jimmy Nederlander, their competitor, has always been friendly and respectful of Kevin and me in our roles as booking agents. If the Shuberts behave like feudal lords, Jimmy is more like a crap shooter from *Guys and Dolls*. He loves talking about what's selling on the road, and what might sell in the future.

Nederlander has several large houses that are not right for our show and one medium-size house, the Nederlander, which is a run-down theater on derelict West Forty-first Street. It hasn't had a hit show since Lena Horne starred in *The Lady and Her Music* in 1981. My first fall in New York, I attended the Nederlander to see a musical of *Raggedy Ann* by composer Joe Raposo, the man who wrote *A Wonderful Life* with Sheldon Harnick. It closed three days after it opened.

We walk down to Forty-first Street, one block south of the porn houses on Forty-second Street, to check it out. Beyond the peeling paint, tattered carpeting, and strong smell of mildew, a large orchestra section and single balcony come into focus. It seats 1,180 people with no second balcony. The seats fan around the stage in a way that builds intimacy and community. It feels right.

We go up to see Jimmy; his son, Jimmy Jr.; and their deputy, Nick.

"So, fellas, I hear you have a big fat hit," says Jimmy Sr. in his high-pitched Midwestern accent. Jimmy, like all the Nederlanders, is from Detroit. None of them ever lived in Cardboard Village.

"We think we have something special, Jimmy," says Kevin.

"My son says it'll run for years," says Jimmy.

"From your mouth," I say.

"Nick tells me you want to rent the Nederlander, you know I named it after my father, David T. Nederlander."

"It's a good place for our show," says Kevin.

"I had a big hit there with Lena Horne," says Jimmy. "Nice lady. Only wouldn't perform if the air conditioner was running. Boy, did it get hot in July."

"Jimmy, listen to me," says Manny. "You should be kissing their feet. You haven't had a booking at the Nederlander in fifteen years."

"So, what do you want?" he asks.

"Free rent until recoupment," says Manny.

"What else?" says Jimmy.

"We share the interest on the advance, fifty-fifty. And you have to do all the work to get the theater ready."

"The theater's yours, boys. I've always liked you."

Playing at the Nederlander, on a dingy block south of Forty-second Street, feels like a perfect way to keep one foot downtown and one foot uptown. We're embracing our bohemian spirit while occupying a theater on the fringes of Broadway.

EIGHT WEEKS TO GO!

ON SATURDAY NIGHT, my friend Tom King is visiting from Los Angeles, and I take him to see the show. He's a star reporter for the *Wall Street Journal*, and his beat is Hollywood, where his fearlessness and sense of humor are respected. Every major player takes his calls; most share the juiciest gossip and confidential information—particularly when it might hurt their adversaries. At intermission, he spots David Geffen, one of his prized sources, in the audience and brings me over to meet him. I've idolized David since college. He was the first entertainment mogul to earn a billion dollars when Universal (of which David owned a huge share) was sold to the Japanese. He produced *Dreamgirls* (with Michael Bennett) and *Cats* (with Cameron Mackintosh and Andrew Lloyd Webber), and created Arista Records and Geffen Records in the 1970s. Now he has created the most important new Hollywood studio in a generation, DreamWorks, with his friends Steven Spielberg and Jeffrey Katzenberg.

"It's a great show," says David. "But let me tell you something, you need to cut it. You've got to be tough, that's your job. I mean, the first act, it's just too long," he says.

David is exactly like he sounds on Barbra Streisand's *Broadway Album*. She featured him giving her business advice in the song "Putting

It Together." I always remember him saying, "It's just not commercial," which in this instance means, *Jeffrey, if you want your show to be commercial, then you must cut it.*

He goes on to tell me how much he hates the Shuberts and how he once sold his house in East Hampton to his friend, Michael Bennett. He's the ultimate macher. What makes him even more remarkable to me is that he has proven that a gay man can be respected, and powerful, in a business of many straight men. He can be seen. Because he's relentless at getting what he wants, and he isn't afraid of anybody.

"If you're interested, I'll do the album," he says. "We'll do it on our new DreamWorks label."

"That's amazing," I say.

Tom calls me at home the next morning and says David wants to talk to me. He gives me his number and tells me to call him.

"Look, Jeffrey's in Deer Valley for the weekend with his family, but he doesn't ski, just works all day, he's dying to see the show. Steven's gonna see it on his next trip to New York and he'll decide if he wants to make a movie. I'll call Cameron and introduce you. He'll do it in London."

"That's amazing," I say, cringing because I say "amazing" too much.

"Come over tomorrow at noon, we'll get some pizza."

On Monday, the day of our lunch, I get a scratchy throat. I try to ignore it.

We meet at David's apartment on Fifth Avenue and Sixtieth Street, where he talks about all the movies they're making at DreamWorks. It's hard to keep up with his fast monologue and the many players in the movie that is his life. We finally get to *Rent*.

"It all comes together in the second act," he says. "But you gotta clean up that first act."

"I know what you mean," I say.

"You're a hundred percent right," says Kevin. "We're working on it."

"So if you want me to make the album, I'll make the album."

"Thank you," I dribble.

"It'll be a great double album," he says.

"I was thinking, maybe we should do what you did with *Dreamgirls*, you know, make an amazing single album to sell more records," I say.

"We wanted to sell it like a pop album, and it worked. 'And I'm Telling You' was the first song to chart since 'Send in the Clowns.' But this is better for *Rent*. People want the whole thing. And we'll make twice as much money because we'll sell twice the discs."

"David, can you help us find a great graphic artist?" I ask. "We need a logo as iconic as *Cats* or *Phantom*."

"Hang on," he says.

He calls his assistant and says, "Get me Robin." David speaks like the Pharaoh in *The Ten Commandments*: "So let it be written, so let it be done."

Robin Sloan is his longtime marketing pro who produced the artwork for all his albums since he founded Geffen Records. Robin tells me I'm going to love a guy named Drew Hodges, who owns his own art studio and creates album covers, book jackets, and logos. She'll call Drew tomorrow.

As we eat pizza and salad and hear David's stories, I start to feel my chest constrict, which means an infection is coming. Why is my childhood nemesis, bronchitis, fighting me now? I won't let it stop me.

On Tuesday, feeling awful with a temperature of a hundred degrees, I go to the doctor for a penicillin shot and antibiotics, then I go to bed. On Wednesday, I make plans to meet with the cast before the show.

My voice is hoarse, my chest pained, but I get in a taxi and travel to East Fourth Street, which has become like my new office. I'm nervous.

I stand stage left with Jim Nicola and Jonathan's father, Al, present. The cast is seated on the metal tables, some in red chairs, some standing. Wilson (Angel) and Fredi (Joanne) are holding each other. They look at me. Are they apprehensive? Are they suspicious of this guy wearing a Michigan sweatshirt? Are they hopeful?

"I'm a little sick tonight but, what the fuck, right?" I say. The cast laughs. "I'm pretty excited tonight because I'm standing on the hottest stage in New York with the hottest cast anywhere in the world. And I applaud you."

Everyone claps.

"You guys have become a shot in the arm for the American theater. People who love musical theater and who have become cynical in the last few years have called me to say, 'Thank you, thank you for giving us something to look forward to.' People are excited about musicals again.

"Over the last several weeks, we've been trying to listen to the show, listen to the audience, we've been trying to figure out what's best for *Rent*. We've thought through every option and debated the pros and cons of every option. But in the end, all we can say to ourselves is, 'We want to go to Broadway.'"

A cast member yelps, others laugh and clap.

"Because if we are not a Broadway show I am packing it up and going home. We are a kick-ass Broadway show the people have been looking for, for years.

"Our first preview is April 16 and we open April 29. And tomorrow we're going to announce it to the world."

Many screams and cheers. Tears drip down actor Jesse Martin's face.

"There's going to be a revolution on Broadway this spring," I say. "It's called *Rent*."

Many activities now happen simultaneously. Paul Clay, who heretofore was a downtown sculptor, needs to design the set for a bigger space. The entire theater must be plastered and painted, with new carpeting. The bathrooms need new stalls, toilets, and fixtures. Many holes in the ceiling need to be repaired. The entire stage electrical system needs to be replaced to accommodate the newest lighting equipment. When Paul tours the theatre, he says, "Don't repaint the ceiling. Just leave the exposed plaster. It looks cool unfinished."

Paul chooses leopard carpeting for the floors. Around the proscenium, he installs a mosaic of broken ceramic art inspired by the lampposts in the East Village.

For the mezzanine bar, Kevin recruits his artist friend, Billy Miller, to paint the nine ceiling squares with his quirky black-and-white scenes of life and people in the East Village.

Costume designer Angela Wendt, who designed the off-Broadway production with a couple thousand dollars and fashioned much of Mimi's wardrobe from Daphne Rubin-Vega's closet, submits her Broadway budget. It's two hundred thousand dollars. Allan Gordon throws a temper tantrum.

"How can a bunch of schmattes cost $200K?" he says. "She's obviously ripping us off."

Manny Azenberg explains the way the union shops work and that we must now build costumes that will last a year and clothe the principal cast as well as understudies. We are all getting a graduate degree in Broadway economics. Our $250,000 off-Broadway musical is now a $3.5 million musical.

I meet graphic designer Drew Hodges to talk about the logo. Drew has heard a little bit about the show and expresses a certain amount of skepticism.

"People aren't sure if this show is the real thing or just another downtown wannabe," he says. "People raise their eyebrows when they hear rock musical."

We get him into the show immediately and talk the day after.

"I loved it, but it's definitely not rock. What it really is, is great theater. It's true to itself."

"What does that mean for advertising?"

"The goal is to embrace who you are and what you are. Don't try to make it something it's not. This isn't Pearl Jam. It's still musical theater but it's absolutely of today. Those characters are real. I know people like Maureen and Angel."

Drew provides a fresh perspective about the show and how to communicate its essence. With a team of talented designers, all working out of his apartment on Sixth Avenue and Twenty-eighth Street, he goes to work to design a logo.

He comes in a week later with ten different ideas. Each idea uses the vernacular of downtown posters that you might see for shows at CBGB. They are all black and white, bold, and raw. We all get up and look at each poster individually. We quietly stare for a few minutes. I feel as if I'm at a great art show.

One logo, pinned up in the middle, is a black spray-painted stencil. The letters R E N T are the white space inside. It reminds me of the POST NO BILLS stencils that are spray painted on plywood walls at construction sites.

With the scattershot residue of spray paint and masking tape that's been ripped off, our four letters—R E N T—are bold and simple. It's unlike any logo for a musical I've seen. And it matches the double meaning of the word. It's the one.

Drew goes away to design the full-page ad announcing the on-sale in the *New York Times*.

Three days later, a large envelope is delivered to my office. I open it with anticipation and care, as if it's a birthday gift.

I pull out a big piece of white paper. It has two words in a typewriter font in front of the *RENT* logo: TICKETS FOR

"That's it?" I think to myself. It's not what I expected.

It's so minimalist, so raw, it looks almost ugly. Under the logo is the author and director credit; the phone number is on the left side farther down; the theater and address are on the bottom left. It looks homemade, as if the words were typed, then cut and pasted, then copied on a Xerox machine. It looks like an ad Mark and Roger made for one of his shows. It reminds me of what I saw the first time I walked into the theater and saw the minimalist set. It captures the time, place, and people of this show.

My initial reaction has given way to a new feeling: I love it.

One of Kevin's great arguments for Broadway was that *more* seats would enable us to sell *cheap* seats. Our top price is $65, the same as all musicals, but we only charge $35 for the rear mezzanine, less than any other show. We also want to sell some twenty-dollar tickets for people with little money, which would have included us just a couple of years ago. My first fall in New York, there was a new musical in previews called *Smile*. A promising collaboration between Marvin Hamlisch and Howard Ashman, it had just received a big story on *60 Minutes*, and I was dying to see it. After work one Tuesday night, I went to the TKTS booth to buy a half-price ticket, but they weren't selling any. I never saw the show, which got negative reviews and closed quickly after opening. If the producers had worked harder to get young people like me in the door, they may have had a better chance of building word of mouth and overcoming their crummy reviews.

Though Cameron Mackintosh, the producer of *Miss Saigon*, had employed a "student rush," the tickets were in the rear balcony and only reserved for high school and college kids.

"What about all the poor people who aren't students?" I say.

"Let's flip it," says Kevin.

"What do you mean?"

"We'll put them in the first two rows."

"That's it!" I say. "We'll sell the first two rows for twenty dollars—but to everybody."

"It'll be like a wave," says Kevin. "The people in the first two rows will start a wave that spreads to the back of the theater."

"And we'll sell them on the day of the show, which will guarantee there's a line in front of the theater every day."

We have a plan.

I say, "I can't believe I'm producing a Broadway show and three years ago I couldn't afford to see one."

"See, I told you," says Kevin.

"Told me what?" I ask.

"That if we stayed together, great things would happen."

I pause. I feel tears coming out of my eyes.

"You were right."

On Sunday, March 17, the *New York Times* Arts & Leisure cover features a half-page color photo of the company arrayed around actor Jesse Martin, playing Collins in his orange vest, at the end of "La Vie Bohème." The giant headline says, "Birth of a Theatrical Comet." Our full-page ad—"TICKETS FOR RENT"—is on page three. There are three big articles on the show: a history of the development of the show, a mini feature on every cast member, and another think piece by their Sunday critic. Jealous theater industry colleagues call the section "Rent & Leisure."

Kevin and I head to West Forty-first Street for the box office opening at nine a.m. When we get out of the taxi, we see our illuminated marquee that went up the previous day. The signage company mistakenly printed it on clear plexiglass instead of opaque white. Tubular fluorescent vertical lights are visible behind the logo.

"This is a disaster," says Kevin.

I look at it again. "It looks like our show," I say. "Everything's exposed. It's perfect."

We tell them to leave it.

A hundred people are lined up to buy tickets. Jimmy Nederlander Sr., the seventy-five-year-old theater owner, still hobbled by a stroke he suffered five years ago, shows up to serve coffee to the customers.

"My father made me work in the box office, boys. Best training I ever had," says Jimmy. "This theater's named after him, you know."

Our young box office treasurer, Johnny Campise, walks over to us shaking and sweating. "You're not going to believe this, but I can't get the system up. It won't turn on."

My heart skips a beat.

"I'm going to be fired by Mr. Nederlander on my first day," he says.

Meanwhile, Jimmy is having a ball talking to the patrons who are lined up patiently to buy tickets the old-fashioned way. Fifteen minutes later, Johnny reboots the system and sells his first pair of tickets.

Our first Broadway show is on sale.

Kevin and I walk with Manny to Ticketmaster on Fifty-seventh Street to check out the action in the phone room.

Sixty young women are sitting at open desks answering calls and taking orders on a bright floor the size of a gymnasium. At the front is a computerized tally board. We stand under it and watch the operators take orders for *Rent*. The tally board behind us passes $400,000, then $500,000. It's amazing. I feel like I'm standing next to Jerry Lewis at his telethon when he says, "Tiffany, what does the board say?" and then the orchestra plays "What the World Needs Now" as they pass another milestone.

We sell $750,000 worth of tickets on that Sunday and reach one million by the end of day Monday.

I receive a call from producer Cameron Mackintosh, who suggests starting the show in London at the Donmar Warehouse. Andrew Lloyd Webber calls and offers to fly Kevin and me on the Concorde to London to look at a theater he would like to buy to house *Rent*. "Do you like theaters?" he says. "What if we bought one for you?" I can't believe that the composer of *Evita* is calling me.

Another music business legend named Ahmet Ertegun calls. He's the founder of Atlantic Records. I explain to him that we're already working with David Geffen. He calls Allan Gordon, who is happy to receive some attention. Allan sets up a meeting at his office with Ahmet. I feel like a traitor going to the meeting.

Allan has placed many packs of Marlboro cigarettes on the table in the conference room. Ahmet is a famous chain-smoker. He is also a Turkish gentleman—kind, gracious, and generous with his compliments. He'll do just about anything to get this album away from David Geffen, who he explains was his protégé. He says that he'll bid more than David and work harder on promotion. "And I'm going to get you the best producer in the business, my friend Arif Mardin, who has made more hit albums than almost anybody."

He is not the only mogul calling. Kevin and I are invited to meet with Terry Semel and Bob Daly, the heads of Warner Brothers, at their Rockefeller Center headquarters. They talk about the benefits of using all their platforms to cross-promote an album, a movie, and a show. Fox sends us their CEO, Peter Chernin, who comes to our office to explain the benefits of being in the Fox family. He goes out of his way to explain that he's a progressive Democrat and that Rupert Murdoch doesn't interfere with his work. We're taken to dinner by Danny DeVito and his producing team from Universal. He explains the virtues of working with an independent outfit like his that will protect us from the big bad studios: "Jeffrey, they will squash you like a BUG!" says Danny. "But I won't let that happen. We'll fight those mothers and protect your movie." Danny is as funny and entertaining in person as he is in his movies. Then Robert De Niro and Martin Scorsese join the party. They make a bid to produce and Scorsese dangles the possibility that he might direct.

What we glean from these meetings is that we have the hottest show in all of entertainment and everyone wants a piece. But it's also clear that none of them give a shit about the live show. They only care about movies. Kevin and I resist the temptation to get seduced. We need to stay focused on our musical.

Ahmet and Atlantic make a huge offer that exceeds the Dream-Works offer. Allan Gordon, eager for a win for his efforts, wants to take it. If David Geffen is going to get this album, he's going to need to raise his offer.

I gather courage. I rehearse what I'm going to say and then I call David from my office on a Sunday afternoon. He always answers.

"David, I need to talk to you."

"So talk."

"I'm calling because Ahmet Ertegun made a huge offer for the album."

"What?" he says incredulously.

"Atlantic Records put an offer on the table and it's higher than yours."

"This is unbelievable. We had a deal."

"We didn't have a deal, David. We had great conversations, which I appreciate. And your lawyers made a good offer."

"Well, then we're done," he says.

"But Ahmet made a better offer."

"You're using Ahmet to leverage me?"

"That's not what happened."

"Why were you talking to Ahmet?"

"He called my partner."

"Ahmet has one goal, to try to take things away from me. Because he's old and he wants to be relevant again."

"He also promised that Arif Mardin will produce it," I say.

"If you want Arif to produce it, then we'll get Arif to produce it. You can have anybody you want. Ahmet doesn't own Arif."

"There's still the issue of the advance," I say.

"Advances don't mean anything if you have a hit album. It's all about the future, Jeffrey."

"David, I have partners. And the Larsons have to approve any deal we make."

"What do you want?" he says.

I take a breath.

"You need to raise your advance to $1.5 million and raise the promotion budget to $300K."

"I don't believe this," he says.

"I really want to make this album with you, David, but you have to beat the Atlantic offer."

"I need to call Mo." David is referring to Mo Ostin, another music industry legend who now runs DreamWorks Records. "Stay right there."

Click.

I put the phone down. I'm drenched with sweat.

Five minutes later, David calls back.

"You've got the 1.5 for the advance. Now, do we have a deal?"

"Thank you."

"Let me tell you something, Jeffrey, this is not the way you treat people in this business. It's all about relationships, it's all about your word. There's nothing more valuable than that. You're going to have a long career, don't break others' trust."

"Thank you. I'll run this by the team and get back to you."

"So we have a deal." He says this as a statement even though it's a question.

"I need to get the Larsons to approve it."

"Then call the Larsons. Right now."

"One more thing, Ahmet also said Atlantic would pay for the opening night party."

"Pay for your own party."

Click.

I'm rattled. I'm sweaty. But I've negotiated the largest advance in history for a Broadway album with the toughest mogul in the business.

OPENING NIGHT

IN TWO WEEKS OF rehearsal before Broadway, Michael tightens staging, focuses choreography and musical numbers, clarifies plot. He makes one cut, a small song called "The Door/The Wall" in Act One in which Mark and Roger bemoan the ways we are trapped inside ourselves. It's overkill; it slows down the momentum of the act. He sharpens the opening of the show. But there's still something missing from the ending. Kevin complains that the final beat of the show, in which all the actors are scattered throughout the stage as they sing, "No day but today," is cold. Michael resists at first, then comes in the next day and changes the blocking. On the last phrase, he brings all the characters together—one family in a group surrounding Mimi and Roger—for the final tableau. The final character to join is Angel. These are all micro-changes for greater clarity and momentum, to express more love and connection.

It's raining and cold on the day of our first preview. The performance is sold out. Will anyone show up to buy the twenty-dollar tickets? Around six p.m. we walk over to the theater, where there are a handful of people lined up. By curtain, we sell all thirty-four tickets, but this opportunity isn't yet popular. Not enough people know about it.

At 7:59 p.m. I'm sitting with Kevin in row G. There is excitement in the air—1,203 people are about to see a show they've heard and read about for two months. Does it live up to the hype? Is it going to be real or phony? Will they be happy to say, "I was at the first performance of *Rent* on Broadway"? I hope so. I take a moment to let it sink in that less than two months ago, we had our dress rehearsal with Jonathan standing in the back. Now we're on Broadway without Jonathan.

"Well, he's actually here," his friend Victoria tells me at intermission. "I put some of his ashes backstage, because, let's face it, Jonathan was a true Broadway Baby."

Witnessing 1,203 people watch a show is a wholly different experience than 199 people watching a show. On Broadway, the audience lets go: They laugh and cry and cheer and go wild. Entrance applause greets the cast when they take the stage. A huge ovation follows the opening number, "Rent." The next applause opportunity is "Today 4 U," Angel's introduction, and the crowd's response grows bigger. Daphne's fierce performance of "Out Tonight" may as well have been at Madison Square Garden. Tonight proves our instinct that this show belongs on Broadway.

A week into previews Jonathan wins the Pulitzer Prize for drama. Kevin announces it to the cast during an afternoon rehearsal. Moments like this reinforce the victory and sadness that pervades every day at *Rent*. Jonathan has joined the handful of musical authors to ever win a Pulitzer Prize, the last of which was won by his hero, Stephen Sondheim, for *Sunday in the Park with George*. At the same time, this leads to tears and sadness and guilt that we are all here enjoying this journey. Jonathan is not.

It's a quick jump to April 29, opening night.

The street is closed to traffic to allow all the opening night guests to congregate. Mom and Dad are here along with my brother, Aaron (who is now nineteen), and my sister, Laurie. Aunt Fern and Uncle Bob are here, with Bob wearing a yellow and black jacket that makes him look like a bumblebee—it's his version of cool bohemian. Uncle Sy and Aunt Amy are here, and she stands in the lobby taking photos on her Kodak Instamatic of all the celebrities: George Clooney, Patrick Swayze, Kevin Bacon and Kyra Sedgwick, David Geffen and Barbara Walters, Christie Brinkley, and Isabella Rossellini.

My date is my best friend, Andrew.

Dad and Mom are sitting next to me. Dad walks across the aisle and introduces himself to George Clooney, who is kind. He understands this unique intersection of family, theater-folk, and Hollywood royalty and plays his role graciously. Dad pulls Mom over to George, and they all take a photo.

Just before the show starts, Victoria, seated in front of me, turns around and hands me a thin tie. "This is an opening night gift from Jonathan. It was his favorite tie."

I take hold of a little bit of Jonathan and squeeze it tight.

When the cast takes the stage there is a long roar from the audience. Anthony Rapp looks at the audience and absorbs this wave of love. He pauses and then says, "We dedicate this performance and every performance of *Rent* to Jonathan Larson." More applause. Then, in the first row, Aaron stands up. The whole audience follows this standing ovation for Jonathan.

And then the show begins. When Mark says, "We begin on Christmas Eve," I try to watch as if I've never seen it before, as if I never knew Jonathan, or criticized the development of Mark or Roger or Mimi. Tonight is special. This unique assembly will never happen again. I'm transported to the East Village on a tide of passion, talent, and exuberance. Watching Collins and Angel sing "I'll Cover You," I care deeply for these two men, and appreciate how Jonathan wrote not only a gorgeous love song using a perfect metaphor, but also an action song that propels character and plot: Angel is buying a new winter coat for Collins after his coat was stolen in the first song. When Collins sings "I'll Cover You" again at Angel's funeral in Act Two, we are brought full circle in the journey of this remarkable couple, who, for me, are the heart of the show. When the cast comes together on the metal tables for the last five notes—"No day but today"—the theater explodes in adulation and joy.

A euphoric performance ends with a gigantic party at the Chelsea Sky Rink—we've covered the entire ice rink with a floor—amid a blur of happy meetings, celebratory conversations, enthusiastic handshakes, and loving hugs. David Geffen introduces me to Barbara Walters and then says, "You know, Jeffrey, it's all about your next show." My aunts and cousins have the time of their lives watching young cast members like Taye Diggs and Wilson Heredia take over the center of the dance floor.

Six days later, we are at Sardi's for the announcement of the Tony Awards nominations. Kornberg hands me a copy of *Newsweek*, which has Adam and Daphne on the cover, something that happens on Broadway every five years or so. We receive ten nominations. The two most expensive shows of the season, *Victor/Victoria* and *Big*, aren't nominated for Best Musical.

In the middle of May I receive a call from a *Wall Street Journal* reporter who wants to interview me. I call my friend Tom King, who works at the *Journal*, and he assures me that the writer, Jeffrey Trachtenberg, is an ace business reporter. I call Kornberg and put him in charge of this story.

We meet at my office a few days later. He asks numerous questions about the business of this venture: What was the initial investment? What is the Broadway capitalization? How many tickets have been sold? How much money can the show earn in a year? Over ten years? He's curious about my background. I glean that he's interested in how two young guys wound up producing the biggest hit on Broadway. I know how to spin this story for maximum impact. He interviews other people in the business to get a longitudinal perspective. He interviews Kevin and I advise Kornberg to make sure he talks to Allan Gordon.

After a couple more phone conversations, a *Journal* editor calls and ask for a photograph that their artist will use for their traditional line drawings. I tell Kornberg to send a joint photograph of Kevin and me and to ensure that they send one of Allan Gordon as well. Another editor calls to fact-check the story. We're on the phone for a long time. I get the sense that this is going to be big.

On the Thursday before Memorial Day, the lead article on A1 of the *Wall Street Journal* says, "How to Turn $4,000 Into Many Millions; The Story of *Rent*." Under the first paragraph is a fantastic line drawing of Kevin and me.

The piece is dramatic, dynamic, and accurate. Its focus is money and business. It's good for us, it's good for the show, and it's good for Broadway. It's not good for our partner, Allan Gordon. It refers to him as a "Wall Street financier." It does not include his picture, and he goes berserk. He screams at Richard Kornberg, he screams at the reporter, then he calls the editor and publisher and threatens to sue. It's an unfortunate example of the jealousy and internecine warfare that sometimes plays out in the tiny world of Broadway. Allan feels disregarded and embarrassed. In his circles he has acted as if he's the principal producer of the show. In fact, the article has perfectly characterized our roles and relationships, which has popped the bubble of his delusions and exaggerations. He was hoping to be perceived as young, creative, and integral; instead, he was called "a money man in his fifties (he wouldn't give his age)." After this incident, our relationship is poisoned, and we never do another show together.

THE TONY AWARDS

I WATCHED MY FIRST Tony Awards ceremony in eighth grade in 1978, when *Ain't Misbehavin'* beat *On the 20th Century.* Though I hadn't seen either show, I cared. I've watched the broadcast from numerous couches every single year ever since. Why? Because musicals unlock feelings inside of me that no other experience can. Because musicals radiate unique aural and visual stimulation. More laughter. More tears. More goose bumps. More yearning and longing and hope than other forms of art. Because musicals make me feel good in a way that no other experience can, except sex. There, I said it. Musicals and sex. I can't live without sex; I can't live without musicals. And the Tony Awards are our Super Bowl. This year, I'm watching from the fifth row.

The Majestic Theatre has played host to *The Phantom of the Opera* for the past nine years, but tonight it will be home to the 1996 Tony Awards. At the morning rehearsal, when all the shows run their numbers, I show up with my dad. Nathan Lane, currently starring in *Forum*, is the host; he's working hard to master all the details of the show. He is gracious when I introduce him to my dad. The producer of the telecast, Gary Smith, greets us warmly.

"You're a good son, Jeff, bringing your dad to 'work' with you."

"You know, he used to bring me to 'work' with him. Right, Dad?"

"Nothing better than serving papers with you, son."

I smile.

"You were my good luck charm."

"Maybe you're *my* good luck," I say.

For the first time, I'm not ashamed in the presence of my father. I'm proud to share this experience with him, which he appreciates and loves.

In a theater with Andrew Lloyd Webber, Liza Minnelli, Bernadette Peters, and Nathan Lane, Kevin and I schmooze with the other nominees.

The Lincoln Center Theatre producer, Bernie Gersten, hands me a huge handful of candy to get through the three-hour evening. "I've been bringing brown bags of candy to the Tony Awards since 1976," he says proudly.

Jonathan wins for Best Book and Best Original Score, and Julie Larson accepts the awards on his behalf. Wilson Heredia wins Best Supporting Actor, and ends his speech saying, "To a new generation on Broadway." How right he is.

We present our number, "La Vie Bohème" followed by "Seasons of Love." Watching, I remember being introduced to *Evita*, *Dreamgirls*, and *Sunday in the Park with George* on the Tony Awards. Though I'm in my seat, I feel as if I'm flying many feet above the audience. How many young people are being introduced to *Rent* right now?

I watch the stage and look at my watch, counting minutes and awards until we reach the last award of the night: Best Musical. I hold my anxiety, my nervousness, my excitement. When we finally get to 10:57 p.m., Andrew Lloyd Webber takes the stage holding the shiny black cardboard booklet that contains the winner. As he opens it, I hear the tape break, and hold my breath. He smiles. "And the Tony Award for Best Musical goes to *Rent*."

Kevin and I jump out of our chairs as if springs bounce us onto the stage. Lloyd Webber hands me the award and whispers in my ear, "Well done, my boy." Standing at the microphone, the same words come out of my mouth that I formed the night after Jonathan died: "Thank you, Jonathan Larson."

The celebratory night ends; I'm home in my bed, still hepped up. My gratitude and love for Jonathan don't stop pouring out: Thank you, Jonathan, for *Boho Days* and *Tick, Tick . . . Boom*. For writing stories for our generation. For giving voice to those who are unseen and unheard. For music that sent electricity up and down my spine and expanded my capacity to feel. And thank you, Jonathan, for taking a chance on a young producer who had big ideas and big dreams.

THE DAY AFTER

WHEN I WAKE UP on Monday morning, I do what I do every day: Eat a bagel and Grape Nuts, drink orange juice and tea, and read the *New York Times* while simultaneously listening to NPR. But today is different because instead of consuming the news, I'm making the news. Both outlets lead with stories about our victories. After getting dressed, I take the train to Times Square. The office is like my backyard woodshed: a place for work, play, and adventure. My whole life has been preparation for producing *Rent*.

In the months after the opening, Mom and Dad get a new personalized license plate for their car. It has four letters: R E N T. They also get a new home. Their security and well-being are essential to me and I'm happy to finally take care of them. Mom still works filling prescriptions at a hospital pharmacy. Her feet and back sometimes ache, but she enjoys the camaraderie of her coworkers, and the job gives her a reason to get out of the house every day. Dad is on disability and works part-time greeting customers at Meijer's Thrifty Acres. We don't talk on the phone a lot, but he regularly writes letters describing his progress and his interest in my life:

> *It has finally, truly, SUNK-IN! A steady blood sugar is the*
> *GOAL . . . . . . I'm still very, very interested in your HAPPENINGS—*
> *Post me, Love Dad.*

Warmth, intellect, and humor come through his words on the page in a way that's impossible in person. It's as if the real Mark Seller has found a way to break through his memory loss and diabetes. This new form of communication unlocks new affection for him. Over the next fifteen years I will collect hundreds of his letters.

Oh, I buried the lede: I also get a new address. My romance with Riverside Drive, which started ten years ago when I saw the movie *Parting Glances*, leads me to an apartment *on* Riverside Drive at Seventy-eighth Street in which the summer sunset washes my bedroom with glorious orange light. I don't yet have a boyfriend with whom I can run through the park, but I will work on that.

Walking up Broadway after work on a warm night in August, I look in the windows at Tower Records and see that the *Rent* recording is their #1 album. The show is sold out for the rest of the year. The first national tour opens in Boston in November. When I reach Seventieth Street, I stop in front of David's Cookies. Standing here ten years ago, right after moving to New York, I looked up at the old apartment buildings and imagined being a producer on Broadway, living on the Upper West Side. The buildings are the same tonight, but my vantage point is different. I'm not outside looking in. For the first time in my life, I'm inside looking out.

It's a long way from Cardboard Village, where I return one spring day years later. I pull up in front of the house on Redwood to find a middle-aged man sitting outside in a plastic chair smoking a cigarette.

I get out of my car and gently walk toward him. I say hello and tell him I once lived here. He welcomes me warmly and explains that he has a hard time with English. He's Arabic. He gestures for me to come inside to meet his family. I'm hesitant to intrude, but he insists.

I step into the living room where my family and I watched *60 Minutes*; where Dad exploded in tears of rage and hurt; where Mom told me she was pregnant; where we ran for the "spray" and dodged Dad's farts; where Naomi Lippa, Andrew's mom, sewed the dresses that paid for her family to have a better life. Today there's another lady: She's listening to a cassette tutorial on English. Two young women, her daughters, are working on laptops. They explain to me that they are students at Wayne State University, and that their family immigrated from Iraq, escaping the recent war. This house is their haven, their launching pad to a better life. For them, this house is good. They are grateful.

I get into my rental car and look back one more time. This house is where I'm from. Where I climbed the maple tree in the backyard and pictured soaring through the sky; where I wrote *Adventureland*; where I listened to *Pippin*, *Evita*, and *Dreamgirls*; where I imagined a better life in the theater. Cardboard Village was my launching pad. And for that, I too am grateful.

ACT THREE

Chapter Twenty-Eight

UNLIKELY

October 16, 2023

I turned fifty-nine years old today.

It's been twenty-eight years since Rent *opened on Broadway. That was fast.*

I ask myself, Where am I? *which really means,* Where have I been, where am I now, and where am I going?

I had a loving, complicated, long-term relationship that recently ended. My former partner, Josh, and I raised two wonderful children who are now young adults. My own existential question—where do I come from?—was answered when I searched for my biological family and had powerful, emotional visits with relatives.

Sitting at my desk looking out the window on Riverside Drive, I watch the sharp waves of the Hudson River flicker under an autumn sun that's turning the maple leaves waxy spotted yellow. The beautiful avenue with which I fell in love in 1987 has been my street for many years. The Hamilton fountain, a marble watering trough for horses that was gifted to New York City by a great-grandson of Alexander Hamilton, is steps from my front door, which is a long way from Cardboard Village.

After all these years, I've come to believe that my life and career were unlikely.

My birth mother might have had an abortion instead of placing me for adoption. The career path for a theater kid from Oak Park who excelled at English and social studies but was crummy at math and science should have been a teacher, lawyer, or journalist.

Becoming a gay dad to two unique, kind people in the first few years of the twenty-first century was unlikely.

Rent, *a musical about downtown bohemians—gays, lesbians, drug addicts—seeking love, joy, and meaning in the age of AIDS was unlikely.*

Avenue Q, *a musical puppet show, was unlikely.*

In the Heights, *a passionate family musical about a tight-knit community of Dominicans, Puerto Ricans, and Cubans, all sung to the music of rap and salsa, was unlikely.*

And Hamilton, *a musical about America's first treasury secretary, was unlikely.*

All won the Tony Award for Best Musical and found wide audiences.

The greatest producer-director in modern Broadway history, Hal Prince, whose successes stretched from The Pajama Game *in 1953 to* The Phantom of the Opera *in 1988, fervently believed in luck, which is perhaps the sister of unlikely. Since the opening of* Rent *in 1996, I've been lucky to call myself a Broadway producer, a spouse, and a parent.*

What follows are reflections on some of the unlikely experiences that helped shape the last twenty-eight years.

Chapter Twenty-Nine

"*AVENUE Q TONY COUP*"

I N THE SPRING OF 2000, I received a call from my friend Robyn Goodman, who presented the original two-night engagement of Jonathan's *Boho Days* at Second Stage in 1990. "I just saw a reading at BMI"—the musical theater workshop for developing writers—"of something called *Avenue Q*," she said. "It's inventive and full of potential. And the characters are puppets!"

"It's a puppet show?"

"It's a musical with puppets. Just go."

The creators presented a reading in the basement theater of the church under the Citicorp building on Lexington Avenue. I showed up and sat in the back next to the great Freddie Gershon, owner of Music Theatre International, the largest licensor of musicals. The creators, two guys named Bobby Lopez and Jeff Marx, welcomed the audience and explained that they were developing a TV variety show, kind of like *Sesame Street* for adults. Out came a troupe of young performers with vivid puppets on their arms who looked vaguely like Muppets.

A puppet named Nicky had a roommate named Rod. They were parodies of Bert and Ernie. Nicky was a free spirit, Rod a fastidious closet case. Nicky began a simple song encouraging Rod to come out:

If you were gay, that'd be okay.
I mean cuz, hey, I'd like you anyway.

Because you see
If it were me
I would feel free to say
That I was gay
(But I'm not gay).

Sung by a puppet, the song made me laugh so hard I literally fell off my chair. In the next sketch, the entire company owned up to their own biases in a song called "Everyone's a Little Bit Racist." I was roaring again. These guys were eliciting laughs through puppets who told simple truths that no human was willing to say out loud. A character called Trekkie Monster, a parody of Cookie Monster, sang "The Internet Is for Porn" with the closing couplet, "grab your dick and double click." Sheer laughter. These puppets surprised and transported me.

I stuck around to meet the authors, Jeff and Bobby, after the show. Jeff greeted me and reminded me that he, too, went to Michigan, then called Bobby over. "You guys are hysterical and I'm really lucky I was here tonight," I said. "This is an ingenious show."

"Wow, thank you," said Jeff. "We really admire your work."

"I don't do TV but if you ever decide you would like to make it into a musical, give me a call. I'm interested."

They called the next day.

Kevin had not seen it, so I invited them to the office to talk, and reached out to Robyn to see if she wanted to work together. She was enthusiastic. On the day of the meeting, Bobby and Jeff arrived along with their puppet creator and performer, Rick Lyon, who had a very chatty and persuasive Trekkie on his arm. Trekkie seduced Kevin in about two minutes.

"OK, we're doing this show," said Kevin.

We were off and running but we didn't yet have a musical. We had a series of sketches about young New Yorkers who lived on a fictional Avenue Q somewhere in Brooklyn or Queens. The characters were wildly different from the characters in *Rent*—nerdy, square, not cool, but they

also shared similar questions: They were young people in New York trying to figure out what to do with their lives. They were in search of
meaning. The guys needed to transform a variety show with a theme
into a musical with a plot.

"I loved every one of your funny songs. But comedy songs won't
sustain a whole musical. You gotta write a story," I said.

"We get it. And we can do that," said Jeff.

"And here's another big question: Can you write a love song?"

When they came back with "There's a Fine, Fine Line," I knew we
had the beginnings of a musical.

They continued collaborating with the man who wrote their
sketches. He was a veteran of *Sesame Street* and a good guy. Six months
later, in early 2001, we planned a reading.

Readings are tough. We rely on them for development, and yet the
audiences are a combination of people who are *too* supportive because
they're connected to the show, or *too* judgmental because they are seeking their next investment opportunity. No one is there to simply experience a new show, so I had an idea: "Let's find some people who just
want to be entertained." We handed out flyers around the TKTS booth
inviting folks to attend a free reading from the producers of *Rent* and
recruited about fifty people, a real audience.

Their vocal reactions and body language were clear. They loved the
songs. New ones like "For Now" were winners and elicited squeals of
delight. But the silence during the long book scenes was deadening. The
audience went limp. As a result, there was no momentum. The energy
went up and down, up and down, which is not what you want. You want
up, up, up, climax, and a whoosh down.

Reading the audience is one of the essential talents and skills of
being a theater creator. Can you watch and listen to the audience and
understand what they're feeling? They don't tell you. They show you.
Are you honest enough to admit when they don't like it? That night at
Avenue Q was a good example of reading the audience.

One potential investor showed up and said, "I liked it but I just don't know who the show is for." When he left, I turned to Robyn and said, "Not him."

Meeting with Bobby and Jeff after the reading, we were gentle but clear: "We need to find a playwright to write a book as brilliant as your songs." With pain, they agreed. Peter Franklin, an agent at William Morris who represented many artists from Terrence McNally and Arthur Laurents to Steve Flaherty and Lynn Ahrens, recommended a young writer named Jeff Whitty who had created an unproduced parody of *The Laramie Project* called *The Plank Project*. Reading it, I howled with laughter for the second time that year. After a series of meetings with Jeff and Bobby, this new team forged ahead.

Our last addition was director Jason Moore, the resident director on *Les Misérables*. He came in with an ingenious concept for staging *Avenue Q*. He spoke with inspiration and insight about integrating puppets and real people onstage in a simple way. He listened to the authors' ideas and expanded upon the possibilities inherent in the piece. He won our trust.

The show started to click at a two-week workshop at the O'Neill National Music Theater Conference in Connecticut. Except for the opening number, most of the other pieces of the puzzle were in place, including a new song for Princeton, the protagonist, called "Purpose," which expressed the major dramatic question with a winning melody. It was a classic "I Want" song—it told the audience the motivation of the leading character. Think "If I Were a Rich Man" from *Fiddler on the Roof* or "One Song Glory" from *Rent*. It set the path for the entire show.

We left the O'Neill still needing an opening number, our version of "Tradition" from *Fiddler on the Roof*. About a month later, Jeff and Bobby sent us a tape of "It Sucks to Be Me." They used the melody from the last song in the show, "For Now," for a new lyric, "It sucks to be me," which adroitly introduced the community of *Avenue Q* and relayed the overall theme. Thus, the first melody of the show was also the last melody. When you hear it at the end, it's already familiar.

We forged a partnership with the Vineyard and the New Group to produce it off-Broadway in March 2003. The production cost 400,000 dollars (twice the cost of *Rent* at New York Theatre Workshop in 1996). Kevin, Robyn, and I contributed 250,000 dollars in what is called an "enhancement" because we were paying for a large portion of the production but earning none of the box office revenue. In return, we owned the commercial rights and all the physical assets of the production, which in our case meant the puppets—the largest line item in the budget. These deals had become essential for the development of new musicals. No resident theater company could afford to mount a musical on its own. As with *Rent*, we imagined it as an off-Broadway show that would play in a five-hundred-seat theater, like *Little Shop of Horrors*.

And, like *Rent*, we watched the show over and over during previews and read the audience, which delighted in the characters, the music, and the story of *Avenue Q*. We realized that, although this is a small musical, it's about big things: "What am I going to do with my life?" was the major dramatic question. The final song, or anthem, "For Now," felt ambitious enough to gain a wider audience. Though I originally feared that a show with puppets would not play to the back of a large theater, I was wrong. These puppets had human-sized heads, with eyes, noses, and mouths that were bigger. Made of felt, with vivid and simple colors, they had more contrast, less detail. In fact, they were easier to see than human heads. This revelation prompted the question: Could these puppets play Broadway? Kevin liked to say that the audience told us where to go. He was right.

But first we had to open off-Broadway. The review in the *New York Times* was warm, fuzzy, and affectionate, appropriate for a musical starring puppets; however, it was not a rave that had "Broadway" written all over it. It appeared the day after the United States invaded Iraq and was buried on page five of the Arts section.

We weren't discouraged. Our guts told us this show could find an audience on Broadway, that we could sell five thousand seats a week, which would be the minimum necessary to sustain a run. We rented the Golden Theatre, an intimate playhouse with one balcony, and planned to open in late July. The capitalization was the same as *Rent* seven years earlier, 3.5 million dollars. Drew and his colleagues at SpotCo created a great logo inspired by the NYC subway graphic, and our first full page ad featured a photo of Trekkie Monster on a train. It was a unique, cheeky ad. We wrapped $22,000, or about four hundred tickets. That's not a lot of tickets when you're performing eight shows a week in a theater that holds eight hundred people.

Sales did not improve.

We started previews in July 2003 with a $220,000 advance (the value of all tickets sold for future performances). That was less than half of one week's capacity. By comparison, *Rent* started previews with a $3.5 million advance. We "papered" the house, which meant giving away five hundred tickets every night. The mission of our marketing team was to fill the seats with the right people—young people who would relate to the story and stimulate word of mouth.

Though the audiences weren't paying, they were having a raucous time. Playing to about seven hundred people per night meant more laughs, bigger applause, huge responses. It was rare for a musical comedy to sustain laughs during both the songs and the scenes. In the case of *Avenue Q*, the laughs were equally big in both.

Over the next two weeks, our daily wrap doubled every two days. It was like lighting a campfire with two sticks. Rub them together enough, and you just might catch a flame. Daily sales rose from $8,000 to $15,000 to $35,000 to $50,000. That meant that word of mouth was working. People were telling their friends, "Go see this." If we sold $50K per day for seven days, that equaled $350K and that's what our show cost to run every week. That was breaking even. But we were hardly a hit.

When the *New York Times* critic Ben Brantley returned to see the show on Broadway, his enthusiasm for the show grew: He compared the song "Purpose" to "Something's Coming" from *West Side Story* and called it a "breakthrough musical." Sales increased, but only modestly. We started doing 70 percent business. We were making a modest profit of about $60–70K every week (the profit is used to pay off the $3.5 million capitalization; thus sixty weeks of $60K would pay off $3.6 million).

It wasn't accelerating like a hit, and we assumed it was because people thought it was a puppet show for kids. Our advertising campaign tried to show our funny bone. Every ad said, "Warning, Full Puppet Nudity." Our mission was to inform consumers that it's a show for adults that would reveal something about their lives *and* make them laugh their asses off. After running for about twelve weeks, the advance finally broke a million dollars. A hit musical would normally have an advance greater than five million.

We continued to wrestle with the problem of what we called "puppet prejudice." This is what we knew: The show was great. The reviews were stellar. The *New Yorker* hired Richard Avedon to do a photo shoot with our puppets and actors. Word of mouth was growing ticket sales, one small step at a time. The advertising campaign was funny, irreverent. Only one other tool would propel us over the top.

Winning the Tony Award for Best Musical.

We were the first new musical to open in the 2003–04 season with about four more on the way. Rosie O'Donnell was producing a musical called *Taboo* about Boy George that had already run in a fringe theater in London. The rising movie star Hugh Jackman was coming to Broadway in a musical about Peter Allen called *The Boy from Oz*. A new musical comprising Jerome Kern songs called *Never Gonna Dance* was trying to emulate the success of *Crazy for You*. And finally, there was the new Stephen Schwartz musical, *Wicked*, which had sold out its pre-Broadway run in San Francisco. The concept was brilliant, it starred Kristin Chenoweth and Idina Menzel, and it had great songs. It was potent. Later, the new musical *Caroline, or Change* by Tony Kushner and Jeanine Tesori would enter the fray after opening at the Public Theater.

We started strategizing in September for an award show in June knowing two things:

1. We were a long shot. Little musicals almost never win the Tony.
2. Opening in July meant we would have to keep the show in voters' minds for ten months. Not easy.

One of our admen, Jim Edwards, hatched an idea to place a satiric ad in the *Times* congratulating every new musical on its opening day. Our puppets would be the welcoming committee. *The Boy from Oz* featured Rod, the gay Republican, under the headline "The Boy from the CLOZET. *Avenue Q* welcomes *The Boy from Oz* to Broadway." For *Wicked* we featured Lucy the Slut with the headline "Meet the Wicked Witch of the Chest." These ads both delighted the theater industry and kept *Avenue Q* top of mind. They reminded anybody who had anything to do with the Tonys—nominators, voters, press—that *Avenue Q* was the funniest show on Broadway. They also reinforced a fundamental pillar of the musical: Puppets can say things and do things that people can't.

By December all five shows had opened, and journalist Michael Riedel was already handicapping the Tonys. *Wicked* had opened on Halloween with mixed to negative reviews, but it didn't matter because the audience loved it and business was growing. It was becoming a blockbuster that grossed more than twice as much as us every week. Riedel proclaimed *Wicked* the easy front-runner. He wasn't wrong.

Tony voters want to vote for hits. They don't want to save a show. We got a big break at the end of 2003 when *Entertainment Weekly*, at its circulation peak, said "AVENUE Q is the #1 show of the year." We put this message on an enormous billboard in Times Square and used it as our primary advertising message for the next six months.

In April we had more good news. With weekly profits in the $70K range, and a few bigger weeks around the holidays, we were on the verge of recouping our initial capitalization. This would prove to the world that we were a Broadway hit. The *New York Times* published an article titled "The Puppets That Made a Profit on Broadway," which reported that *Avenue Q* had recouped after forty weeks.

The Tony season would begin with the nominations the first week in May.

It was 2004, a big election year was upon us between Senator John Kerry and incumbent George W. Bush, whose name was a lyric in the final song of the show—"George Bush is only for now"—which received thunderous applause every night.

"Everybody campaigns, but no one will admit it," I said to the team. "Let's admit it."

"You can't do that," someone said. "It'll backfire."

"You're right, we can't do that, but the puppets can," I said. "It'll be an old-fashioned political campaign."

"I love it," said Vinnie, the creative director. "You know, red, white, and blue, with buttons and bunting and flags."

That concept gave Bobby and Jeff the idea of writing a campaign song about elections that never mentioned Tony Awards, Broadway, or any shows. In their new song, "Rod's Dilemma," Rod had to vote for the rotary club president. He went around to all his friends to seek their advice on whom he should vote for: the cute guy he has a crush on, the most popular person, or the best person for the job. The answer he received was, "Vote your heart," which was the snappy chorus. That was the message we wanted to convey to the Tony voters.

THE TONY SEASON IS a race for publicity, votes, and ultimately gold medallions. The show that received the most nominations would be the lead of every news story all over the country. We knew we wouldn't get the most nominations because our designs were modest next to the bigger shows. *Wicked* would win the most.

The same day the nominations were announced, we sponsored a lunch at John's Pizza on West Forty-fourth Street for presenters from all over the country—the people who bring the national tours to their cities. They were also Tony voters. Then and there, we kicked off our "political campaign." The restaurant was decorated with the red, white, and blue banners and bunting like a Democratic National Convention. We passed out buttons with slogans like "Don't Suck, Vote for Q." And the cast of *Avenue Q* performed the new original song, "Rod's Dilemma," which surprised and delighted the crowd. We handed out the CD to all the presenters as they departed and sent it to all 750 Tony voters.

Wicked's ten nominations dominated the twenty-four-hour news cycle. But every day thereafter *Avenue Q* was in the conversation. The industry assumption that "*Wicked* will win for sure" changed to "Could *Avenue Q* beat *Wicked*?"

Broadway pros live for the Tony Awards. To say we all work hard on our shows is an understatement. They become our children, our lovers, our best friends. They become our lives. We fight for their success, and we want to win. It's not just business. It's our emotions, our hearts (no pun intended), our self-esteem. While our heads might say, "the Tony Awards don't matter; it's just a game," we don't believe it. We feel it, live it, breathe it. Rightly or wrongly, we perceive the Tony Award as the affirmation of our efforts.

The co-lead producer of *Wicked*, David Stone, was one of my best friends in our twenties. We worked together at the Weissler office. I went to Passover seder at his mother's home and slept in his brother's bunk bed. David was at my thirtieth birthday party and received a small percentage of *Rent*. I had admired Stephen Schwartz since seeing *Pippin* in the eighth grade and listened to its album every day. I loved *Godspell* in high school and attended every community theater production I could find. Years later, he invited me to the first reading of *Wicked*, after which he asked me for my observations. While I never talked to either man during this period, tension wafted through the air, and everyone felt it.

I was in the park one afternoon in late May with my two kids—May (aged nineteen months) and Tommy (an infant in a stroller)—when I received a call from my press agent, Sam Rudy, who was reporting a challenging development. Insiders were whispering that our song was causing a "backlash" and that any chance we had of winning even one Tony for Best Original Score was kaput. Juggling a press agent, a toddler, and an infant, I lost track of the toddler and started running around furiously to find her. I was panicked that she had been kidnapped while I was trying to win a Tony. She turned up on a slide nearby and I realized that this competition was taking over my mind.

Two days before the Tony Awards, dozens of media outlets made predictions. A site called Gold Derby aggregated many opinions, and said *Wicked* had a one hundred percent chance of winning the Tony Award for Best Musical. Another site listed the predictions of twenty different publications. All twenty said *Wicked* would win. The *New York Times* said *Wicked* would win.

My heart and my head were at odds. Kevin wouldn't accept it, which reflected his indomitable fighting spirit. He was always optimistic, even when the world was indicating otherwise.

The Tony weekend often coincided with one of the Triple Crown horse races—the Belmont in Queens. The day before the Tonys, a long-shot horse named Birdstone won. Kevin called me.

"Did you see Belmont?" he asked.

"What's that?"

"The horse race. It's the last race in the Triple Crown."

"Kevin, do you think I was watching a fucking horse race?"

"The horse won against 36–1 odds," he said.

"That's worse than our chances," I said.

"I'm telling you, this is a sign."

"From your mouth," I replied.

The phone rang again.

"It's David."

I was a little shocked that the producer of *Wicked* was calling. "How are you feeling?" I said.

"I just want you to know I don't trust any of these predictions that say *Wicked*'s gonna win."

"David, less than ten years ago, we sat in your apartment and talked about how impossible it would be to ever produce a Broadway musical. And look where we are now, getting ready for the Tony Awards because we both produced hit shows."

"This isn't easy," he said.

"It's what we came for."

"Easy for you to say, you already have your Tony."

"And you'll have one tomorrow. I'll just be happy if Bobby and Jeff win a Tony for Best Score and we put a great number on national TV."

"We'll see."

"David, try to enjoy this. It's supposed to be fun."

"See you tomorrow," he said and hung up.

Walking to our seats at Radio City Music Hall, I ran into the president of the Broadway League, Jed Bernstein. "It's going to be a good night," he said to me, smiling. I asked myself, *Why did he say that? Was that also a sign?* I had no idea if the president of the League was privy to the winners. But it made me feel like he was secretly telling me that *Avenue Q* was going to win the Tony.

We all sat down. Kevin and his wife, Lynnette, were on the aisle, followed by Robyn and her partner (and our set designer) Anna Louizos, then Josh, and me. Hugh Jackman, the host, began the opening number, "One Night Only," from *Dreamgirls*. He danced with the Rockettes and brought out the casts of every musical, including our puppets. It was a blast. It reminded me that I was a participant in the biggest night on Broadway and I was surrounded by everything I love. That was the first time I cried that night.

A half hour in, Harvey Fierstein entered to present the Tony for Best Book of a Musical. My heart started beating as fast as if I were on a run. He told the tried-and-true joke that a hit musical is always the work of the composer, but the flop is always the fault of the book writer. Then he turned to the nominees. He was focused and fast.

"And the 2004 Tony goes to Jeff Whitty, for *Avenue Q*."

Shocked and thrilled, Kevin and I looked at each other and, in that moment, said to ourselves, *We're gonna win the Tony.*

Fifteen minutes later, in a canny act of theatrical opposites, LL Cool J appeared with Carol Channing. At eighty-four years old, she was still all glasses, sequins, and legs. In her effervescent, inimitable gravelly voice, Carol, with LL, announced the nominees for Best Score. Then LL Cool J opened the booklet, looked down, and said, "And the American Theater Wing's Tony Award goes to *Avenue Q*."

Bobby and Jeff rushed to the stage like two college kids and had a brief hugfest with LL and Carol.

"When we started writing *Avenue Q* four years ago, Jeff was an intern, and I was a temp. Our lives kind of sucked and we wrote a show about people whose lives kind of suck," said Bobby.

"But things get better. LL and Carol just gave us a Tony Award," said Jeff. The crowd roared.

Over the next hour we lost the next three awards, though I was thrilled when Idina Menzel won Best Actress in a Musical for *Wicked*.

Our Tony number, "It Sucks to Be Me," was the last nominated musical to perform. CBS didn't want to put words like "suck" in the nine-to-ten p.m. hour. It received a funny and spirited introduction by Jimmy Fallon and looked great on the TV monitors, thanks to our director, Jason Moore, who staged it like a song on *The Muppet Show*. We asked the cast to hang out backstage after the number just in case we won for Best Musical. "If we win the Tony you're coming out with the puppets," I said. I was thinking about the best visual images for news stories the next day.

Producing a new musical necessitates waiting for the last award of the night, which comes around 10:58 p.m. It's thrilling, it's exhausting, it's nerve-racking. Nathan Lane and Sarah Jessica Parker arrived at the microphone center stage, holding the black booklet that contained the winner. He made a joke about Donald Trump and then they compared their crushes on Hugh Jackman. I felt like I was going to have a heart attack. Sarah Jessica Parker announced the nominees. Nathan Lane said, "And the 2004 Tony Award for Best Musical goes to . . ." He opened the book; he looked down, he paused for a tiny sliver of a second. With a face of surprise, he said, "*Avenue Q*."

I was floored and jubilant. This win felt like the greatest victory of my career.

The audience stood up. The puppets converged on us. In the *New*

York Times the next day was a photo of Robyn and me on stage at Radio City being hugged by a puppet of my likeness that leading actor John Tartaglia was holding. The headline: "*Avenue Q* Tony Coup Is Buzz of Broadway." In the end it was the ingenious songwriters who conceived the show and labored over its creation who handed us our most potent campaign tool.

This was not supposed to happen. It was unlikely.

It ran six years on Broadway and another nine years off-Broadway. It played in Vegas for a year and toured for four years. I called it "a perfect musical" because it was a flawless execution of its goal—to be the *Sesame Street* for adults. The book, music, and lyrics were in perfect sync. Every scene, every song, every character was an inspired manifestation of the central theme.

I'm often asked why I only produce unconventional musicals.

It's true that I developed a specific aesthetic awareness from an early age. I was attracted to contemporary music and stories, not to traditional, old-fashioned music and stories. The second musical I saw was *Pippin* and, though the story was from the Middle Ages, it was told through contemporary gestures, ideas, and music. Under Bob Fosse's direction, it was the epitome of the modern musical. The next show I fell in love with was *A Chorus Line*, which was a breakthrough musical for many reasons, one of which was that it was about real people revealing intimate truths. You can draw a line from the first musical I ever saw—a teenage theater troupe's contemporary rock musical of Rumpelstiltskin called *Rump*— to *Rent*. It's also noteworthy that three of my four Tony Award–winning Best Musicals were contemporary, and the fourth, *Hamilton*, used contemporary music and gesture; all four took place in New York City.

But I don't look for unconventional musicals. I look for musicals to fall in love with. I'm looking to cry, to have the hair on my arms stand up, to hear something aurally different than anything I've heard before, to laugh my ass off. I'm looking to be surprised. I have no idea what the audience will like. At the end of the day my hope is that, if I love it, then others will love it as well.

Chapter Thirty

CAN WE DO BETTER?

WHILE *AVENUE Q* WAS in previews in the summer of 2003, our sound designer Nevin Steinberg ran into Kevin on the 1 train and told him about a reading he was working on that he thought had potential. A group of guys from Wesleyan University were developing a new musical called *In the Heights* and were presenting their early draft at a small theater on Forty-second Street. Kevin showed up, sensed an energy in the room, and called my cell phone.

"Hey."

"Where are you?" he asked.

"I'm standing on Forty-second Street."

"Me too. I'm at the Fairbanks. There's this reading and I'm pretty sure something cool is about to happen and I think you need to get over here right now."

"I think I'm getting bronchitis," I said. "I feel like shit but I'm on my way to see *Zanna, Don't!* It's supposed to be sweet."

"Can't you just come here instead?"

"They know I'm coming. That would be rude."

My mistake.

Kevin was mesmerized by a young man named Lin-Manuel Miranda who was playing the narrator of his own musical about Washington Heights, and the eclectic score that wrapped rap music around salsa, merengue, and Broadway pop.

The next day, Kevin said, "We're doing this show. I saw Roy Furman"—a colleague and producer—"there and his daughter, Jill, and Jill and I decided we'd do it together."

"We'll see," I said. Kevin was like the father who came home every day with a new pet. Most didn't last.

A week later, a gaggle of young guys who looked like they were still in college crammed onto the couch in Kevin's office. He introduced me to the author, Lin-Manuel, a kid with a baseball cap on his head; his director, Tommy Kail, a guy with so many curls that he could audition for *Annie*; and their partners. They were winning and charming.

"So, what's your story?" I asked.

"We have a little theater company in the basement of the Drama Book Shop," said Tommy. "They give us the space for free."*

"Smart," I said. "What's it called?"

"Back House Productions."

"How did you guys meet?" I asked.

"We went to Wesleyan together. After Lin graduated, I asked him to play me the score of his musical, and then I offered to develop it here."

"We've been working on it for the last year," said Lin.

"How do you make ends meet?" I asked.

"I'm a substitute teacher at Hunter," said Lin.

These guys reminded me of Andrew, Jonathan, and me.

Kevin started working on the show with producer Jill Furman, who was also helping the guys produce their improv rap show, *Freestyle Love Supreme*. Lin needed a book writer for *Heights*, and they recruited a young playwright, Quiara Hudes, who recently had an off-off-Broadway success called *Barrio Grrrl!* She and Lin collaborated like loving siblings. Over several months they restructured and expanded the story. When I asked Kevin for updates, he'd say, "Just wait."

---

* In a wonderful "full circle" moment, Lin, Tommy, and I, along with Jimmy Nederlander Jr., bought the Drama Book Shop in 2019 and reopened it with a beautiful new design by David Korins in 2021 post-Covid. Lin still shows up to write in the basement.

In the fall of 2004, we produced a twenty-nine-hour reading, a workshop in which actors, creators, and a music director work together for a week to read and sing the show out loud from music stands. Actors' Equity Association requires that the actors work no more than twenty-nine hours over the course of the week. I sat down in the front row to discover what Kevin was so excited about. I heard the opening syncopated rhythm—*dun dun dun, dundun, dun dun dun, dundun.* An infectious clave. Lin sang,

> *Lights up on Washington Heights, up at the break of day*
> *I wake up and I got this little punk I gotta chase away*
> *Pop the grate at the crack of dawn, sing*
> *While I wipe down the awning, hey y'all, good morning.*

I had no history with rap music. I didn't understand its melodic appeal. I didn't relate to it. But I was instantly transfixed by the warm words of this young man singing "Hey y'all, good morning." Then the sound of a glorious chorus rose behind him, singing "In the Heights, I wake up and start my day"—and I had the visceral response that certified *this is for me.* A sound I had never heard before—rap music surrounded by Broadway choral music—pricked my ears. Invigorating, stimulating, and thrilling, its many characters were teeming with heart, humor, and gorgeous music. An infectious song called "96,000," in which everyone in the community fantasized about winning the lottery, bowled me over.

I loved the narrator, Usnavi, played by Lin. I loved the young college student, Nina, portrayed with a sense of warmth and yearning by Mandy Gonzalez. The neighborhood matriarch, a seventy-five-year-old woman named Abuela Claudia, rose from her seat and sang out, as if from a bell tower,

> *Calor . . . calor . . . calor . . .*
> *Ay mama!*
> *The summer's hottest day!*
> *Paciencia y fe! Paciencia y fe!*

At that moment, the musical became next-level—transcending from entertaining and joyous to profound. One of the most gorgeous arias I had ever heard was transpiring in front of me. The struggle of an older Cubana who moved to the city as a young girl, forced to learn a new language, a new culture, a new sensation called winter, and then make a living as a maid, was heart-wrenching. Claudia sang,

Polishing with pride, scrubbing the
Whole of the Upper East Side
The days into weeks, the weeks into years, and here I stayed.

She was like my mother working at Cunningham's Drugs for five dollars an hour so I could have braces. I was overwhelmed with feelings and tears. And then, in a theatrical coup, Abuela Claudia surprised the audience in the final couplet revealing the winning lottery ticket for $96,000. How did a twenty-four-year-old composer understand the life experience of a seventy-five-year-old woman? This was the first time I wondered if Lin's gift was divine. And I'm an atheist.

Our process from that moment forward was to guide Lin, Quiara, and Tommy as they dramatized the best stories of this community. They changed focus, cut characters, scrapped songs, and added new songs.

We solidified our camaraderie with this band of young theater makers at Josh's and my home in Sagaponack, New York, with a weekend getaway of beach time, swimming, and an epic Ultimate Frisbee game in our backyard. Kevin, Lin, and Bill Sherman (our co-orchestrator and Lin's college roommate) played on one team, and Tommy, Alex (Lac) Lacamoire (our music supervisor), and me on the other team. No one was a varsity Frisbee player, but we all played to win. Our producing partner, Jill Furman, hosted us at her parents' home for a beautiful dinner.

Another residency at the Eugene O'Neill National Music Theater

Conference proved essential. Part of the process at the O'Neill was for another composer to see the show and conduct a notes session with the creators. The O'Neill asked Andrew Lippa, who said to Lin, "You don't have one song in three, every song is in four. You need more variety."

Lin was both annoyed and inspired by the challenge. He wrote "Breathe."

The question that I asked over and over through this process: "Can we do better?" The show needed to go deeper in dramatizing Nina's challenges as a working-class Latina in the white affluent world of Stanford University. It needed to strengthen her relationship with Benny, a childhood friend who didn't go to college. And it needed songs from the parents to express their motivations and conflicts. We planned to open in early 2007 in a new off-Broadway theater complex called 37 Arts on West Thirty-seventh Street and Tenth Avenue. Kevin and I were co-owners of the complex.

In the Heights opened in early February to a warm review from Charles Isherwood in the *New York Times*. "Light and sweet are actually just the words to describe this amiable show, which boasts an infectious, bouncy Latin-pop score by a gifted young composer, Lin-Manuel Miranda."

The other reviews were fine, if less enthusiastic, and the show's sales were fragile—slow but steady. "Amiable and bouncy" didn't sell many tickets. Daily sales improved by single digits. To use the phrase "building momentum" would be overstatement. We consistently sold about three hundred seats in a house of five hundred. Every morning, right after yoga class, I checked the wrap and said to myself, *Come on, can't we sell a few more seats?* Checking wraps immediately after a hot yoga class was a bad idea.

Word of mouth was spreading slowly and softly, not unlike the first months of *Avenue Q*. If the sales weren't yet encouraging, the makeup of our audience was: middle-aged and older Jewish ladies at Saturday matinees; young couples who consistently raised their flip phones like lighters during "Blackout"; more Latinos than I'd ever seen in a theater before, thanks to the sales efforts of Lin's dad, Luis Miranda, who was a longtime political consultant, media owner, and Latino community leader.

The general manager complained to me one day that the afternoon performance was interrupted when a teenager eating too much candy threw up during the first act. He was part of a large group of teens and tweens celebrating a bar mitzvah.

"You're telling me this kid's bar mitzvah party was at our show?"

"Yes."

"This show can run on Broadway," I said.

"What do you mean?"

"It's teenagers, it's matinee ladies, young couples, Latinos. Our job is to get more of each of those groups. Our audience is wide; now we gotta make it deep."

A new musical from off-Broadway with nice reviews, no name recognition, no stars. When Kevin and I went to see Jimmy Nederlander to book one of his theaters, he said, "Boys, I haven't seen the show, and you know I love you, but they tell me it's a flop. For Christ's sake, it's only doing 60 percent business."

"We know, Jimmy. But we'll get an audience on Broadway," said Kevin.

"What you need is a star. Can't you get Chita?"

"That's not what we do, Jimmy. This is like *Rent*."

"Well, that worked out for us," he said.

"And this will too," I said.

"I don't have a theater, boys, I'm sorry."

"We were hoping for the Rodgers," said Kevin.

"Marc Platt's doing *Pal Joey*. How do I turn down a show by Richard Rodgers?"

What he also meant was, how does he turn down the coproducer of *Wicked*, Marc Platt? We felt betrayed. Nederlander made a fortune from *Rent*. We rehabilitated the derelict Nederlander Theatre. Bottom line: They made even more money from *Wicked* and Marc Platt, which meant he got first dibs. No yelling or screaming. We knew we would make new deals on new shows in the future.

Time to scramble. The Shuberts offered us the Imperial, but we would have to move out after six months to make way for *Billy Elliot*. They guaranteed we could move to the Longacre, which was not a good theater for musicals—two balconies and not enough seats in the orchestra. This was a poor solution. Moving a show from one theater to another would cost a million dollars and force us to suspend performances for two weeks. With no other options, we agreed.

After closing off-Broadway in July, we regrouped and prepared for a Broadway opening in February. It was the biggest new musical we had produced—bigger cast and bigger orchestra, which meant the weekly break-even would be higher; we had to sell more tickets than *Avenue Q* or *Rent* to pay our weekly expenses.

We knew advertising would be essential to building a new brand. Re-enter Drew Hodges, our advertising guru. While we would do traditional things like direct mail and a full-page ad in the *New York Times*, we needed to make a splash. Every day, we talked about ways to reach our audience. Drew had a motto: "To pierce the veil of indifference," which I posted on the board behind my desk.

A fantastic TV spot would reach the widest possible audience. It was (and still is) hard to shoot a TV commercial in the theater and make it not look hokey. We decided to shoot on location on 185th Street in Washington Heights.

Lin said, "We've got this beautiful neighborhood, why not use it?" Our corner had a bodega, a fire escape, and a wide avenue for dancing.

He and his music team, Alex Lacamoire and Bill Sherman, took three different songs from the show, "In the Heights," "When You're Home," and "Finale," and, in his words, "squished them together into thirty seconds of greatest hits coming at you."

We made something that looked like this:

As the sun rises over the George Washington Bridge, Lin juts down the aisle of a bodega singing "Lights up on Washington Heights." He opens his door, and the screen explodes with children running by and the ensemble dancing to the opening chorus. Some extraordinary jumps by dancer Seth Stewart lead to water blasting from a fire hydrant as the whole company dances in the street to Chris Jackson singing the refrain of "When You're Home." It ends with fireworks and the final words of the show, "you're home."

Then we got lucky. *Pal Joey* canceled. Nederlander offered us the Richard Rodgers Theatre and the Shuberts were gracious in letting us off the hook.

We launched our campaign with the kinetic, colorful, sexy commercial. The dazzling visuals worked if you were at the gym and couldn't hear it. The catchy music worked if you were in the kitchen and couldn't see it. It expressed how the show would make you feel, which was the mission. It sold tickets, which meant playing to at least a thousand people a night during previews. Once fifty thousand people have seen a musical, it's on its own trajectory—it will either succeed or fail based on the word of mouth generated in those early weeks. Thus, the job of the producer is to find the first fifty thousand.

While advertising kicked in, we still faced the question "Can we do better?"

Lin returned to my house that summer to work on the show. He expanded and enriched "Carnaval del Barrio" to make it a more rewarding production number and wrote the mother's song in Act Two, "Enough." When our next-door neighbor Kurt Vonnegut stopped by one afternoon for an informal lunch, I asked Lin to play him the opening number. Kurt's response: "He's better than Dylan."

Some journalists compared the show to *West Side Story* because it also portrayed the lives of Puerto Ricans. I didn't agree and thought the comparison lazy. I argued that we were actually doing *Fiddler on the Roof.* I handed every member of the creative team a book called *The Making of a Musical,* by Richard Altman, who was Jerome Robbins's assistant director on *Fiddler on the Roof.* It was an excellent handbook for a young team of musical makers. In one chapter, Altman described how Robbins transformed the song "To Life" into a showstopper. I read the section to the team and said, "See how he did 'To Life'? Do that with '96,000.'" And that is, indeed, what choreographer Andy Blankenbuehler did in the transition from off-Broadway to Broadway.

I met Andy Blankenbuehler when he was in the first class of Dance Break in 2001, a workshop created by the Society of Directors and Choreographers to give visibility to young choreographers. He staged a number from *Parade*, which I didn't like when I saw the first production in 1998 at Lincoln Center Theater. But his choreography was unlike anything I'd seen before. It changed my opinion of what *Parade* could be. He was in the back of my head when we started working with Lin and Tommy, so I brought them to watch him choreograph a class. His work had syncopation, precision, and muscularity. We hired him to choreograph the show, and then gave him a workshop before we went into rehearsal so that he could work with Tommy on the opening number and develop the physical vocabulary of the ensemble. Andy's contribution was like adding the fourth leg of a chair: Dance was as integral to this musical as book, music, and lyrics.

Something happens when an off-Broadway musical moves to Broadway. It breathes, it expands, it grows up. At the Richard Rodgers Theater, with seating that rises like an amphitheater, making it the best house in which to watch choreography, *In the Heights* was funnier, warmer, more infectious.

The answer to the question "Can we do better?" was yes.

The audience response was explosive from the first performance. And the box office grew every week. But it still wasn't a smash like *Wicked* or *Jersey Boys*, the two blockbusters of the decade. It was, in baseball lingo, a "double," which meant it had to win the Tony to continue selling tickets and stay for a long run.

This time, the path was a little clearer because the competition in 2008 wasn't as formidable. Another strong musical called *Passing Strange* moved to Broadway from the Public, but it was unconventional even by my standards. A musical memoir by a powerhouse singer-songwriter named Stew, who also starred in the show, it was an exploration of the making of an artist. A half-dozen excellent costars illuminated his journey that took audiences into the German avant-garde. It would only last for six months.

As the Tony Awards approached, I was once again focused on maximizing press. What photo would be in the papers (and on websites) all over America when they announced the winner for Best Musical? The day before, Kevin and I assembled Lin, Tommy, Chris Jackson, and Seth Stewart at Andy Blankenbuehler's dance studio. Andy staged the moment: Kevin and I would hoist Lin onto our shoulders with the help of Chris and Seth.

"*That* will be the photo for the 2008 Tony Awards."

Indeed.

Chapter Thirty-One

WHO IS MARK BELANGER?

WILL I LIVE MY whole life without ever knowing where I came from? Or more specifically, who I came from?

That question wouldn't stop chasing me as I passed forty years old and became a parent of two beautiful adopted children. Both were open adoptions. Josh and I knew our kids' birth parents. We were present at their births and, when the time was right, our kids would know their origin stories and their biological parents. And yet, I never acted on my own story. I was afraid of being rejected by my biological parents. For the second time.

In 2006, with May turning four and Tommy about to turn three, I decided it was time. The State of Michigan had a long-standing law that all adoption records were sealed in perpetuity. Locked inside a file room in Pontiac, Michigan, was my original birth certificate with the name my birth mother gave me, as well as her name and my birth father's name. I was barred from seeing it. But a new policy was enacted in the late '90s that allowed adoptees and birth parents to request "identifying information" through a court-appointed social worker. Upon receiving the request, the social worker would open the file, contact the other party, and ask if they would like to exchange information. If both agreed, then the social worker made the connection.

I filled out a simple one-page application that was to be mailed to the Oakland County adoption director, Marilyn McAllister. Even though signing the form was easy, placing it in the mailbox was not. It felt like my existence was on the line. My whole life had consisted of interviews, auditions, and applications—for plays, colleges, jobs, apartments, boy-friends. I closed that mailbox lid and realized that everything always seemed to come down to one question: Was I in or out?

Ten days later, sitting at my desk, the receptionist announced, "Jef-frey, Ms. McAllister on line three." What blew through my mind in the short space between the announcement and my answer were past re-ceptionists announcing Jonathan Larson, or my physician Dr. Naiditch calling with HIV results. Blood drained from my head. I inhaled.

I said hello to a woman who exuded the warmth of a kind aunt. Yet I was filled with fear. What if my birth mother said no, she's not willing to talk to or meet me? I once had a friend, also adopted, who discov-ered the name and address of his birth mother. When he showed up at her home, she wouldn't open the door. In the gentlest way possible, Ms. McAllister told me that my biological parents had died. Then she said that I have two half brothers and that she had spoken to one of them, and he was happy to exchange contact information.

"His name is Kevin Belanger," she said.

I started crying at my desk. I have a brother named Kevin and he wants to talk to me? I was so scared of rejection that this sentence from a nice lady named Marilyn felt like a life force shooting through my body. Then she told me that the name given to me at birth was Mark Belanger.

I had a different name? Jeffrey Seller is really Mark Belanger? Or is Mark Belanger really Jeffrey Seller? I felt dizzy.

"Really?" I said. "That's my father's name."

"Well, actually your father's name was Jerry Avison. He was of the Jewish faith, born in Russia in 1911. Unfortunately, he died in 1982."

"No. I mean my father. My real father," I said.

"I know this can be confusing."

"What was my mother's name?" I asked.

"Your mother's name was Barbara Belanger. She was born in 1929. She died in 2002."

"That's a nice name," I said.

"It says here she was Irish and Catholic."

Marilyn gave me Kevin's email address and cell phone number. He lived near Chicago. That my biological brother shared the same name as my longtime business partner and friend was poetic.

"Thank you, Marilyn, you are very kind."

"It makes me feel so good when I can bring people together."

I took a moment to take all this in. *My original birth certificate says my name is Mark*. I shivered thinking about it. What does it mean to be named twice? I had the same name as my adopted father. That's not where the coincidences would end. Soon, I would learn that I had another sibling whose name was Jeffrey.

How do I start a conversation with a brother with whom I've never spoken, and whom I've never known? Kevin made it easy. He was warm and accessible. He expressed pride at my accomplishments and patience with my questions. He enjoyed telling me how much our mother loved theater; that she took him to see *No, No, Nanette* on Broadway when he was young, which was so much fun. He told me that our mother was very pretty and wore beautiful dresses; she loved being taken "out on the town."

"When Marilyn called me, I was kind of, I don't know how to say it, you know, just shocked," said Kevin. "I never even knew mom was pregnant. I guess a six-year-old wouldn't notice, maybe because she was so small. None of it made sense. So I called my aunt Joan and asked her, 'Do I have a younger brother?' And she said yes. So I guess everyone knew but us."

Kevin also knew my birth father, Jerry, who was in a relationship with my mother after her divorce. Kevin had vivid memories of Jerry, who was a frequent guest at their home and sometimes brought Kevin with him to the apartment buildings he owned. Jerry was a self-made, successful builder.

"He would pay me a few bucks to pick up the litter, then take me to his country club, and I got to swim in the pool while he played golf. I remember he had one of those accounts where you can order anything you want. He was a nice guy."

This story made me think about Jerry's achievements and mine. Builders and producers have a lot in common. I was happy to learn that my drive and success may have had a biological component.

When Kevin was around ten years old, he and his (our) mother moved to Long Island, where they lived for a while with Barbara's sister, Aunt Joan.

"I never knew why we left Royal Oak," he said.

"Hold on, you lived in Royal Oak?" I said. "That's like two miles from the house I came home to in Oak Park."

"That's freaky," he said.

"But you said you moved."

"Yeah, Mom took me with her but didn't take Jeff and David, our two older brothers. They went to go live with my dad. We wound up in Rego Park—in Queens—and mom got a job with Chubb. I used to go back to Detroit for summers and that's when our brother Jeff was hit by a car riding his bike on Woodward Avenue. He was so popular, and I remember there were so many kids at his funeral."

"I don't even know how to process that."

"He was the greatest kid."

Kevin and our mom, Barbara, eventually moved to Chicago, where Barbara continued working for Chubb as an underwriter. He wondered if they moved so much because she wasn't happy, because she was lonely. Eventually, she moved again, this time to Phoenix, where she lived again with her sister, Aunt Joan. And that's where she died in her early seventies of heart disease.

Listening to my mother's life story made me feel lightheaded, as if I might faint for the first time in my life. For forty years I knew nothing about this woman, and now I was being flooded with information.

Kevin sent me many photographs. Mom was, indeed, beautiful. I studied her for signs of me. Was I in there? Was I in her eyes, her hair, her hands? Kevin sent me a photo of his high school graduation. He had a mass of long, curly blond hair, just like me at age eighteen. It felt good to look like my mother and brother.

We planned to get together in Phoenix with Aunt Joan and my oldest biological brother, David, who both lived there. Kevin explained he was a bit of a loner. Joan invited us all to her house for dinner.

"Do you think you could maybe go with me?" I asked my partner, Josh. I didn't want to force him—we had two young kids at home.

"Of course, honey. This is huge. I want to be there right next to you."

"I can't believe this is finally happening."

On a Friday in February, we flew to Phoenix and checked into the Frank Lloyd Wright–inspired Biltmore Hotel. This felt like another seminal life event—like my bar mitzvah, or the day I came out to Andrew, or moving to New York. The hard part was over—they acknowledged me. They accepted me into their lives. But I was still churning inside from the anticipation that, in a couple of hours, I would be in the presence, for the first time in my life, of three relatives with whom I share DNA. After forty-plus years, I had finally found my tree.

Joan's condo was a few miles from our hotel. We turned into a bland boxy complex with one dead-end street. Beige stucco attached houses with garages sticking out were on either side of the street. Her unit was on the left. We were ten minutes late.

"You OK?" asked Josh.

"I guess so," I replied.

I knocked. Kevin answered, shook my hand, and greeted Josh and me with a warm smile. The first thing I noticed was that he was taller than me.

"Can we hug?" he said.

"Sure, yeah . . . of course," I replied.

"You two totally look like brothers," Josh said.

"Except I have way less hair," said Kevin.

"Did you get lost?" said Joan, a small, sturdy old woman who walked to the door from the living room. Her face had strong creases; her short hair was still brown. Warm and fuzzy, she was not. David, my oldest brother, came to the door as well and said hello in a sweet, quiet voice.

We walked into a condo shaped like a shoebox—long and narrow. Off the entrance hall was a small alcove leading to two bedrooms that were opposite each other.

"That was your mother's bedroom," said Joan, pointing to the front bedroom.

A small kitchen had a pass-through that opened onto the oval dining room table and living room. Burgundy and beige floral curtains covered the windows, blocking out the dark February night. The apartment was airless, glum except for a lineup of framed photos on the living room wall. In the corner at the far end of the room was a dark recliner.

"You see that chair right there?" said Aunt Joan, pointing. "That's where your mother died."

I scrunched my face. Her words stung; her tone was unkind. There seemed to be pleasure underneath her words.

"I'll bet it was her favorite chair," said Josh. "I wouldn't mind that."

"Heart failure. One minute she's sitting there, next minute she's gone."

"It's sweet that you lived together," said Josh.

"Had nothing for retirement. Where else was she gonna go?"

"That's not exactly what happened," Kevin said gently to me.

"How many times did I have to save Barbara?" said Joan.

Kevin backed off.

Two empty highball glasses sat on the oval wood table. We missed cocktail hour. Joan did not. Cheap white wine was plentiful. David spoke little but drank a lot. He was a little bit chubby and had dark brown, straight hair. I didn't see myself in him, except for his eyes. We shared the exact same shade of blue-green.

"I hope you like pork tenderloin," said Joan. "I know you're Jewish."

"We love pork," said Josh.

"You know, Jerry was Jewish," she said, referring to my birth father.

Josh looked at me as if to say, *Anti-semite?*

"I know," I said. "My parents were also from interfaith marriages."

"Well, it certainly didn't work for Barbara and Jerry."

Josh was scanning the photographs that lined the wall. I followed him. There were many photos of Barbara and Joan—drinking, dancing, having a good time. Cocktails and cigarettes were ubiquitous.

"Joan, what can you tell us about these photos on the wall?" said Josh. "It looks like you and Barbara were the life of the party."

"Well, I'll say this for my sister, she could be a lot of fun. Loved to dress up, you know, the fake jewelry, the hats, the shoes. She was quite a looker."

"Do you have any children, Joan?"

"Nope. Never could. You know, when all this happened, I said, 'Fertile Myrtle, she can't stop getting pregnant.' I told your mother I would adopt you, but she said no."

I didn't know what to say. Buried underneath her bitterness was a small expression of charity and desire. Maybe she wanted me. I looked at Josh, who gently took my hand and squeezed. We sat down for dinner. He put his hand on my knee. He was shielding me.

Aunt Joan poured white wine.

"No thanks," said Josh. "I don't drink."

"Doesn't drink," said Joan, rolling her eyes.

The pork tenderloin was dry, the green beans slimy, which didn't matter to Joan because she wasn't eating. Her dinner was the wine. One empty bottle became two, which became three. We searched for small talk. I asked David some questions about his auditing job at Charles Schwab. Josh talked about our children. Joan didn't ask me any questions.

"From all these beautiful photos it seems like you and our mother were close," I said.

"Well, when your parents pick up and leave, and you're sleeping in the back of a car, you get close."

"What do you mean?"

"They left us—my brother and sister and me. No place to live, it was the Depression. We spent a few months living in the back seat of a car.

332

That's why I think your mother got together with Jerry. He was much older than her, you know. I think she always wanted him to take care of her."

Aunt Joan seemed to be hosting this dinner out of a sense of obligation. Her sour, "tell it like it is" manner was less honest and more cruel. I was starting to feel defensive on behalf of a mother I had never known.

Kevin told sweet stories about growing up with our mother in Royal Oak. He was engaged, affable. Joan continued telling stories that showed how much she resented her sister.

"Your mother was in the hospital, getting her appendix out. I went to see her and there was Jerry visiting. Always Jerry. And she was still married to a different man! And then when she finally divorced her husband and got pregnant, Jerry leaves her. Guess he didn't want kids."

I needed to get out of there. Josh found a way to exit graciously by claiming jet lag. Back at the hotel, I flopped down on the bed and Josh laid down next to me.

"Your brother Kevin is a sweetie pie. Know what, you guys are a lot alike. You're gonna have a very sweet relationship."

"What about her?" I said.

"She's a meanie," said Josh. "She's still angry and jealous of your mother because she was the pretty one. She was the one who made beautiful babies—like you."

"Thank you, honey." Tears had been building behind my eyes since I saw the chair in which my mother died.

"I'm sorry Joan was such a bitch. You know what she was supposed to say? That your mother loved you very much and never stopped loving you. So I'm saying it for her."

"How do you know?" I said, tears streaming down my cheek, breaths getting caught in my chest.

"Because I know you. And she knew you. You are part of her."

"I need you to lay on top of me. Hold me." Embraced by Josh's strong, beautiful body, I felt like I was releasing Joan's bile. He was squeezing the pain out of me while hugging me with his affection.

"I love you," he said. "And your mother loved you."

"I need you to hold me like that. It's exactly why I love you and why I'm so happy you came here with me."

"Honey, I'll always be here with you. It makes me love you more."

Coming home to two cuddly kids jumping into my arms shouting "Daddy" was the antidote for the bombardment of a bitter aunt. Josh was affectionate and understanding. And yet, over the next months I sank—I lay in bed feeling glum and didn't know what to do with myself. It was like someone had died. I was mourning the death of my mother even though I never knew her.

A few months later, I had a wonderful dinner with Kevin and his wife and two kids at his home in suburban Chicago. They attended my shows in Chicago, and I could tell he was proud to say he was my brother. His wife, Nancy, said that my gestures, facial expressions, and movements were "uncanny," just like my mother. My niece talked about how much she loved her grandmother. Knowing that I came from somewhere, from someone—from a pretty, vivacious, independent, and yet, lonely woman named Barbara Belanger helped me feel whole.

Chapter Thirty-Two

THE HAMILTON MIXTAPE

I N 2011 I TOLD Kevin McCollum I wished to end our business partnership. After twenty years, I didn't want to ride a tandem bicycle anymore. I wanted to ride solo. I wanted to make my own decisions and live by them, whether they resulted in success or failure, pleasure or pain. It felt like a natural transition at age forty-seven, which I figured was the halfway point in my career.

I also wanted to streamline my communication with authors and directors. Over many years and many new musicals, I learned that a creator is more responsive to one producer's voice offering suggestions and criticism.

Kevin was hurt by this and, even though I was sure this was what I wanted, it felt like getting a divorce. A separation made even more difficult since it occurred only a few months before Lin was ready to initiate a production plan for *Hamilton*, his new musical inspired by Ron Chernow's biography *Alexander Hamilton*.

I heard the first batch of *Hamilton* songs in the summer of 2010. Lin and his girlfriend and future wife, Vanessa, came out to Sagaponack for a weekend of pool, beach, wonderful meals cooked by Josh, and some epic games of "Celebrity."

On a Monday night, after Vanessa had gone back to town to work, Lin and I had some chicken and ribs at TownLine BBQ, and then returned home, where he shared demos of his new work, *The Hamilton*

Mixtape. With piano, electronic beats, and his voice, Lin played "Alexander Hamilton," "My Shot," and "Right Hand Man." Each song was its own fierce wallop. If the aural landscape of *Heights* was a warm, enveloping Caribbean breeze, then *Hamilton* was a series of theatrical missiles. A Fourth of July fireworks show. One additional song, "Helpless," was a sweet, catchy R&B tune—pure love.

"I want to make an album," he said.

"I'll help you do anything you want," I replied. "If you want me to go raise the money, I'll raise the money. Just keep going."

I didn't hear anything more for a while. Tommy Kail wanted to advance the possibility of a musical. After an extraordinary partnership on *In the Heights*, he was Lin's closest collaborator. In the summer of 2011, he persuaded Lin to accept a one-night booking at Jazz at Lincoln Center's American Songbook cabaret for January of 2012. Tommy figured if he could get him to do two songs a month, they'd have a dozen songs by the new year, plus a compelling case for a stage musical.

In January of 2012 with Alex Lacamoire at the piano and a company of actors that included Chris Jackson, Jon Rua, and James Monroe Iglehart, they performed twelve songs in front of the shimmering glass curtain overlooking Columbus Circle. The electricity and drive of the music, the bullet-like motivation of the title character, and the eclectic score that included "You'll Be Back," sung by Gavin Creel wearing a Burger King crown, proved to me—and everyone in the room—that this was a unique musical in formation.

Stephen Holden wrote the next day in the *New York Times*, "Is 'The Hamilton Mixtape' a future Broadway musical? A concept album? A multimedia extravaganza in search of a platform? Does it even matter? What it is, is hot."

Then, just like I wrote Jonathan a letter in 1990, I also wrote to Lin and Tommy:

Dear Lin and Tommy, though I've expressed to each of you separately my enthusiasm for HAMILTON, I thought it good to tell you both today that if I become your producer, I will be a passionate advocate, cheerleader, sounding board, constructive critic, and barker. I have a new company name: Adventureland. It's the name of the play I wrote in the 4th grade about my two best friends and I journeying through a land filled with fun, danger and plenty of adventure. It was where I wanted to be in the 4th grade and it's where I want to be now. It's where you guys often toil and no doubt it's where Alexander Hamilton traveled for much of his life. I look forward to getting back in a room with both of you to start talking about a new musical. I'm ready.

Best wishes, Jeffrey.

The question was, what did Lin want to do? His answer was to continue writing his musical while developing a "concept album" in the way that Andrew Lloyd Webber made albums first of *Jesus Christ Superstar* and *Evita*.

My job was to say yes, to nurture the artist, not to tell the artist what to do. To be there when the artist asked for suggestions. Twelve years of psychoanalysis taught me to *listen.* Artists want to feel heard. And eventually they are going to say, "What do you think?" This is where a dialogue begins that requires the producer to weigh what to offer and when to offer it. Many practitioners focus on the hard skills of producing—optioning the play, raising the money, booking the theater—but they don't think about the soft skills—giving an author a place to write, making them lunch, showing up without demands or pressure, sending the right note at the right time.

Hiring a book writer was our first discussion because Lin had worked so successfully with Quiara Hudes on *In the Heights.* We gave it a try with a gifted young playwright. It didn't work. When we did our first reading for ourselves, we discovered that every time the actors started talking, the show fell to the ground. The air went out of the balloon. It wasn't the fault of the book writer. This musical just didn't need talking. I called Tommy the next morning. We both agreed that there was a simple answer: "Lin's gotta write the whole thing." With one gulp of gumption, Lin agreed.

We booked a one-week workshop at New York Stage and Film for July of 2013, in which Tommy, Lin, and music director Alex Lacamoire would put together a reading of the first act. The theatrical narrative was compelling and muscular. The piece exploded off the page. I sat next to Andy Blankenbuehler, who was practically choreographing in his chair.

We all agreed that we wanted to open at one of the resident theater companies in New York City, like the way in which *Rent* and *Avenue Q* opened. On a steamy day in August (Yes, another hot day! Why do so many important events take place in summer?), I took Lin and Tommy on what they called their "college tour." We started on the West Side visiting the Atlantic Theater Company, then worked our way to New York Theatre Workshop. By my quiet design, we ended at the Public Theater. As we turned the corner onto Lafayette Street, Oskar Eustis, the artistic director, was standing on the front steps eager to welcome us.

Oskar wanted this show. Passionately. I had quietly fantasized about opening this show in the same place *A Chorus Line* opened. I wanted the history and reputation of the Public to help spark the ball of fire for an original new musical that, at first sight, might seem quixotic. After a tour of the Newman Theatre, and a terrific conversation with Oskar about the scope and power of the show, Lin and Tommy seemed interested. They walked down the steps smiling.

Tommy, Lin, and I went to lunch at Cafe Luxembourg the next day to make a plan. Lin said he wanted to go to the Public provided they could start rehearsal by the end of 2014.

"Lin, you haven't even written Act Two yet," I said. I thought it might be harder to write Act Two because there's no revolution ("Winning is easy, young man, governing is harder"). And I knew how long it took to write Act One—four years.

"Don't worry. I'm writing it at your house this fall," he said.

My job: Say yes!

"Can I please make one suggestion?" I said.

"Of course," said Lin.

"Cut 'the mixtape.' Just call it *Hamilton*."

He smiled. "I'll think about it," he said.

Lin started on a tear—he wrote at home, he wrote in cafés, and he went to my house with his dog, Tobi, for a week, where he hatched a new song on the front porch, "The Room Where It Happens."

In January of 2014, we read Act Two at a rehearsal studio on East Fourth Street. Lin and Tommy recruited actor Leslie Odom Jr. to play Aaron Burr. Though I had seen him on the TV series *Smash*, I felt like I knew him from *Rent* but that didn't seem possible—he was too young to have done *Rent* all those years ago. When I said hello, he reminded me that he joined *Rent* as a swing and Benny cover when he was a senior in high school in the late '90s. Amazing. Leslie wore a navy blue three-piece suit. Sharp and smart. He wanted this part. This part wanted him.

"What Did I Miss" gave way to the first "Cabinet Battle," which gave way to "Say No to This," which gave way to "The Room Where It Happens." I was in awe. At the end of the read-through I said to Lin, "It's better than Act One."

A month later, we read the whole musical in front of about sixty people, which demonstrated its cumulative power; in May we launched a six-week workshop where Andy and Tommy started exploring ways to physicalize, or stage, the show. David Korins, the set designer, experimented with platforms and moving panels; Paul Tazewell, the costume designer, experimented with costumes that incorporated the fashion of the late eighteenth century with twenty-first century flourishes like sleeveless vests that showed shoulders, arms, biceps. We planned to share this work in progress with an audience of about 150 folks at four run-throughs on a Thursday, Friday, and Saturday (we did two on Friday). Andy choreographed almost all of Act One; Act Two was still performed with music stands.

What transpired on the stage on Thursday was so unique—a musical so compelling, so enthralling that I'm not sure I took a breath for the entire first act—that I called Mike Nichols, acquaintance, supporter, friend, and asked, "Are you free tomorrow at two p.m.?"

"Mr. Seller, if you're asking me to be free, then I'll be free."

On Friday afternoon, I waited for Mike by the door—he was eighty-three and needed a health aide by that point—and he was one of the last people to arrive.

Walking in, he turned to me and said, "Can I invest?"

"Mike, watch the show first!"

Mike flipped for the show because Mike was always about what's next. One of my great pleasures was watching Tommy Kail meet his idol, Mike Nichols, face-to-face in two theater seats, on that special afternoon. The first investor check I received was from Mike Nichols. He died while the show was still in rehearsals, but I always considered his investment a good luck charm.

After the workshop, two people from different generations and different parts of my life said, "That was the best thing I've ever seen." Over twenty years of producing, I had never heard anything like this. The first was Kimberly Belflower, my kids' babysitter, and a playwright from Georgia who would later have her first success with a terrific play called *John Proctor is the Villain*. The second was more unlikely: Drew Hodges, my longtime advertising collaborator, who had seen and/or worked on one hundred musicals since he designed the *Rent* logo in 1996. What they were both expressing was the notion that something unlikely was upon us.

If you pulled out of your wallet a ten-dollar bill in any city in America and asked a person on the street, "Who is that?" they would probably say "I don't know." Upon closer inspection of the bill and the name under the drawing, they'd say, "Oh, that's Alexander Hamilton." And if you said, "Who was that?" they might say, "Wasn't he the guy Aaron Burr shot in a duel?"

Creating a rap musical from the eight-hundred-page biography of America's first Treasury Secretary, who never became president—the principal architect of our financial system and new government—was unlikely. But it was also the result of years of preparation. Every play, every song, every dance that Lin, Tommy, Alex, and Andy created prior to *Hamilton* was preparation. Every musical Lin consumed from childhood forward was preparation. The videotape of every major musical that Tommy studied at the New York Public Library for the Performing Arts was preparation. Each of these young creators was at the top of their game.

The engagement at the Public Theater was sold out before our first preview. Why? Because six hundred people who saw the workshop told their friends and families to go see it, which is how every hit show in the history of theater was made. This proved to me, once and for all, that word of mouth is responsible for 90 percent of sales. Good marketing—advertising and press—can make a great show a little bit more successful. It can't help a mediocre show. It can't make a hit or cause a flop.

A triumphant opening in February was followed by a celebratory opening night on Broadway six months later. The fireworks over the Hudson River that accompanied opening night were a perfect manifestation of the enthusiasm that *Hamilton* generated, not just on Broadway, but all over New York City. Ben Brantley suggested "mortgaging your house and leasing your children" to obtain hard-to-get tickets. Lin, cast members, and special guests performed live #Ham4Ham preshows in front of the Richard Rodgers Theatre every day of previews to accompany the lottery of the first row of ten-dollar tickets. These mini shows became social media sensations.

Because we opened in August and the Tony Awards would not happen until June, our post-opening mission was to keep feeding the flame that was *Hamilton*. It wasn't hard. I thought about it like the "Twelve Days of Christmas"—we needed a blast once a month. These included the release of the original Broadway cast album, which spread our music faster than any show before thanks to streaming on Spotify, Apple, and YouTube; a performance of the opening number on the Grammy Awards live from the Richard Rodgers Theatre, another first; a concert performance in the East Room of the White House for President and

First Lady Barack and Michelle Obama; the kickoff of our Hamilton Education program; and then the triumphant Tony Awards in which the Obamas introduced the show and Barbra Streisand awarded us the Tony Award for Best Musical.

But we still didn't rest. With one month left before the departure of the original principals, we shot the live film of the musical over three days in late June 2016, with two shoots in front of a live audience and two days of shooting without an audience for close ups, "dolly shots" and other tricks. When it was all over Lin, Vanessa, and their baby son, Sebastian, came out to Sagaponack for a week of rest and decompression.

Hamilton had become the Obama-era musical. Its values reflected those of our first Black President. Back in 2009, when Lin was still conceiving the initial album, he performed the first song at the White House. President Obama joked to me, "Jeffrey, I feel like I'm a coproducer, because I did the first workshop!" But it wasn't just for Democrats. The second vice president to shoot another civilian (!) also showed up and enjoyed the musical: Dick Cheney. Conservative columnists Peggy Noonan and David Brooks wrote columns on how *Hamilton* reflected America's best impulses and values as a nation. The former director of the National Endowment for the Arts, Rocco Landesman, said, "*Hamilton* isn't just a show. It's a national trust. It belongs to everybody."

Lin and his team created a show that ignited our latent patriotism. It may have even inspired patriotism in some young people and people of color for the first time in their lives. It allowed every American to feel like part of our nation, our story. It impacted our political culture. The Republican-controlled state legislature in Utah passed a bill to pay the full cost of our education performance in Salt Lake City. It saved the image of Alexander Hamilton on the ten-dollar bill. It positively affected numerous spheres of public life.

Hamilton depicted America at its best: who we can be, who gets to be included, what kind of a nation we can build—a nation that sustains disagreement, conflict, and imperfection, *and* manages to progress, sometimes slowly, toward the values set forth in the Declaration of Independence and the Constitution.

With the 2016 election season upon us, we sold a fundraiser performance to the campaign of Democratic candidate Hillary Clinton and believed that we would take another step forward when we elected the first female president of the United States. We were going to heed Angelica Schuyler's phrase from "The Schuyler Sisters" and "put the woman in the sequel."

The election of Donald Trump on November 8, 2016, was also unlikely.

With the votes of about 80,000 people (less than one tenth of one percent of all votes) in the states of Wisconsin, Michigan, and Pennsylvania, our country elected a misogynistic, racist, ignorant narcissist who expressed admiration for some of the world's most violent fascists but didn't even know that Abraham Lincoln was a Republican. He won the presidency with three million fewer votes than Hillary Clinton.

We were punched in the gut. His election was inconsistent with everything we thought the Obama years had achieved. It extinguished our hopes for progress and exacerbated our fear that we might live in a country that tolerated, if not encouraged, discrimination against people because of their skin color, sexual orientation, or religion; fear that this country would interfere with a woman's right to control her body; fear that the leader of our country would band together with dictators like Vladimir Putin and Kim Jong Un, and disregard sixty years of partnership with our allies.

Each of us experienced our own form of shock and despair the night of the election. My twelve-year-old son woke up the morning after, scrunched his face, and asked, "Did he win?" I was ashamed as a father to say yes. I was ashamed as an American citizen to say yes. How could we have done this? Then I asked myself, "How is our company going to perform at two o'clock today?" I called a voluntary meeting for 12:30 p.m. to talk, to share, to cry. It felt like someone had died.

I welcomed the group and acknowledged the moment. One wardrobe crew member became upset, tears rolling down his face, and said, "I don't feel like I can even be in this country anymore. As a gay man I'm afraid for my very existence." Mandy Gonzalez, a Mexican-Jewish American, said, "I feel fear as a Mexican walking down the streets." Anthony Ramos, our young firebrand, said, "Now we know! We know who we're dealing with. At least he came out and said it. We're gonna have to fight."

When the show went up that afternoon, the audience response seemed to have grown deeper. We learned that the message of *Hamilton* wasn't dead, it was more important than ever. *Hamilton* showed us what we must hold on to.

Ten days later, the following Friday, I was exhausted. I decided to leave the office early and go to a movie. I took the 2 train to 72 Street and started walking south on Broadway toward Lincoln Plaza Cinema. My phone rang. It was Nick Scandalios, the theater landlord, who said, "Jeffrey, you're not gonna like this but we just received a call from the team of Mike Pence, and he wants to come to see the show tonight. I'm not responding until I talk to you."

"Fuck" was the first word that came out of my mouth.

What that word contained: Why does this man have to come see our show now, when our emotions are so raw? How can I ask the cast to perform for a man who has argued against gay marriage, abortion rights, and affirmative action? For a man who has silently stood by Trump's many cruelties? And how can I say no? One does not say no when the vice president–elect of the United States who is the governor of another state wants to see a show. That would be disrespectful to the office.

And yet, I also believed that these were not "normal times," and "normal behavior" was not suitable for this situation. This election was not comparable to feeling distraught when George W. Bush was declared by the Supreme Court to be the winner of the 2000 election. This was not comparable to George W. Bush being rewarded with four more years after his misguided and disastrous invasion of Iraq. To me, this election and its aftermath felt like a fight for the character of our country.

Therefore, while I had to say yes, that didn't mean that this wasn't an opportunity to make a point. After all, the vice president–elect was asking for something special—last-minute house seats (the seats held by the landlord for VIPs). His team was asking for treatment that is unavailable to regular citizens. I decided right then and there that, if he wanted special treatment, we deserved the right to speak to him and express our concern for the future of our country.

I walked the five blocks to Lincoln Plaza Cinema. I met Josh, and we sat down in our seats. I told him what happened, and then immediately jumped up and exited the theater. In the public plaza behind the theater, I wrote the following words on my iPhone:

Dear Mr. Pence, we welcome you. Before we start our play tonight, we wish to express to you that we are African American, Puerto Rican, Dominican, gay, female. We are immigrants. We are America. We are the Americans who are anxious and scared that you and your new administration will not protect us, defend us, or uphold our inalienable rights. We are afraid you will not protect our planet. Our children. Our parents. We hope this play will help you help us.

I thought, *Lin and Tommy will never go for this—too disrespectful, too combative—but I gotta try.* Lin was in London shooting *Mary Poppins Returns* and was five hours ahead. I got Tommy on the phone first and explained the situation. I read him the draft. He said, "Get Lin on the phone." We patched Lin in, where he had just returned home from work. Lin said, "OK, get my dad on the phone." Luis Miranda, Lin's dad, had been a political strategist for thirty-five years. He had worked for Mayor Koch, written countless speeches, and was a canny tactician. We found Luis and he said, "Cut this, move that, and make it simpler. Less!" Thus, the four of us edited the speech and created a plan. We would ask

Brandon Victor Dixon, a Broadway veteran, and our new Aaron Burr, to give the speech.

Brandon immediately agreed. The entire production team met at my office at five p.m. We debated the question of timing: Should we address Mr. Pence before or after the performance? Before would present a distraction from the play. After would risk his leaving before we had time to address him. We decided to go after, which would also give me more time to get TV cameras there, and I talked with Brandon about pushing the speech forward in the curtain call.

The managers called the cast and crew in early for a meeting in the basement. Tommy and I explained what we wanted to do; Brandon read the speech out loud. Anthony wanted it to be stronger. He was our rebel on the barricade. With one exception, the cast was excited to be taking a stand. One person was not aligned, but not for political reasons. "My father works at a factory in Ohio," he said. "You don't know what it's like out there." He was worried for his father's safety, but reluctantly agreed to participate.

I didn't want the plan to leak, so I waited until six p.m. to call Michael Paulson at the *New York Times*.

"You need to come to the theater tonight. Pence will be there."

"I can't, but can I send Pat Healy?" Patrick Healy was a veteran political reporter.

Then I asked our press agent, Sam Rudy, to invite the TV stations. It was late notice, but I figured some would show up by the end of show. I was thinking again about the opening night performance of *42nd Street* in which David Merrick announced that Gower Champion died. My goal was to maximize impact.

Was I doing this for political protest or for publicity?

Both.

Yes, I knew this event would create enormous publicity for the show and would generate sales. But I also believed it was essential to protest this terrible development in our country. I believed it was my duty as a gay man, parent, and Jew to stand up and say, "This is not right." I was buoyed by the courage of my partners, Lin and Tommy. I called and warned my two producing colleagues, Jill Furman and Sander Jacobs. "Oh boy. You better think this through, Jeffrey. I know that guy"—he meant Trump—"and he's not gonna like it. But you're going to do what you're going to do." I thanked Sander for his input and said I had to do this.

When Pence entered the theater before the show, there were some boos, some cheers, some clapping. His presence heightened the emotions of the entire performance. When Hamilton and Lafayette sang the lyric "Immigrants, we get the job done," a standing ovation ensued. When King George III sang "when people say they hate you," the sustained applause stopped the show.

During Act Two, Tommy and I anxiously stood in the alley behind the theater along with John Buzzetti, his and Lin's agent.

We listened to Hamilton and Burr exchange their last argument, "Your Obedient Servant." As these founding fathers counted years of acrimony, we counted minutes until the speech.

"What do you think?" John asked Tommy.

"This is before," said Tommy. "In fifteen minutes, we'll find out what after looks like. It's not going to be nothing."

We entered house left as the show came down at 10:48. Three news cameras were set up at the back of the orchestra. I saw Pence stand and applaud with the crowd. He was smiling. Then he and his daughters stepped into the aisle with two Secret Service agents and started walking out. Before he reached the exit door, Brandon Victor Dixon adroitly, gently, charmingly said, "We have a guest in the audience this evening, and Vice President–elect Pence, we see you walking out but hope you will hear us for just a few more moments." The audience was a cacophony of cheers and boos. "There is nothing to boo here, ladies and gentlemen, we're all here sharing a story of love. We have a message for you, sir, and hope that you will hear us out." Mr. Pence stopped and listened. Brandon invited the audience to video his words.

"Vice President–elect Pence, we welcome you and we truly thank you for joining us here at *Hamilton*, an American musical, we really do. We, sir, are the diverse America who are alarmed and anxious that your new administration will not protect us, our planet, our children, our parents or defend us and uphold our inalienable rights, sir. But we truly hope this show has inspired you to uphold our American values and to work on behalf of all of us. All of us. Thank you for attending this wonderful American story told by a diverse group of men and women of different colors, creeds, and orientations."

Mr. Pence exited. The cast exited. The orchestra playout began.

The *New York Times* posted a digital article later that night, which was followed by a story in the print edition on page 10 of the Saturday paper. CNN jumped right in, followed by every media company in the country. When Trump started posting multiple tweets on Saturday morning—"They need to apologize," "they were very inappropriate," "highly overrated"—the story multiplied and spread around the world.

Hamilton was the lead news story on every cable, network, and digital channel on Saturday. The story snowballed through the weekend. Pence weighed in on Sunday. "I wasn't offended by what was said," he commented. "I nudged my kids and said, 'that's what freedom sounds like.'"

Friends in Tel Aviv, Zurich, Florence, and even Kabul texted to say they heard the story. Many Broadway companies sent letters and gifts of appreciation to the cast. Artists and celebrities tweeted support.

A handful of Trump supporters, including Bikers for Trump, threatened to protest in front of the theater and interfere with the show. We hired a security team and reinforced our safety measures for the next four years.

It was one the earliest public protests of the new Trump era. Our voices rose in the most respectful manner possible. And yet, it was a controversial decision. I received an angry letter from a progressive lawyer and Hillary voter who thought our actions were inappropriate and disrespectful. His opinion pained me. It is hard to be criticized by allies. But it was still my proudest moment as a producer.

IT IS RARE FOR a Broadway musical to affect culture, and it is even rarer for a musical to affect politics. *Rent* and *Hamilton* did both.

Rent had a measurable, positive impact on the health and lives of young people. I saw this firsthand. A couple of years into the run, we created a program to do a handful of matinees each year for high school students. On a Wednesday morning, twelve hundred kids from the tristate area came to the Nederlander Theatre and participated in a workshop in which cast members spoke, a music director taught the entire audience "Seasons of Love," and representatives of each school performed from the stage. Kids presented songs, monologues, scenes, poems, and dances that related to the themes, characters, or story of *Rent.* These performances manifested talent, insight, and courage. I witnessed young men and women come out, talk about suicide and family conflict, and express camaraderie with the characters. The morning workshop was followed by the *Rent* performance in the afternoon.

Numerous articles and dissertations showed anecdotal evidence that *Rent*, along with the AIDS Memorial Quilt, helped reduce stigma around HIV and increased testing. At speaking engagements, teens approached me to say, "*Rent* saved my life." It helped teens experiencing thoughts around suicide. It helped teens who felt like outsiders— because they were gay, trans, or just other—to feel part of something.

The *Rent* student matinees became the inspiration for the groundbreaking Hamilton Education Program, known as #EduHam, in which more than 250,000 young people from Title I schools (schools in which most students qualify for a free lunch) studied American History along with *Hamilton*, and then congregated at our theaters to share their performance pieces, learn about the show, and dialogue with the cast. I fervently believe this program will result in greater civic participation, more education, and contributions to the arts. The *Hamilton* experience may inspire the next community leader, mayor, or congresswoman; the next teacher, air force pilot, or football coach; the next poet, songwriter, or performing artist.

During the 2020 election cycle, when Covid shut down all live performance, *Hamilton* cast members used their popularity and reach to present live Zoom events that raised millions of dollars for presidential candidate Joe Biden and Georgia U.S. Senate candidates Raphael Warnock and Jon Ossoff; conducted live letter-writing parties that increased voter turnout in two pivotal states: Wisconsin, where Biden won by 20,000 votes, and Georgia, where Biden won by 12,000 votes. *Hamilton* made a difference.

While our 2016 protest didn't affect Trump's cruelest impulses, I believe it helped spark more protest, which may have affected the millions of civil servants who have kept our nation, our states, our counties, and our cities operating. Over the last four years, we learned that many of these civil servants often acted in the best interests of our country—of our people—against the dictates of the forty-fifth U.S. president.

How did *West Side Story, Fiddler on the Roof,* and *Hair* affect us? These great musicals enriched our culture, our civility, our community. They manifested the power of theater to show us who we are; to change us for the better.

What *Rent, Avenue Q, In the Heights,* and *Hamilton* have in common is that they all expanded the notion of what kind of musical could play on Broadway. Without *Rent,* none of those shows would have existed, and to that list you can add *Next to Normal, Dear Evan Hansen,* and *The Book of Mormon.* Because what *Rent* did was to, as Jonathan Larson put it, "create a Broadway that was about our characters, our stories, our music." It has been my good fortune to help advance that mission.

I still love musicals.

I still want to produce another good one.

I'll always be a theater kid.

ACKNOWLEDGMENTS

M Y SIBLINGS, Laurie Gates and Aaron Seller, who shared the bathroom, the tumult, and the love. The writing coaches and readers who imbued me with confidence and courage, Ari Shavit, Michael Sokolove, Oskar Eustis, Maja Thomas, Tommy Greenwald, Jim Nicola. The high school English teachers who taught me to write, Leslie Ann Pomerantz, Barbara Goldsmith, Shirley Citron. The extraordinary agents who helped shape the manuscript and never stopped believing, David Kuhn, Nate Muscato, Helen Hicks. Publisher and editor Jonathan Karp and Maria Mendez, for their enthusiasm, support, and guidance. Colleague and friend Drew Hodges, for his art direction; two amazing illustrators, Peter de Sève and Michael Byers. Early employers and industry giants Fran and Barry Weissler, Susan Weaving, Miles Wilkin, Paul Blake, Emanuel Azenberg. Former assistant Jason Arnold and colleagues Tori Lynn, Michael Maier, and Maggie Brohn. Stellar Adventureland marketing team Laura Matalon, Shane Marshall Brown, Mike Karns.

The artists who created these extraordinary musicals: Jonathan Larson, Michael Greif, Tim Weil, Marlies Yearby; Bobby Lopez, Jeff Marx, Jeff Whitty, Jason Moore, Stephen Oremus, Ken Roberson; Lin-Manuel Miranda, Quiara Hudes, Thomas Kail, Andy Blankenbuehler, Alex Lacamoire, Bill Sherman. The family and friends of Jonathan Larson, Julie Larson, Matthew McCollum, Dylan McCollum, Victoria Leacock,

353

ACKNOWLEDGMENTS

Matthew O'Grady, Jonathan Burkart, Eddie Rosenstein. Producing partners Kevin McCollum, Robyn Goodman, Jill Furman, Sander Jacobs.

Two men who enriched my life, Andrew Lippa and Josh Lehrer, and one man who makes every day joyous, exciting, and full of love, Yuval Sharon.

Finally, two spectacular young adults who have cheerfully and lovingly gone on many adventures with their challenging dad, May Lehrer-Seller and Thomas Lehrer-Seller.

ABOUT THE AUTHOR

JEFFREY SELLER is one of the masterminds behind the Tony Award winning musicals *Rent*, *Avenue Q*, *In the Heights*, and *Hamilton*. His shows have garnered twenty-two Tony Awards, including four for Best Musical, and his Broadway productions and tours have grossed more than $4.6 billion and reached more than 43 million attendees. Jeffrey is the only producer to have mounted two Pulitzer Prize–winning musicals—*Hamilton* and *Rent*. Jeffrey also revolutionized theater accessibility with the $20 ticket lottery for *Rent*, making theater affordable to many. This passion for accessibility underscores his belief in the power of the theater to change lives, which started with his own.